BRITISH RACING PRINTS
1700–1940

BRITISH
RACING PRINTS
1700-1940

CHARLES LANE

∘ THE ∘
SPORTSMAN'S
PRESS
LONDON

Published by
The Sportsman's Press 1990

© Charles Lane 1990

for
CELIA

British Library Cataloguing in Publication Data
Lane, Charles
    British racing prints 1700–1940
    1. English prints. Special subjects. Racehorses, history
    I. Title
    769.4963612

ISBN 0-948253-45-2

Photoset and printed in Great Britain by
BAS Printers Limited, Over Wallop, Hampshire

CONTENTS

ACKNOWLEDGEMENTS

I am very grateful to Mr Julian Armytage who has given me so much encouragement and help in putting this book together, inspired as it has been by his exhibition of racing prints, 'Heritage of the Turf', shown in London in 1986. I am particularly indebted to Mr David Oldrey; Mr Oldrey has kindly gone out of his way to comment in detail on the contents of the book, proposing many changes to the story of racing which would have been far less accurate without his help.

I wish to thank the staffs of libraries, galleries and museums in London and across the country who have answered numerous questions about some of the little known artists who painted the original pictures. I also wish to thank Miss Joan Bailey, lately of the London Library, for all the work she has done in painstakingly discovering the results of obscure races by searching newspapers and other sources.

Mr Armytage, Mr David Fuller of Arthur Ackermann & Son, and the staffs of the major London auction houses have been very generous in letting me borrow so many of their photographs. These, with the sources of other photographs, are acknowledged below with my sincere thanks for permission to use them.

Arthur Ackermann & Son Ltd Plates 1, 3, 4, 6, 8; figures 1, 9, 12, 13, 15, 21, 23, 24, 25, 68, 72, 73, 75, 77, 93.

Julian Armytage Plates 7 (below), 9, 10, 12, 14; figures 2, 3, 4, 6, 8, 10, 11, 14, 16, 17, 19, 27, 28, 29, 30, 31, 35, 37, 41, 44, 46, 47, 48, 50, 52, 55, 56, 57, 59, 60, 61, 62, 63, 64, 65, 66, 69, 70, 74, 76, 79, 81, 82, 88, 90, 91, 94, 97, 98, 103, 104, 107, 109.

Bonhams Plates 11, 13; figure 26.

Burlington Gallery Ltd Figure 5.

Christie's Figures 18, 37, 49, 106.

Christie's South Kensington Plate 2; figures 33, 51, 53, 92, 101.

Fores Gallery Figure 45.

Fox Gallery Plate 7 (above).

Frost & Reed Ltd Plate 16; figure 80.

Parker Gallery Figure 68.

Phillips Fine Art Auctions Figure 96.

Sotheby's Plate 5.

Sotheby's, Sussex Figure 95.

The Lambourn Press Ltd Figure 31a

Tryon Gallery Plate 15; figure 34.

Finally, owners of prints, too many to name individually, have been extremely kind in allowing me to visit them to see an engraving or check a detail which I needed to make this book as complete as I could. I am very grateful to them all.

LIST OF ILLUSTRATIONS

The colour plates are shown in the text as [*Plate 1*], [*Plate 2*] and the black and white illustrations as [*1*], [*2*] and so on.

[7]

12 *The Earl of Abingdon's Marske. Stipple engraving after George Stubbs.*

13 *Colonel O'Kelly's Volunteer. Stipple engraving after George Stubbs.*

14 *Christopher Wilson Esq's Champion. Derby & St Leger 1800. Mezzotint after John Nost Sartorius.*

15 *HRH the Duke of York's Moses. Lithograph by and after James Ward* RA.

16 *Sir M. W. Ridley's Fleur-de-Lis. Mezzotint after Abraham Cooper* RA.

17 *The Duke of Beaufort's Lop. Stipple engraving after Ben Marshall.*

18 *After Running. Aquatint after Jacques-Laurent Agasse.*

19 *Panoramic View of British Horse Racing, the Race for the St Leger Stakes of 1812 on Doncaster Course. Aquatint after Clifton Tomson.*

20 *Ascot Heath Races. Aquatint after James Pollard.*

21 *Sir W. Maxwell's Filho da Puta, with J. Jackson up. St Leger 1815. Aquatint after John Frederick Herring Snr.*

22 *A Steeple Chase. Plate 2. Aquatint after Henry Alken Snr.*

23 *The Liverpool Grand Steeple-Chase, 1839. Plate III. Aquatint after Francis Calcraft Turner.*

24 *The Marquis of Westminster's Touchstone, with G. Calloway up. St Leger 1834. Aquatint after John Frederick Herring Snr.*

25 *J. B. Bowes Esq's Cotherstone. Derby 1843. Aquatint after John Frederick Herring Snr.*

26 *The Start for the Memorable Derby of 1844. Aquatint after J. F. Herring Snr.*

27 *The Duke of Westminster's Bend Or, with F. Archer up. Derby 1880. Aquatint by and after Edwin Hunt.*

28 *HRH the Prince of Wales's Ambush II, with A. Anthony up. Grand National 1900. Chromolithograph after N. Arthur Loraine.*

29 *HRH the Prince of Wales's Diamond Jubilee, with Herbert Jones up. Triple Crown 1900. Chromolithograph after N. Arthur Loraine.*

30 *The Duke of Portland's St Simon. Ascot and Goodwood Gold Cups 1884. Photogravure after Alfred Charles Havell.*

31 *Newmarket Fin-de-Siecle. 'The Birdcage'. Photogravure after Isaac Cullin.*

31a *The Downshire Wall, Punchestown. Colour reproduction after Gilbert Holiday.*

32 *Preparing to Start. Aquatint after Jacques-Laurent Agasse.*

33 *The Finish. (Derby 1923.) Colour reproduction after Cecil Aldin.*

34 *The Grand National (1920). Becher's Brook. Colour reproduction after Cecil Aldin.*

35 *Newmarket – Training; and Ascot Heath – Preparing to Start. Aquatints after Henry Alken Snr.*

36 *Epsom Races, with Horses preparing to Start for the Two Mile Heat. Aquatint after Henry Alken Snr.*

37 *Racing from Newmarket Heath; and Racing. Aquatints after Henry Alken Snr.*

38 *The High Mettled Racer. The Foal. Aquatint after Henry Alken Snr.*

39 *The High Mettled Racer. In Training. Aquatint after Henry Alken Snr.*

40 *Grand Leicestershire Steeple Chase, on the 12th of March 1829. Plate III. Aquatint after Henry Alken Snr.*

41 *Fores's Steeple Chase Scenes. The Brook. Aquatint after Henry Alken Snr.*

42 *The Last Grand Steeple Chase at the Hippodrome Race Course, Kensington. Aquatint after Henry Alken Jnr.*

43 *Mr W. Chifney's Priam. Derby 1830. Lithograph. Anon.*

44 *Henry Padwick Esq's Virago, with J. Wells up, accompanied by his trainer John Day and groom William Goater. Aquatint after Thomas Barratt.*

45 *John Day Snr's The Hero, with portraits of the jockey Alfred Day, and the owner. Aquatint after William and Henry Barraud.*

46 *Newmarket Scenes. Waiting for the Trainer. Aquatint after John Alexander Harington Bird.*

47 *Newmarket Scenes. The Trial. Aquatint after John Alexander Harington Bird.*

48 *Ascot. The Royal Enclosure on Cup Day. Photogravure after Henry Jermyn Brooks.*

49 *The Bibury Welter Stakes, 16th June 1801. Mezzotint after Henry Bernard Chalon.*

50 *Mr G. Crompton's and the late Lord Rous's Quiz. Mezzotint after Henry Bernard Chalon.*

51 *Barbarossa, bred by Lord Spencer Chichester in 1802. Mezzotint after Henry Bernard Chalon.*

52 *Stanlake Batson Esq's Plenipotentiary. Derby 1834. Lithograph after Abraham Cooper* RA.

53 *Life of the Race Horse. Backing the Colt. Lithograph by and after John Doyle.*

54 *Morning Exercise, Newmarket. Colour reproduction after Lionel Dalhousie Robertson Edwards* RI, RCA.

55 *The Earl of Jersey's Riddlesworth, with J. Robinson up. 2,000 Guineas 1831. Aquatint after John Ferneley.*

56 *The Celebrated Mare 'Beeswing' with her First Foal 'Old Port' by Sir Hercules. Lithograph after John Ferneley.*

57 *The Derby Day. Line engraving after William Powell Frith* RA.

58 *Denis O'Kelly Esq's Soldier. Aquatint after George Garrard* ARA.

59 *Extraordinary Steeple-Chase. Aquatint after Edward Gill.*

60 *William Scott's Sir Tatton Sykes, with the owner up, led by Sir Tatton Sykes. St Leger 1846. Aquatint after Harry Hall.*

61 *Henry Jones Esq's Prince Charlie. 2,000 Guineas 1872. Aquatint after Harry Hall.*

62 *The Marquis of Westminster's Satirist, with W. Scott up. St Leger 1841. Aquatint after Charles Hancock.*

63 *Mr Irwin's Foig-a-Ballagh, with F. Bell up. St Leger 1844. Aquatint after Charles Hancock.*

64 *The Earl of Jersey's Glencoe. 2,000 Guineas 1834. Aquatint after Charles Hancock.*

THE STORY OF RACING

I

SETTING THE SCENE
1660–1727

Horses have been raced in England from time immemorial; the Romans certainly raced at Chester and York among other places. Stock had been imported at various times from Spain and elsewhere long before the thoroughbred was created by the fusion of Eastern blood with native stock in the seventeenth and eighteenth centuries. The Royal Studs probably began in this context in the reign of Henry VIII and numerous records exist during the second half of the sixteenth century when they were under the control of Elizabeth. However, it was members of the House of Stuart who, as far as they were able, gave consistent encouragement to the gentleman's recreation of racing. James I came to Newmarket to hunt. Although not a natural horseman, he enjoyed riding over the flat heathland in pursuit of the hare and the quarry of the hawk. His more agile courtiers raced their horses against each other to while away the hours when they were not expected to be in attendance on His Majesty. From the day of his succession in 1625 Charles I had relatively little interest in sport and, in the later stages of his reign, committed all his energy to saving his crown which a civil war finally wrested from him, taking his head as well.

The importance of Newmarket gained a fresh momentum at the Restoration of Charles II in 1660. This signalled the renaissance of the enjoyment of country pursuits after more than a decade of suppression due to well grounded fears that such gatherings were likely sources of Royalist discontent. Charles's interest in and fondness for horses stemmed from his eleventh birthday when William Cavendish, Duke of Newcastle, an acknowledged authority on all aspects of horsemanship excepting racing, was appointed his Governor.

One of the first acts of the King on regaining the throne was to appoint James D'Arcy as Master of the Royal Studs, which had been dispersed under the Commonwealth (to the considerable advantage of several leading Parliamentarians). A beneficial result of the dispersal was to spread the blood of some of the best horses in the land more widely, achieving a small improvement in the quality of the country's stock as a whole. On 7 March 1661, after the fall of the Commonwealth, King Charles attended the first recorded race meeting on Epsom Downs, but it was not until 1665 that he visited Newmarket. However, during the next twenty years he imprinted his enthusiasm for racing and sport so firmly on that place that he can be fairly described as the founder of what was to become the home of the turf. Unlike his grandfather he was an accomplished horseman so that, beside giving silver bells, bowls and cups (Plates) for prizes, settling arguments over wagers or the results of matches, he rode in races himself and sometimes won. One of his favourite horses was named Old Rowley, a nickname the court at Newmarket gave to their sovereign and which became the title of the course still used for the Guineas, the Rowley Mile.

It is sad that the King's interest in Newmarket is not recorded in a painting or print so far as I am aware. There is however an engraving of Charles II watching a race beneath the walls of Windsor Castle, [1]. This print is a line engraving on copper after a drawing by Francis Barlow. It shows the King with his courtiers in a small stand, the front hung with carpets below which there are the scales (the clerk with marvellously bouffant hair), watching four dock-tailed racehorses being ridden by their jockeys towards a finishing post. A cartouche with the Royal supporters of the Lion and the Unicorn at the top of the plate describes the scene as 'The Last Horse Race Run before Charles the Second of Blessed Memory by Dorsett Ferry near Windsor Castle' on August the 10th, 1684. 'Drawn from the Place and Design'd by Francis Barlow, 1687' is engraved in a wreath of laurel between four laudatory verses below the image; the latter date is two years after Charles II's death.

[13]

1 *The last Horse Race Run before Charles the Second of Blessed Memory. Line engraving by and after Francis Barlow.*

Within three years of succeeding his older brother, James II was in exile. Despite being a good horseman he had few opportunities to enjoy sport of any nature after his accession. The arrival in the West Country of William of Orange and his advance towards Oxford led to James's precipitate flight in 1688. William III improved the Royal Studs and went to Newmarket the following year where he was well received by the little town which was becoming used to seeing its prosperity rise and fall with successive monarchs. In later years William raced his own horses on the Heath, but while his interest in the turf was considerable it lacked some of Charles II's *joie de vivre*. Royal encouragement of racing was revitalised by Queen Anne, the younger daughter of James II, when she ascended the throne in 1702. The Queen, often accompanied by her equally enthusiastic consort, George, Prince of Denmark, presented a number of Plates, attended meetings and ran her own horses with success at Newmarket and York. She is remembered most of all, however, as the founder of Ascot. She directed a course be laid out on the Heath and from the first race on Saturday 11 August 1711, the Ascot meetings have attracted a succession of Royal patrons. Queen Anne died in 1714,

two days after her horse Star won a £40 Plate at York on 30 July. So ended a hundred years of Stuart patronage of racing, a patronage which helped to establish the sport sufficiently to carry it through the lean years of limited Royal interest which followed.

Racing at the turn of the seventeenth century lacked official regulation except for sporadic Statutes passed by Parliament to put right some aspect which was plainly going wrong. Fifty years were to pass before the Jockey Club came into being as a social club which soon acquired control of the conduct of racing at Newmarket. The owners of racehorses training at Newmarket organised their sport as they wished and a certain continuity was provided by a remarkable character from Dorset, Tregonwell Frampton. He was born in the reign of Charles I, was probably a rider and owner in the lifetime of Charles II, and was the keeper at Newmarket of the 'running horses' of William III, Queen Anne and George I. This wily and often unscrupulous jockey, gambler, trainer, breeder, owner, arbiter and juror of all racing matters at Newmarket who died in March 1727, was known in his later years and ever since as the Father of the Turf. No doubt a sharp eye will spot the ageing Frampton among the spectators in the set of engravings by Claude du Bosc and Joseph Sympson Snr after the work of Peter Tillemans showing a 'View of a Horse-Match over the Long-Course . . . . .'; a 'View of the Round-Course or Plate-Course with divers Jockeys and Horses . . . . .'; or a 'View of the Noblemens and Gentlemens several Strings or Trains of Running Horses taking their Exercise . . . . .' [2] at Newmarket. An engraving of Hunting makes up this set of four double copper plates published in 1723. In 1914, Messrs Fores published a photogravure, also after a painting by Tillemans, of 'King George I at New-market' (in 1722), in which Frampton features. As the King's trainer and by his acknowledged position as 'Mr Racing', he could order with almost royal authority all aspects of its conduct on the Heath each spring and autumn.

In the seventeenth and eighteenth centuries some races and matches were run as a single heat but usually there were too few horses to provide a full or worthwhile day's entertainment unless a race was run in a series of heats. An incidental 'advantage' of racing in heats was the additional opportunity to gamble on each stage. Since heats were very different to the system we know today, some explanation is needed to understand how they were arranged. Essentially, all the horses entered in a race, four-year-olds or older carrying weights appropriate to their age, and raced usually over a distance of at least four miles, took part in as many heats as it required for one of them to win two outright. This horse was the winner of the race. To run four heats, sometimes five, and six in an afternoon was not unknown, requiring stamina in man and beast, and the employment of tactics to make best use of a horse's qualities. It might be that in the opening heat a certain jockey would be content to let his mount take it easy while the first and second fought out an exciting finish. This jockey would then win the next two successive heats from the exhausted opposition, or even win the second heat, rest in the next and win the fourth, whilst having to see that no other horse won two heats in the meantime. To prevent a horse simply walking a heat

2 '*A View of the Noblemens and Gentlemens Severall Strings or Trains of Running Horses taking their Exercise up the Watering Course on the Warring Hill at New Markett*'. *Line engraving after Peter Tillemans.*

which, for tactical reasons, its jockey had no intention of trying to win, a post was set in the ground 240 yards short of the finishing line. Any horse which was to go forward to the next heat had to be 'within the distance' (the 240 yard post) as the heat winner finished. In a slightly different context this is the origin of the term 'winning by a distance'. If two horses passed the finishing line together the heat was declared void or 'dead', from which 'dead heat' arises. In the early days if a horse won the first and second heats it was required to carry its weight again within the distance in a third heat run primarily to decide the runner-up, possibly to save the second horse's stake.

An example of how exhausting the whole system could be is the tale of the five-year-old bay horse Leonatus belonging to the Duke of Grafton. Leonatus was entered for a £50 plate run in two-mile heats at Huntingdon on 31 July 1770. Five horses were entered. Leonatus won the second heat and by the start of the fourth there were only three horses left in. Leonatus came third in this heat and was placed overall in that position behind Titus and Last. Two days later, Leonatus came out again for another £50 plate run in four mile heats also at Huntingdon. The winner of the first heat fell in the second, (won by a horse named Sportsman, owned by the Earl of March who was later know as Old Q, Duke of Queensbery) with Leonatus second of the five starters. Leonatus won the third heat in front of the remaining runners, and then only he and Sportsman turned out for the fourth heat which resulted in a dead heat! Sportsman won the fifth heat. Hardly surprisingly, Leonatus never ran again. On each occasion these plates were the only race of the day. By 1800, racing in heats, despised for some time at Newmarket, was dying out as more and more horses were entered for races; however, at some provincial meetings this form of running continued to fill out an otherwise slim card. By 1850 the practice had stopped altogether.

It was only natural that when gentlemen wished to test one of their horses against another's, a bet would be made on the result. This straightforward transaction between owners quickly attracted gamblers who arranged their own wagers, sometimes with the owners but more usually with those of their own ilk. Betting posts were erected on racecourses to act as rendezvous for those who wished to make or take bets. For a person outside the circle of those who knew the qualities and form of the horses in training, it was often difficult to decide which animal to back. The importance of this type of information led to deception. There are many stories of owners deceiving each other, resulting in some of the more rash among them being ruined, as were some professional gamblers. The group to suffer most was the hoi polloi with their irresistible urge to gamble but no means to choose where best to place the little money they had; destitution sometimes followed. In fairness to the nobility, owners and breeders who organised racing at this period, they did not set out to entertain anyone but themselves. However, the openness of Epsom Downs, Newmarket, Ascot Heath or wherever racing took place allowed large crowds to gather and gamble. The considerable sums of money so wastefully employed by the aristocracy and the opportunity provided for the poor to further beggar themselves led to widespread and often warranted criticism from moralists. In Queen Anne's reign Statutes were enacted to limit the amount of money an owner could win by betting on his own horse, but such measures were more honoured in the breaching than keeping. The malign influence of betting erupts at regular intervals throughout the history of racing.

Eastern horses, Arabs, Turks and Barbs, the names given to those small fiery animals from the hinterland of the Mediterranean shores stretching from Turkey to Morocco, began seriously to be imported into England in the reign of James I. The first of the three great Eastern sires from which all thoroughbreds descend in the male line was the Byerley Turk who arrived in 1688; then followed the Darley Arabian, bought in about 1704; and a stallion to be named the Godolphin Arabian was sent over from France in 1730. There were other Eastern horses who played a major role in the development of the thoroughbred. The names of the Leedes, Cullen and Devonshire Chestnut Arabians; the D'Arcy White, D'Arcy Yellow, Akaster and Lister Turks and the Morocco Barb occur again and again in the pedigrees of the notable horses painted by contemporary artists. The value of their lines was not fully recognised until the first half of the eighteenth century; however, breeders soon found that mixing English and Eastern blood usually resulted in progeny with speed and stamina far superior to pure-bred Arabs or English running horses. Also a weakness in the conformation of one horse could partly, and sometimes wholly, be eliminated by judicious mating; like the alchemist's gold, perfection seemed attainable, if not often achieved.

When speaking of English horses there is a school of thought, supported by some visual evidence from paintings and sculpture, that the best were essentially

Iberians imported over the years from Spain and Portugal as chargers and weight carriers for Royalty and the aristocracy who could afford them. Another view is that the thoroughbred evolved from crossing the native Galloway with Eastern stallions. What is sure is that Arabs played a very significant, perhaps dominant, part in creating the thoroughbred racehorse of the past two hundred years.

The science of breeding was developed in Yorkshire where some of the best strains of English horses were reared. James D'Arcy (the son of Charles II's Master of the Royal Studs) petitioned William III for six Barbary or Arab stallions since such quality could not be found elsewhere in England to serve his equally high class mares in Yorkshire. Unfortunately there are only patchy records of the ancestry of these early race-horses, so vital to the art of breeding; the Arabs had been keeping the pedigrees of their horses for centuries. Another difficulty experienced by the student of history today is that in the seventeenth century horses were often renamed when they changed ownership. Scraps of information (sometimes conflicting) can be gleaned from journals, letters and even paintings and prints, but they are like parts of a jigsaw puzzle for which you have no picture – impossible to put together either quickly or with complete conviction.

Before 1727 there was no annual record of racing, merely details for certain meetings and of major events. However in that year John Cheny of Arundel published *An Historical List of all the Horse-Matches run, and all the Plates and Prizes run for in England and Wales (of the value of Ten Pounds or upwards) etc.* This list and those which followed provide us with the first reliable record of the names of horses and who owned them. In a fashion, this linking of race meetings across the country started to give the turf a cohesive identity. Heber took over this record and with others provided a variety of lists, or calendars, of racing until 1773 when James Weatherby, Keeper of the Match Book at Newmarket, first published the long-running *Racing Calendar*. Between 1741 and 1754, Thomas Butler of Pall Mall and, again, John Cheny published a series of engravings of famous racehorses whose careers fall within this period. The majority of these prints are after the work of James Seymour and Thomas Spencer, but I suspect some of the early plates were from paintings by John Wootton, Tillemans' contemporary. Each of these somewhat crudely drawn racehorses with jockeys up are surrounded by a long and useful description of their pedigrees and performances. The typical detail from the plate of Bay Bolton

increases our understanding of the state of the turf at the beginning of the eighteenth century:

Bay Bolton, Originally call'd Brown Lusty, and afterward Whitefoot and Bay Bolton. This Horse, Eminent both for his Figure in Running & likewise as an Excellent Stallion; was Bred by the late Sr. Mathew Piearson of Yorkshire. His Sire was a Large Grey Horse bred by a Former Sr. Wm. Strickland of that County, call'd Hautboy, He being a son of Mr. Wilks's Hautboy, of late Years distinguished by ye Style of Old Hautboy, Bred by the Darcy Family, & got by the White Darcy Turk. Bay Bolton's Dam was a Black Mare of Sr. Mathew Piearson's got by Makeless a Horse of great Eminence Especially as a Stallion. He was got by an Arabian of Sr. Thomas Oglethorp's of Scotland and His Blood Esteem'd as Excellent as any not entirely Foreign. Bay Bolton's Grand Dam was got by Brimmer, His great Grand Dam by Diamond. His great great Grand Dam was full Sister to the Dam of Old Merlin. At York in 1710, Bay Bolton, then a 5 Year Old, & ye 1st time of His Running, won a 60£ Gold Cup, against 8 Six Year Olds, a case Exceedingly rare, especially at a place so eminent, & in a Country renown'd above all others in these Kingdoms, for Producing high bred Horses, & ye greatest Numbr. of them. He also Won ye Subscription Purse at Middleham Moor & ye Rich Prize at Quainton Meadow, & becoming ye Property of his Grace the late Duke of Bolton, He was brought to Newmarket, where He won a match against ye Duke of Somersets Windham, one against Sr. M. Piearsons Merlin, & two against Mr. Framptons Draggon, and afterward a Stallion to their Graces ye late & present Dukes of Bolton, & died at Bolton-Hall in Yorkshire, at upward of 30 Years Old about 17 Years ago. He was ye Sire of ye Duke of Boltons Sloven, Fearnought, Starling, Cyphax, Camilla, and Gypsey; the Earl of Godolphins Whitefoot and Morrat, and many other fine Horses.

At the time of the deaths of George I and Tregonwell Frampton in 1727 Newmarket was recognised as the home of the turf, with York the second most important centre of racing. Meetings of varying regularity, organisation and quality also took place annually in the rest of Britain. An enthusiasm for breeding faster race-horses with greater stamina was aroused by the intrinsic merit of improvement, by the rewards of winning Plates and Prizes and the chances of making large sums of money by betting. In the same period, the late seventeenth and early eighteenth centuries, the distinctive genre of sporting painting first appeared, practised initially (with exceptions to be counted on one hand) by artists who came to England from the Low Countries. Although outside the strict date confines of this book, the Barlow print of King Charles II watching racing at Dorsett Ferry in 1684 is included (see page 14) since the style of the more sophisticated engravings of Newmarket after Tillemans can be traced back to it. In turn, the Tillemans' composition was followed by later artists and with only slight changes remained the model for the painted racing scene until the late nineteenth century. Similarly, portraits engraved in the early eighteenth century begin to provide a visual record of the famous racehorses of the day. To start with they are of little value in anatomical terms due to the crudeness of their drawing but, within a few years they begin to add more realistic flesh and bones to the written anecdotes and pedigrees of the giants of old. From 1700 to 1940 these portraits and racing scenes were made in a variety of ways, culminating in the use of the camera when the photographer replaced the engraver and to some extent the artist as well.

For prints of this period, see:

BARLOW, Francis, page 85
SEYMOUR, James, page 162
SPENCER, Thomas, page 168
TILLEMANS, Peter, page 173
WOOTTON, John, page 185

2
FORMATIVE YEARS
1727–1765

King George II was no more interested in racing than his father, but he kept the Royal Studs and continued to employ Masters of his Running Horses. One, named Thomas Panton, was rather uncharitably described by Horace Walpole as a 'disreputable horse jockey'. Happily the momentum of racing created by the Stuarts was maintained by the nobility who bred and owned racehorses during this period. The names of the Dukes of Ancaster, Bolton, Devonshire, Grafton, Portland, Rutland and Somerset, the Earls of Godolphin, March, Portmore and lesser lights appear regularly in the limited annals of racing of the first half of the eighteenth century. To this list must be added the King's third son, William Augustus, Duke of Cumberland. He was much preoccupied as a soldier throughout his life, not least in playing a part in the War of the Austrian Succession. He received a somewhat ignominious baptism of fire at Dettingen in 1743, being shot in the thigh by an Austrian officer who mistook the Duke for a French cavalryman as he rode back to the lines of the Pragmatic Army after his charger had run away with him. George II led the Army during the battle once cynically described as 'the Glory of which was forced upon us by the French'. In 1744 Cumberland was made Captain-General of the Allies and later achieved greater renown by the destruction of the Jacobite uprising of 1745. The year before Culloden, he was appointed Ranger of Windsor Great Park, took possession of the Ranger's Lodge in Windsor Forest (later called Cumberland Lodge) and there formed a stud which produced two of the great sires in the history of racing from which all horses descend in the male line: Herod (foaled in 1758) and Eclipse (1764).

A Captain Robert Byerley of Middridge Grange in County Durham commanded a troop of horse in the Duke of Lorraine's army fighting the Turks. This officer took possession of a smart young stallion at the Seige of Buda. Two years later he rode the horse when commanding a regiment of Dragoons with King William at the Battle of the Boyne in Ireland. By virtue of his charger's speed, Colonel Byerley is said to have avoided capture by James II's cavalry during the fight. The Byerley Turk never raced, but once safely home proved outstanding at stud. His grandson, Partner (foaled in 1718), won a number of Plates at Newmarket before in turn becoming an excellent stallion. King Herod, more usually known as Herod, bred by Cumberland in 1758 was a son of Tartar and grandson of Partner. At the death of the Duke, Herod was bought by Sir John Moore Bart, of Neather Hall, Suffolk. He was an outstanding horse but inclined to break blood vessels, and is remembered now as the crucial link in the descent of the male line from the Byerley Turk to Classic three-year-olds in the following century. His line only really flourished in France by the second half of the nineteenth century becoming almost extinct in England until reintroduced into this country by Roi Herode in 1909.

The direct male line of Eclipse runs straight back through Marske, Squirt and Bartlett's Childers (a brother of Flying Childers) to the Darley Arabian. Thomas Darley, the consul in Aleppo, sent a stallion home to his father's stud at Aldby Park in Yorkshire in 1704. The Darley Arabian stood at Aldby until his death in 1730, and his blood is represented by more thoroughbreds in the direct line than that of the descendants of the other two Arab founding sires. An argument about whether Flying Childers, who appears in many early engravings, was a superior horse to his brother's great grandson Eclipse can be sustained for some time! At the sale of the Duke of Cumberland's horses, Eclipse was bought by a butcher, Mr William Wildman, who owned stables at Mickleham in Surrey. Eclipse first ran on 3 May 1769 in a race of four-mile heats against Gower, Chance, Trial and Plume. When Eclipse won the first heat easily, an Irishman named

Denis O'Kelly with a flair for gambling and an erratic lifestyle which culminated in attaining the rank of Lieutenant Colonel in the Middlesex Militia, offered to place all the runners in the second heat in their finishing order. His bet was taken up and he gave his terms as: 'Eclipse first, the rest nowhere.' Eclipse outclassed the other four runners to win the race with ease and O'Kelly his bet, there being no other horse which 'saved his distance' and thus was placed. A year later the Irishman bought Eclipse from Wildman. The horse was never beaten, winning eighteen races including eleven King's Plates. He went to stud in 1771, dying of colic in 1789. His immediate offspring (among them three Derby winners) won more than £158,000. George Stubbs painted Eclipse at least once, from which picture(s) a number of engravings were made, including one for the *Turf Review*. J. N. Sartorious also painted Eclipse (and Herod) basing his work on that of Stubbs. In 1832 William IV gave one of Eclipse's feet, suitably mounted, with £200, to be run for annually at Ascot by horses owned by members of the Jockey Club. The race was short-lived and in 1837 The Eclipse Foot was presented by the King to the Jockey Club itself.

> *Immortal foot – eternal toe –*
> *Of Hoofs the A to Z!*
> *Sole relic of our lost Eclipse,*
> *The quickest of the dead.*

It still occupies a place of honour in the middle of the dining room table at the Club's premises in Newmarket High Street.

The third of the founding Arab sires, to be known as the Godolphin Arabian, came to England in 1730. As a young man Mr Edward Coke spent a number of years in France. In Paris he found an Arab stallion and brought him over to Longford Hall in Derbyshire where he was establishing a new stud. Three years later Edward Coke died; only thirty-three, and perhaps with a premonition of an early death, he had made a timely Will in which his brood mares and horses in training were bequeathed to Francis, 2nd Earl of Godolphin, also the recipient of Tregonwell Frampton's estate. Coke's stallions were left to a Mr Williams, and from him Godolphin bought the Arabian to whom his name was thereafter attached. Lord Godolphin held the sinecure of Governor of the Scilly Isles from 1733 until his death in 1766. While obviously knowing what he was doing at his stud in Cambridgeshire, he was otherwise described as 'an insignificant man'. Lord Chesterfield said that he came

to the House of Peers only to sleep, 'and that he might as well sleep on the right as on the left of the Woolsack', such was his lack of interest in Whig or Tory politics. There is a rare mezzotint of the Godolphin Arabian after a picture presumed to have been painted from life by David Morier, a Swiss who came to England in 1743. This plate was published in 1753. The stallion was painted much later by Stubbs, perhaps from the Morier picture or some other contemporary work or written description. The latter painting was engraved by his son George Townley Stubbs [*Plate 1*] and also included among the prints of the shortlived *Turf Review*.

Lord Godolphin's Arabian covered Coke's famous mare named Roxana on a number of occasions and from these matings came two particularly good foals; the racer Lath and the stallion Cade. Lath was bought by the Duke of Devonshire but was not successful at his stud at Chatsworth; Cade raced little, but as a stallion fathered Matchem (1748) whose blood runs today in many outstanding thoroughbreds in England and America. Indeed, he is the vital link in the chain of descent in the third and final male line still in existence anywhere in the world. Matchem stood 15.1 hands high (the Godolphin Arabian was 14.1½ hands) and although rather a plain horse won nearly all his races, remaining in training until he was eight years old. His stud fee of £5 was soon increased to £50 as his offspring started to race, winning an eventual total of £151,000 in stakes during their careers. John Wootton and several other artists painted Matchem but, as far as I am aware, the only contemporary engraving is of his victorious match with Trajan engraved after Thomas Smith in 1769 as Plate VI in a set detailing the career of a thoroughbred. There is also a photogravure of the Wootton portrait published by Mr Fores in about 1900 in a series of eight 'Famous Sires'. The publication of these reproductions was partly a quid pro quo for helping Mr William Woodward to form his famous collection of sporting paintings in America which includes the five Woottons (Darley Arabian, Byerley Turk, Flying Childers, Matchem, and King Herod) and three Stubbs (the first titled the Godolphin Barb, Eclipse, and Diomed) reproduced by Messrs Fores.

We sometimes criticise early portraits of racehorses, even those painted by Stubbs, since the physical characteristics of the animals look odd to us today. It is however wrong to dismiss such work solely on this score since apart from the idiosyncrasy of the small painted head (thought beautiful), racehorses were

3 *Mr Martindale's Sedbury. Mezzotint after James Seymour.*

4 *The Duke of Somerset's Bald Charlotte. Mezzotint after James Seymour.*

changing shape through breeding. I am confident that even those practising before Stubbs were painting what they saw with reasonable accuracy; although there is no doubt that the patrons of artists rarely demanded warts-and-all portraits of their favourites! This view is reinforced by the many references to the good likenesses achieved which can be found in early commentaries. Even those with less talent such as Thomas Butler, the Pall Mall bookseller and publisher (of Seymour's series of famous racehorses), were not far from the truth in what they depicted. In the 1750s Butler advertised his willingness to undertake commissions to portray 'horses, dogs, living and dead game' in a manner 'more elegant' and in a 'newer taste [more realistic?] than has been yet'. He was not short of business. However, Butler and others were often let down by the limited skills of the line engravers they employed. It is almost impossible to pass judgement on the merits of a horse based on an early outline engraving. It becomes slightly easier to do so when the whole plate is etched with features and landscape giving relative proportion to the subject. The art of mezzotint engraving which began to be practised in this field in 1750 suddenly provides texture, light, shadow and moulding to the subjects. These characteristics of the mezzotint engraving provide a more accurate portrayal of the conformation of racehorses of the period.

Among the prints which give a much better idea than before of how horses looked are twelve plates after Seymour's paintings engraved by Thomas Burford in 1752. Five are presumed to be portraits of racehorses. The first two are of a pair of horses in stalls attended by a groom; a theme continued much later by J. F. Herring Snr. The other three are said to show Flying Childers by a rubbing house, after running; the mare Roxana (Lath and Cade's dam) being led from a training ground; and Miss Slamerkin with her colt Othello. Twelve line engravings of similar subjects published by Bowles & Carver some years later indicate that the first two of their stable scenes are of the Duke of Bolton's and the Duke of Grafton's 'running horses'; another shows racehorses belonging to Sir James Lowther, Bart, and Plate 11 is of Aaron and Driver. The last print records a Give and Take Plate at Maidenhead on 9 September 1754. The hazards of riding are well illustrated by the results of the three heats which comprised the race. In the first, both Mr Roger's Aaron and Mr Lamego's Driver fell 'at comeing in'. Thomas Brett, riding Driver, was injured in the fall but his mount was awarded the heat. In the second, Driver

had David Newcomb up 'who rode him badly and lost the heat'. In the final heat Driver had yet another jockey, Thomas Arnold, and won it and the Plate. Aaron was ridden by Sam Tate throughout. There are other permutations of these hunting and racing line engravings, few of which can be precisely dated.

R. Houston engraved a dozen portraits after Seymour and Thomas Spencer in 1755 and 1756, which were sold by Spencer and a Robert Clee from Panton Street, Leicesterfields, London. These fine mezzotint portraits are bordered by an ornately scrolled 'frame' with a coat of arms at the top and a description of the horse's pedigree and performance at the foot. The composition echoes the surround of the Barlow print of King Charles II at Dorsett Ferry. The names of the horses portrayed: Childers; Old Partner; Sedbury [3]; Dormouse; Crab; Lamprie; White Nose; Cullen Arabian; Babraham; Bay Bolton; Bald Charlotte [4] and Wilson's Chestnut Arabian can be found in the pedigrees of many subsequent thoroughbred winners. Among Seymour's many portraits of racehorses, it would be interesting to know why these were chosen for engraving. No doubt each horse was famous in its day but there were many others as well, or better, known than several of them. As yet, there were no themes for a series of prints such as the long runs of Classic winners which were to provide such a marvellous vehicle for publishers, artists and engravers in the future. Interest in these engravings must have been relatively slight (accounting for their rarity) in an era when human portraiture was enjoying its golden age in England and 'horse painters' were still looked upon askance, among them the late, profligate and wild young man, James Seymour.

The attraction of the engraved racing scene is more obvious and provides much greater interest for us in terms of racing history. The line engraving of the Match between Windham and Bay Bolton, sometimes found coloured by a contemporary hand, is one of the earliest records of a race in progress. The print is after a painting by John Wootton.

A View of a Horse Match at Newmarket; between Grey-Windham (a Horse belonging to his Grace the Duke of Somerset) and Bay-Bolton (a Horse belonging to his Grace the Duke of Bolton) Painted from the Life by that Celebrated Artist Mr. John Wootton, and Engraved by Josephus Sympson Junr. Humbly Inscribed to his Grace Charles, Duke of Somerset.

To the left, a group of mounted spectators gather round a post which Grey Windham is approaching;

his jockey looks back at Bay Bolton being spurred on a length behind. There is a chaise and more galloping riders in the background. A drummer, whose role was probably to attract the attention of the spectators to the start of the race, runs behind Bay Bolton and points to the grey. He is looking out at us as we examine the print. This figure balances the composition and is typical of a device used by Jan Wyck (c1645–1700), Wootton's tutor, who often inserted an incidental rustic to draw the viewer's attention to the principal subject matter. At first glance it seems surprising that the apparent winner of the Match is not given in the title, until one discovers from the engraving of James Seymour's portrait of Bay Bolton that this is the horse who, on coming south from Yorkshire, 'was brought to Newmarket where He won a Match against ye Duke of Somerset's Windham.' The artist's licence of showing Windham in front of Bay Bolton most probably arises from it being the Duke of Somerset who commissioned the painting.

A very similar scene, engraved by R. Rooe after Seymour shows 'A View of the Great Horse Match between Conqueror and Looby that was Run at Newmarket on the 6th of October 1735.' The Match [5] was run over four miles with Conqueror, owned by Thomas Panton, carrying 8 stone 1 pound, beating Looby on 8 stone 6 pounds. Bay Bolton and Looby belonged to Charles Powlett, the 3rd Duke of Bolton. His father was among those who went to Holland and returned with the Prince of Orange in 1688. He was succeeded by his son in 1721. Both were enthusiastic supporters of the turf, but Charles, although fond of

pomp and ceremony, was obviously made of less stern stuff than his father:

> *Now Bolton comes with beat of drums*
> *Tho' fighting be his lothing,*
> *He much dislikes both pikes and guns,*
> *But relishes the clothing.*

In the early eighteenth century a man who managed or was involved with horses was described as a 'jockey', giving rise to a group of influential owners and breeders of racehorses becoming known as the Jockey Club. The members of the Club met at public and other houses in London and first properly came to light when they leased land at Newmarket to build a Coffee Room in 1752. Successive leases were taken by members of the Club whose premises soon expanded in line with the responsibilities they took upon themselves as regulators of racing on the Heath. One of their number was appointed Steward to act as the 'chairman' and provide a focus to whom disputes both at Newmarket and later from elsewhere could be brought for arbitration. The role of the Club evolved slowly since it lacked positive leadership until the young Sir Charles Bunbury was made Steward in 1768. It is possible that Bunbury is among the riders seen in an engraving by Houston after Francis Sartorious of the Marquis of Rockingham's Bay Malton beating Lord Bolingbroke's Gimcrack at Newmarket [6]. This was a Match for 1,000 Guineas held on 1 October 1765. The course in this scene is far more sophisticated than that illustrated in the race between Windham and Bay Bolton

6 *Bay Malton beating Gimcrack in a Match for 1000 Guineas at Newmarket, 1st October 1765. Mezzotint after Francis Sartorius.*

in about 1710. The later print shows two small stands and some rails to control the spectators. The latter seems a little superfluous in view of the Jockey Club's determination to keep racing at Newmarket almost exclusively for its own members' enjoyment.

In 1760 the Duke of Cumberland had resigned all his Army appointments and after a life of active soldiering, retired to his Lodge at Windsor. He was grossly overweight, asthmatic, suffering from his wounds and had quarrelled with his father shortly before the King's death in November that year. However, the very large stud that he maintained was prospering, despite his gambling debts which were always prodigious. In October 1764, against the advice of his doctor, Cumberland travelled to Newmarket to see his horse Herod run a 500 guineas match against the Duke of Grafton's Antinous (Antinous received 3 lb and was favourite but Herod won). He became ill but recovered, and continued to take part in all matters of State to help his nephew, George III, in the early years of his reign. The Duke died suddenly in October 1765. As a successful breeder and the owner of the largest string in the country (he ran twenty-four different horses in the year of his death), his involvement kept the flame of Royal interest alight. This flame was temporarily extinguished at his death until relit with enthusiasm by the Prince of Wales (George IV) when he reached his majority in 1785.

For prints of this period, see:

ANON, page 84
MORIER, David, page 141
ROBERTS, James, page 153
SARTORIUS, Francis, page 157
SEYMOUR, James, page 162

SHAW, William, page 166
SMITH, Thomas, page 167
SPENCER, Thomas, page 168
TILLEMANS, Peter, page 173
WOOTTON, John, page 185

The Earl of Godolphin's Arabian.
Stipple engraving after George Stubbs ARA.

PLATE 1

Epsom – Running.
Aquatint after
Henry Alken Snr.

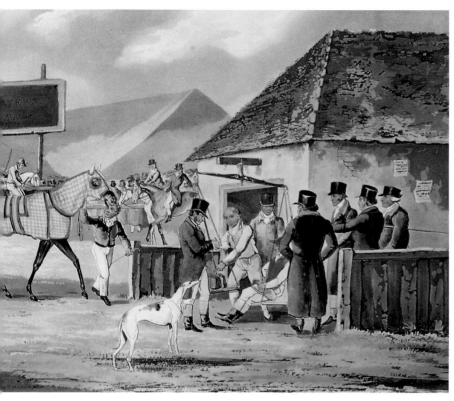

Ipswich – Weighing.
Aquatint after
Henry Alken Snr.

PLATE 2

HRH the Prince of Wales's Baronet, with Sam Chifney up. Stipple engraving after George Stubbs ARA.

PLATE 3

Lord Foley's Pumpkin, with W. South up. Stipple engraving after George Stubbs ARA.

3
'TRAINS OF RUNNING HORSES'
1765–1800

At the age of twenty-one Thomas Charles Bunbury was elected MP for Suffolk, the county he represented as a Whig for over forty years. He succeeded to the baronetcy three years later, in 1764, as Sir Charles Bunbury. His passion for racing started in his youth and his interest in breeding racehorses was in the direction of speed rather than stamina. In the early years of the eighteenth century horses did not race until they were five years old, but four-year-old racing started in the north of England in 1727 and at Newmarket in 1744. Three-year-old racing first took place on the Heath over the last two miles of the Beacon Course in 1756, necessarily a much shorter distance than races for older horses with their greater maturity and strength.

The training of racehorses, and in some cases their treatment when running, was often severe. In a number of engravings horses are shown at work well covered in blankets and rugs (their riders wear thick coats too!). This was to make them sweat profusely, a practice continued well into the nineteenth century although the leading trainer in about 1800, Robert Robson, began the trend away from such ideas. The theory was not quite so foolish as it seems as naturally the horse sweated more in slower work and must to some extent have needed less fast or long distance work. Naturally to run four-mile heats required a different training regime to that needed for racing over shorter distances. After work they were rubbed down vigorously not only to remove the sweat to prevent a chill, but to stop any stale moisture being reabsorbed into the body. Hard training and racing inevitably shortened the careers of many horses. An exception was that of the iron-grey Gimcrack who did not retire to stud until he was twelve years old. This little horse was exceptionally courageous and tough (he twice revenged his defeat by Bay Malton in the Match for 1,000 Guineas at Newmarket in 1765), winning twenty-six of the thirty-six races in which he ran. He

was owned for a time by Sir Charles Bunbury who appreciated his speed and resolution, two characteristics which more than compensated for his lack of size. As well as Francis Sartorius, George Stubbs sympathetically portrayed Gimcrack for the *Turf Review* when the horse was at the stud of Earl Grosvenor.

Racehorses which performed less well or failed at stud were employed in one way or another until the end of their days. The 'Life of a Racehorse' is the theme for a number of sets of engravings. Six early aquatints by Francis Jukes apparently after Charles Ansell but painted by Thomas Gooch in 1783 were published in 1784. They include the plates: 'As a Foal'; 'As a Colt in Training'; 'As a Racer after Running' [7]; and 'As a Hunter going out with Hounds'. Identical ovals, on this occasion correctly shown as after Gooch, were published in 1790 with similar titles as well as 'As a Post Horse' and 'His Dissolution!' The year before, four aquatints titled 'The High Mettled Racer', with verses, engraved by John Hassell after Thomas Rowlandson were published by S. W. Fores. They are of 'The Racehorse', 'The Hunter', 'The Hack', and 'The Cart-horse'. Other series in the same vein followed among which the final plate in Henry Alken Snr's 'Seven Ages of the Horse' is the most grisly. It shows an emaciated corpse being carried away to the knacker on a farm cart!

By 1770 racing was taking place at more than a hundred meetings across the country. Some were badly organised and poorly attended, but where a city or town corporation offered the use of land and sometimes provided money for prizes and trophies, owners and locally appointed stewards organised well conducted meetings. This was often the case in the north of England, particularly in Yorkshire where there was great enthusiasm for the sport. Racing was established at York many years before that at Doncaster but, by the 1750s, meetings on nearby Cantley Common had

7 *Life of a Racehorse. As a Racer after Running. Aquatint after Charles Ansell.*

become well known features of the summer calendar. The first Doncaster Gold Cup (value £80) was run on 25 September 1766. It was a race of four-mile heats using a weight for age scale of 7 st 10 lb for five-year-olds; 8 st 7 lb for six-year-olds; and 9 st for Aged (seven years or older). Of only four runners, Charlotte, a six-year-old chestnut mare belonging to Lord Hamilton, was fourth in the first heat, winning the two following. Ten years later General Anthony St Leger of Park Hill proposed a Sweepstake of Twenty-five Guineas each for three-year-olds over two miles at the autumn Doncaster meeting. There were six subscribers of whom five ran; colts were required to carry 8 st and fillies 7 st 12 lb. Lord Rockingham's brown filly by Sampson won; she may have been named Alabaculia at a later date. This was the first occasion that three-year-olds ran at Doncaster. The race was repeated in 1777, and the following year moved from the Common to Doncaster Town Moor, the present site of the racecourse. Shortly before the 1778 meeting, the Marquis of Rockingham (then out of Office; he was Prime Minister 1765–1766 and again in 1782) proposed at a dinner attended by St Leger that the General's name should be given to the race. The fame of the Great St Leger Stakes as the last of the classic engagements in the calendar for three-year-olds did

not materialise until many years later. This may account for only a handful of the early winners being portrayed by artists of note.

Highflyer was bred by Sir Charles Bunbury in 1774. The colt was by Herod out of a mare named Rachel by Blank. This parentage included the blood of the Byerley Turk, the Darley Arabian and the Godolphin Arabian which augered well for his prowess as both a racehorse and stallion. Bunbury sold Highflyer to Lord Bolingbroke before his first race in 1777; his Lordship sold him on to Mr Richard Tattersall. The young Tattersall came up to London from Yorkshire in 1745 and worked initially at Beevor's Horse Repository in St Martin's Lane. Within eleven years, Tattersall had sufficient capital to bring into being a long dreamt of ambition to establish a centre for selling horses by auction in London. He obtained from Earl Grosvenor a long lease on a plot of land at Hyde Park Corner, and there established first a stables and, later, kennels and stands for his twice weekly sales of horses, hounds and carriages. 'The Corner' as it was known became a fashionable meeting place and a room was provided where Members of the Jockey Club could dine. When Tattersall bought Highflyer [8] the horse had already won a considerable sum in stakes, but his new owner was more interested in breeding than racing. At stud, Richard Tattersall discovered that his stallion's progeny out of Eclipse mares were nearly all successful; he sold much stock young before they were raced, making a great deal of money in the process. Becoming extremely fond of the horse, he named the house he built near Ely Highflyer Hall. When the stallion died aged nineteen, Tattersall placed the following memorial over his grave:

Here lieth the perfect and beautiful symmetry of the much lamented Highflyer, by whom and his wonderful offspring the celebrated Tattersall acquired a noble fortune but was not ashamed to acknowledge it.

Sawrey Gilpin painted a portrait of Highflyer which was aquatinted by Francis Jukes and published by the artist from his house in Knightsbridge in 1788. Another painting of the stallion, by Benjamin Killingbeck, was engraved in mezzotint and published by Laurie & Whittle in 1794. Richard Tattersall died the following year, his successful business and the Highflyer line being passed to his son Edmund.

There were regular spring and summer meetings at Epsom after 1730. Being close to London, visitors found the Downs easy to travel to with the added advantage of sampling the Spa waters and salts, although this aspect of the town's attraction was beginning to decline. In 1773 the young and recently married 12th Earl of Derby took over the lease of a house named The Oaks close to Epsom. Like Bunbury, he was extremely fond of racing, but enjoyed cock fighting even more. Derby was a Steward at Epsom where the early summer meeting comprised races run in heats over two or four miles. In 1778 the Earl and his friends who stayed with him at The Oaks during this week of racing, decided to introduce the following year a race for three-year-old fillies run over a mile and a half – they called it the Oaks Stakes. There were seventeen subscribers and twelve started in the first Oaks in 1779, won appropriately by the favourite, Lord Derby's Bridget. Those staying at The Oaks that year included Sir Charles Bunbury, by now the accepted authority on racing and an almost permanent senior Steward of the Jockey Club. In 1770 the number of Stewards of the Club had been increased to three. Each served for three years and in their final year became Senior Steward, an arrangement continued until the Club received its Royal Charter in 1970.

8 *Highflyer, bred by Lord Bolingbroke. Aquatint after James Barenger.*

Nowadays there are six Stewards and the Senior Steward serves for four years. Due partly to the success of the first Oaks, Bunbury and Lord Derby proposed that a new race open to colts and fillies should be run on the Downs over the distance of one mile in 1780. Again Fortune smiled on one of the promoters, since Sir Charles Bunbury's Diomed, ridden by Sam Arnull, won the first running in a field of nine. The following year The Derby, as the race was named, was won by the Irishman Major Denis O'Kelly's Young Eclipse. The Colonel (as he became) found the winner again in 1784 with Serjeant (also a son of Eclipse) when the course was lengthened to a mile and a half. Lord Derby first won the race in 1787 with Sir Peter Teazle whose sire, Highflyer, provided, like Eclipse, three winners of the race. The importance of the Derby and the Oaks in their own right as well as being valuable indicators of the performance of young horses in betting terms was quickly realised. A further thirty years were to elapse before the 'preparatory' races, the Two Thousand and One Thousand Guineas, were established at Newmarket to complete the five classic three-year-old tests in the calendar.

King George III had little interest in racing and was horrified by its extravagance, particularly that of gambling. His plain, straightforward outlook on life and morals could hardly have been more different to that of his son, the Prince of Wales. Even before reaching his majority, the Prince was heavily involved in the turf. He had a string of racehorses in training at Newmarket, many of them sired by Eclipse, bred by his great uncle the late Duke of Cumberland. In 1788, Sir Thomas, ridden by William South, was the first horse to win the Derby in the royal colours. This joyous occasion was shortlived for the extravagant and flamboyant Prince was deeply in debt and temporarily gave up the turf. A reluctant Parliament came to his rescue and in 1790 he resumed racing on an even more lavish scale than before, but this second burst of activity was also brief.

Despite the King's general aversion to racing, it was in his reign that Ascot, so conveniently close to Windsor Castle, began to rival Epsom and Newmarket in attracting the largest crowds and the best horses. At the end of the century George III gave permission to a Mr Slingsby to erect a stand on the course to house the remarkable number of 1,600 spectators. Another royal connection was that with Frederick, Duke of York, the younger brother of the Prince of Wales, who bought a house near Ascot, Oatlands Park. Frederick gave the Park's name to an extremely valuable handicap race, the Oatlands Stakes. The first running was on 28 June 1791 in the presence of the King. There were forty-one subscribers of 100 guineas each. A number of these declared quarter or half forfeit dependent upon when they scratched. The actual stakes, with nineteen starters, were 2,950 guineas. The Derby had been worth 1,600 guineas six weeks before. The Prince of Wales's Baronet ridden by Sam Chifney won the two-mile race; Express was second and the gambler 'Cripplegate' Barrymore's Chanticleer, third. To the King's consternation (or perhaps envy) the Prince won more than £17,000 on the result. The finish was painted by Francis Sartorius's son, John Nost Sartorius, and a year later an aquatint of the scene was published, engraved by John William Edy [9]. The plate shows four racehorses approaching the judge's box with carriages beyond the far rails and a few mounted and foot spectators in the foreground. During these years there are other prints of racehorses and racing after the work of J. N. Sartorius of which a pair: 'Traveller beating Meteor' and 'Grey Diomed beating Traveller' are particularly fine. In spite of their naivety from today's viewpoint, they give a good feeling of excitement and speed showing the two racehorses at full stretch. Engravings after portraits by this Sartorius are surprisingly stiff, although the conformation of the horses may be accurately depicted.

'A View of the Noblemen's and Gentlemen's Trains of Running Horses taking Their Exercise up Warren Hill, east of Newmarket' [10] is an outstanding plate containing line, stipple and aquatint engraving by Joseph Collyer. It is an extensive landscape seen from Warren Hill which overlooks the little town with Ely Cathedral on the horizon. The Heath is thick with 'trains of running horses' and in the foreground the gathering of noblemen and gentlemen form a pyramidal group topped by the Prince of Wales standing in a phaeton drawn by six greys. The painter of the whole scene is not known but the figures are by Edward Francis Burney. The plate was published by John Bodger of Stilton, Huntingdonshire on 4 June 1791 and sold by him and by Mr Weatherby, the proprietor of the Racing Calendar.

That autumn the results of two minor races on consecutive days at Newmarket led to the Prince of Wales's second temporary retirement from the turf, occasioned by suspicions of dishonesty rather than by overreaching himself financially. Starting at 2 to 1 on, the Prince's horse Escape finished last in a two-mile race against Coriander, Skylark and Pipator on 20

9 (above) Ascot, Oatlands Stakes, 28th June 1791. Aquatint after John Nost Sartorius.

10 (below) A view of the Noblemen's and Gentlemen's Trains of Running Horses taking Their Exercise up Warren Hill, east of Newmarket. Line, stipple and aquatint. The figures after Edward Francis Burney.

October. On the 21st, at 5 to 1 against, Chifney and Escape won a four-mile race from a field of six in which Skylark, the only other runner in both races, came third. The suggestion that the jockey had pulled Escape in the first race together with a rumour that the Prince of Wales had won a great pot on the second persuaded the Stewards to call for an explanation from Chifney. Sam told Sir Charles Bunbury, Thomas Panton and Mr Ralph Dutton that Escape was short of work on the first day and needed the four miles of the second race to show his true form. The Stewards did not accept this story and Bunbury told the Prince that unless he changed his jockey, no gentleman would run a horse against him in the future. To his considerable credit the Prince stood by Chifney, gave up racing and sold all his horses at Tattersalls. Twelve years later, the Jockey Club re-examined the matter and concluded they had been harsh. Perhaps motivated more than anything else by the desire to see the Prince of Wales back on the Heath, they expressed their regret to His Royal Highness who thanked them for their thoughtfulness, but did not return to Newmarket. The scandal had done little for the name of the sport, being just the kind of incident at which those who disliked the turf could wag their fingers while claiming that racing was riddled with scoundrels.

It may have been from a similar stance that Sir William Newcomen demanded that the northern owner Sir Charles Turner give up running his thoroughbreds when he married Newcomen's daughter. Sir Charles was then at the height of his turf success having won the 1795 St Leger and Doncaster Cup with Hambletonian, and all the other races bar one at the Town Moor meeting that year. He sold Hambletonian (a grandson of Eclipse) to Sir Henry Vane Tempest (sometimes Tempest Vane), his neighbour and a leading North country extrovert and owner, for whom the horse again won the Doncaster Cup in 1796. Two and a half years later, not having run at all in 1798, Hambletonian met Mr James Cookson's Diamond in a Match at Newmarket for 3,000 guineas. Diamond had been sold a few years previously to Cookson by Vane Tempest, and the Match proved to be 'the greatest ever since that between Old Merlin and Mr Frampton's horse nearly a century before'. Both were six-year-olds and the Match was run over the Beacon Course, a distance of four miles and one furlong with only one bend. Frank Buckle was riding Hambletonian at 8 st 3 lb and Denis Fitzpatrick rode Diamond at 8 st. The crowd on the Heath on 25 March 1799 was immense. Large sums were wagered on the result for which Hambletonian stood at 5 to 4 on. The second half of the race was run very fast and both jockeys punished their mounts with spur and whip. Contemporary paintings show Hambletonian winning by a short neck. Sir Henry enjoyed the acclaim of the crowd as he rode Hambletonian in Hyde Park a few days later, while Frank Buckle and another famous jockey, William Clift, measured the colt's strides in the last mile of the course, finding them to be a remarkable and consistent eight yards. This is well suggested in the various 'rocking horse' paintings of the scene. No less than four pairs of engravings of Hambletonian and Diamond were published after the work of J. N. Sartorius between 21 August 1799 and 1 March 1800 [11]. Those of the Match in progress adopt the usual formula of the race being followed by mounted owners and their friends, shouting encouragement and passing comments among themselves. Stands, rails and groups of spectators form the backdrop.

Vane Tempest commissioned George Stubbs to paint a small picture of the Match and, more importantly, a large portrait of Hambletonian. The latter is a lifesize study (exhibited at the Royal Academy in 1800) of this brilliant racehorse after running. His ears are back as he is rubbed down by a stableboy; a groom holds his head. As in many of Stubbs's paintings the humblest servants are portrayed 'facing the camera' and, in this case, with the lad peering out from underneath the horse's neck. The activity around Hambletonian's head is neatly balanced by the irritated kicking of his off hind leg. The canvas is obviously big, although a larger one would have given a better proportion to the picture, and the fee asked for so much work on a large scale led to owner and artist falling out. Stubbs had to take Vane Tempest to court to obtain his £300. The smaller picture has never come to light and may not have been painted; only a preparatory drawing exists. Vane Tempest hoped that both paintings would be engraved so that public demand for a memento of his horse and the Match could be satisfied but this hope was not realised. Hambletonian continued to run until 1801 before going to stud. He died in 1818, outliving his owner by five years. A painting of Diamond with Denis Fitzpatrick up by Ben Marshall was also exhibited at the Academy in 1800. A mezzotint of this portrait was published by Thomas Palser in 1811, showing how great was the interest in this match, perhaps the most remarkable prior to the meeting of Voltigeur and The Flying Dutchman some fifty years later.

If the *Turf Review* had been successful and con-

11 *Sir Henry Tempest Vane's Hambletonian Preparing to Start against Mr Cookson's Diamond over the Beacon Course at Newmarket, 25th March 1799. Stipple engraving after John Nost Sartorius.*

tinued after the year when the engravings were first advertised, there is little doubt that Hambletonian would have been among the horses portrayed by Stubbs. Also, if the *Review* had progressed beyond the fourteen stipple engravings published in 1794 and 1796, we would now have a better record 'of every horse of note that started from the year 1750 to the present time'. Stubbs's fortunes were at a low point when he conceived the idea of portraying all the important thoroughbreds of his painting lifetime, and some of the matches and sweepstakes in which they took part. They were to be engraved by his son George Townley Stubbs and published in large and small sizes with the earliest subscribers receiving the best impressions. In advertising this undertaking, Stubbs wrote:

As such an history of an animal peculiar to this country, the horse surely may put its claim to general notice; and although numerous volumes of Cheney and Heber, downwards, may give critical knowledge to the diligent and deep explorer, they certainly do not impart sufficient information to a superficial observer; yet both may regret

that there is not a regular series of paintings and engravings of these horses, with their histories, which have been, or are now, famous .

It is therefore proposed to publish, by subscription, A Review of the Turf.

The amount of information given about the horses portrayed is much less than one might have expected from this advertisement. Sixteen horses were painted: The Godolphin Arabian; Marske [*12*]; Eclipse; Dungannon; Volunteer [*13*]; Gimcrack; Mambrino; Sweetbrier; Sweetwilliam; Protector; Shark; Baronet; Pumpkin; Bandy; Anvil; and Gnawpost with two colts. Fourteen were engraved in small size (Bandy and Gnawpost were omitted) and thirteen large, leaving out the Godolphin Arabian. Some were printed in colour. The plates were published in 'numbers', each costing two guineas and comprising three prints. The small engraving of the Godolphin Arabian was 'presented to subscribers gratis, as a frontispiece to the work'. This plate and the first number were published in February 1794; the next two numbers in May and

12 *The Earl of Abingdon's Marske. Stipple engraving after George Stubbs.*

13 *Colonel O'Kelly's Volunteer. Stipple engraving after George Stubbs.*

December that year; Sweetwilliam was published in July 1796 and the last number, Eclipse, Gimcrack and Marske, on 1 September 1796. Excepting Baronet [*Plate 3*] and Pumpkin [*Plate 3*], the engravings are of the horses in landscapes, sometimes with a groom. Sam Chifney in the royal colours has Baronet at full gallop with characteristically slack rein, and William South is shown on Pumpkin. Sadly the project failed; among the reasons for this were that Stubbs had many critics at this time, and worries about the war in France resulted in there being far fewer subscribers than expected.

The end of the century saw the turf well established with its patrons and a large public following, despite the difficulties of the era and the strictures of those who disapproved of racing. Artists were in demand to paint both human and equine portraits, in many cases the activities of their horses being the reason for the transient fame of the owners. Engravers successfully adapted stippling and mezzotinting to give the light and shadow of the rippling shoulders of racehorses and the distant views of Newmarket or Epsom Downs. The slightly simpler skill of aquatinting, producing a variable ground with less detail, was becoming more popular among publishers who were looking for an effective but less expensive and time-consuming way of reproducing paintings and some sporting water-colours. Jukes, Edy and Hassell were early exponents of aquatinting, a method by which the majority of sporting prints were soon to be engraved.

For prints of this period, see:

4
THE OLD ORDER CHANGES
1800–1840

It is difficult to discover precisely when the term 'classic' was first applied to the Derby, Oaks and St Leger, and subsequently to the one mile races at Newmarket: the 2,000 Guineas (started in 1809) and the 1,000 Guineas for fillies (1814). However, by 1800 the racing of three-year-olds was well established and the first three classics mentioned acknowledged as their main testing grounds.

During the last twenty years of the previous century just under half of the forty or so southern classic races, the Derby and Oaks, were won by horses belonging to three owners: the Duke of Bedford (six); Earl Grosvenor (eight); and the Earl of Egremont (four). In this period the Duke of Bedford only ran one horse in a St Leger and Earl Grosvenor, three. None were successful. Between 1800 and 1837, of the 130 southern classics, again almost half fell to a handful of owners: the 3rd Duke of Grafton (five); the 4th Duke of Grafton (twenty); the Earl of Egremont (five) and his son (one); the 2nd Earl Grosvenor (two); his cousin, General Grosvenor (two); Lord Jersey (eleven); and Lord Exeter (seven). These powerful noblemen had only one success in the St Leger which was that of the then Marquis of Westminster's (2nd Earl Grosvenor's) Touchstone in 1834, who was in any case trained at Malton in Yorkshire. Lord Hamilton, later the 9th Duke of Hamilton, whose Charlotte had won the first Doncaster Cup in 1766, was prominent in the northern racing circuit until his death in 1819. His horses won the St Leger on seven occasions between 1786 and 1814. The Hon. Edward Petre won four St Legers in the period of forty years covered by this chapter as did Squire Watt of Bishop Burton.

These statistics show how much racing was dominated by a relatively small band of grandees, of whom the Dukes of Grafton were perhaps the greatest ornaments of the turf among 'the old order'. Combined with enthusiasm, their straightforward and open ways endeared the 3rd and 4th Dukes to all. They proved that races could be won fairly at a time when dishonesty was increasingly rife and rarely tackled. The father of that kind, courteous politician Augustus Henry Fitzroy, 3rd Duke of Grafton, a great-great grandson of Charles II, died young. Augustus Henry's education, and that of his brother, the future Lord Southampton, was directed by their grandfather, the 2nd Duke. The 2nd Duke's interests were in the hunting field which he only quit after a bad fall at the age of seventy-two in 1755, dying two years later. The 3rd Duke left Peterhouse, Cambridge in 1753 and after a grand tour of Europe became MP for Bury St Edmunds before succeeding to the title in 1757. In the 1760s he was preoccupied with politics, leading the 'Young Whigs' and then becoming Secretary of State in the Administration of his fellow turfite the Marquis of Rockingham. He was made First Lord of the Treasury under the elder Pitt before succeeding him as Prime Minister in December 1767, holding Office until 1770. Notwithstanding these duties, Grafton's passion for racing grew and the foundation of his later achievements was laid when he bought a mare named Julia, bred by Thomas Panton, for his Euston Hall Stud. His stable at Newmarket was managed by John Westall, a friend from his days at Cambridge. As already mentioned, his trainer, Robert Robson, was the first of his profession to stop sweating his horses in long gallops under heavy sheets, pursuing a more enlightened regime. Although the Duke's horses won many races, the classics eluded him until 1802 when his Tyrant, ridden by Frank Buckle, won the Derby. Clift rode his winners of the Oaks in 1804 (Pelisse) and 1808 (Morel). Goodisson was up on Pope to win the 1809 Derby and the following year Clift was again in the saddle at Epsom, winning with Whalebone. The 3rd Duke died in March 1811. Much of his success was based on his excellent personal judgement of horses, and of his stable staff in whom he took a close and friendly interest whatever their position. These

14 *Christopher Wilson Esq's Champion. Derby & St Leger 1800. Mezzotint after John Nost Sartorius.*

triumphs were all the more remarkable since his stud was never very large.

The 4th Duke, George Henry Fitzroy, the eldest of the 3rd Duke's sixteen legitimate children, had all the attributes of a Parliamentarian, was MP for Cambridge from 1784 to 1811, but had no great liking for politics. Inheriting his father's interest in the turf, he devoted all his energy to it. Westall, the Grafton manager, died in December 1811. His place was taken by the Duke's half-brother, the Reverend Lord Henry Fitzroy; Robson remained the trainer. Within a few years the stables began to provide an even longer string of winners, with fillies predominating. Whisker won the Derby in 1815 when the Duke had only nine horses in training (winning twenty-six races). The 2,000 Guineas fell to the Duke on five occasions: 1820–1822; 1826 and 1827; and the 1,000 Guineas every year from 1819 to 1827, except 1824 when Rebecca was second. The Duke's fillies also won the Oaks in 1813, 1815, 1822, 1823, 1828 and 1831. The Reverend Lord Henry died in 1823 and Robert Robson retired five years later. The 4th Duke's enjoyment of racing diminished and at the time of his death in 1844 he had very few of his horses in training at Newmarket. Perhaps this was as well since his son, the 5th Duke, took no interest in racing at all.

It appears that the Dukes of Grafton did not enter a single horse for the St Leger, demonstrating the gap which existed between the north and the south of the country. One of the first to bridge this gap was Mr Christopher Wilson whose integrity and honesty were such that his advice in racing matters was often sought, and his judgement as an arbiter accepted without question. Later in life this son of a Bishop was considered to be the 'Father of the Turf' in succession to the more active Bunbury. Reaching his majority in 1785, he rarely missed a meeting at Newmarket, Epsom, Ascot, Doncaster or York, the last course being near his home, Oxton Hall, Tadcaster. Wilson did not keep many horses in training but raced the first colt to achieve the double of winning the Derby and St Leger in 1800. The horse was Champion, by Pot-8-Os out of Huncamunca. Champion was portrayed with his trainer by J. N. Sartorius and this painting was published as a very fine mezzotint in 1802 [*14*]. A further distinction came in his winning the first 2,000 Guineas at Newmarket with Wizard (who was just beaten in the Derby by the Duke of Grafton's Pope), and the first 1,000 Guineas with another Charlotte five years later.

Newmarket-trained horses seldom ran at York or Doncaster and only the very good northern horses came south, staying for long periods and sometimes for the remainder of their racing careers before returning north to stud. When a horse was to race any distance from home, it walked, sometimes taking two or three days about it. An often quoted exception was that of Lord George Bentinck's Elis. The horse, fancied for the 1836 Doncaster St Leger (entered in the name of Lord Lichfield) was still in his stable at Goodwood four days before the race. The distance between the two sites being too far to walk in time, Bentinck obtained 12 to 1 at the last moment against Elis winning. He had already borrowed from Lord Chesterfield a large cattle waggon pulled by six horses and converted it for his purposes. Putting the colt and a companion in its padded interior, they arrived at Doncaster the evening before the race, quite fresh. The horse won by two lengths from the favourite, the locally owned and trained Scroggins, and Lord George went home with a very long wallet. Some thought this rather dubious practice. It was, however, understandable at a time when the much wider field of owners entering racing, without the apparently limitless means of some of the earlier noblemen, depended upon gambling success to cover the costs of keeping their horses in training.

When the Prince of Wales left Newmarket in high dudgeon in 1791 the loss to this Heath was Ascot's gain. While drastically reducing his racing activities he still had more than one hundred winners between 1800 and 1807. The first Gold Cup was run for at Ascot in the latter year which also marked the death of the Prince's old jockey, Sam Chifney Snr in a debtor's prison. With more loyalty to Chifney's memory than he showed to many of his living friends, the Prince had already engaged Sam Snr's eldest son William as his trainer, and the younger son, another and scarcely less brilliant Sam, became his principal jockey. When he succeeded as King George IV his support of Ascot ensured its growing popularity. In 1822 a stand was erected for the use of the Royal Family, and three years later the King instituted the semi-state Royal Procession by being driven in an open carriage up the New Mile. The cavalcade was preceded by the Master of the Buckhounds who was the Steward of the meeting. At much the same period a Royal Enclosure was laid out to which the Sovereign invited his friends; an arrangement which continues today in a much modified form. The large field for the Gold Cup in 1829 included the previous year's winner, two Derby, an Oaks and a St Leger winner. The race was won by Lord Chesterfield's Zinganee, recently bought in competition with the King from the Chifneys and loyally given up to His Majesty after the race. The second horse was Lord Jersey's Mameluke (Derby, 1827) beaten by a length. A year later the picture was a very

15 *HRH the Duke of York's Moses. Lithograph by and after James Ward* RA.

different one with only four horses starting, due to George IV barring 'common fellows' (not members of the Jockey Club, Brook's or White's) from entering their horses. It also poured with rain and the King was terminally ill.

The closeness of Ascot Heath to Windsor no doubt added to its attraction, particularly among the less eager Royal racegoers. One who did not lack enthusiasm was the Duke of York whose Pointers won the first running of the Wokingham Stakes, in 1813. The Duke's profligacy on the turf rivalled that of his older brother, but he had two winners of the Derby to show for it: Prince Leopold in 1816 and Moses [15] in 1822. His death in 1827 and that of the King on 26 June three years later removed within a short space of time the kind of patronage on which the turf thrived, but on which it was beginning not to have to depend.

With the same conditions as those laid down by the late King, the first Ascot Gold Cup of William IV's reign boasted only two runners! The following year the race was again opened to all owners. The 'Sailor' King's knowledge of the turf was limited to say the least, but he thought that racing had its place as a vehicle for maintaining social intercourse between himself and his subjects. That he was not entirely correct in this hope can be gathered from the diary of the Hon. Charles Greville, Clerk to the Council and inveterate racehorse owner and also manager for others. He describes the King's attendance with typical acerbity:

> with great cortege, eight coaches and four and other carriages. The reception was strikingly cold and indifferent. William was bored to death with the races, and his own horse broke down.

However, showing considerable concern over the low state into which racing at Ascot quickly fell in the early 1830s, the King set about improving the management of the June meeting, first by limiting the responsibilities of the Master of the Royal Buckhounds to those which he understood, and secondly by inviting the Stewards of the Jockey Club to take over all racing matters. This also led to a rapprochement between Royalty and Newmarket, not that William ever visited the small Cambridgeshire town or its heath. The course at Ascot was also improved, new turf put down and plans for another stand considered. Part of the motivation for all this activity was to counter the increasing attraction of racing at Goodwood which was outshining Ascot in its popular and fashionable appeal.

A new course had been laid out in 1801 at Goodwood by the 3rd Duke of Richmond, then aged sixty-six.

The Duke was a contemporary of the 3rd Duke of Grafton with whom he shared a similar life of Court, Parliament and, in his later years, the turf. As Lord March he had ridden his horse Wiggem and been defeated in a Match by Grafton on Driver. In April 1802 racing took place for three days in Goodwood park. The majority of the events were for hunters, organised for the benefit of the Duke's friends. The highlight of the third day, however, was a Match for 100 guineas between the Prince of Wales's Rebel and the Duke's Cedar, which Rebel won. When the 3rd Duke of Richmond died in December 1806, racing at Goodwood temporarily lapsed into the doldrums as a nephew of the Duke succeeded to the title who took little interest in the turf. Thirteen years later the 4th Duke died of rabies in Canada, probably as a result of a bite from his pet fox! His son came from much the same mould as his great-uncle but had been far too busy as ADC and Assistant Military Secretary to the Duke of Wellington in the Peninsular War and later at Waterloo to be able to give much time to reviving Goodwood's fortunes.

The first Goodwood Gold Cup was run in 1812, but there was no race in 1815 or between 1817 and 1824. In this last year there started a long alliance between Lord George Bentinck, a younger son of the Duke of Portland, and the Duke of Richmond. This association was enhanced in part for Bentinck by his falling madly but discreetly in love with the Duchess, an ardour not returned. With the full approval of the good natured Duke, Lord George began revitalising Goodwood with his characteristic zeal and energy, attracting society, owners and the best horses to the annual July meetings on this beautiful course. By 1830 there were no more hunt races. In that year the King's Fleur-de-Lis [16] won the Gold Cup for the second time running, beating two other horses inherited from his brother: Zinganee and The Colonel. In 1835 Elis (nominally Charles Greville's but in reality Bentinck's) won the Molecomb Stakes for two-year-olds, and Mr Theobald's Rockingham won the Cup. The Duke and Bentinck, the Marquis of Tavistock, Lords Chesterfield, Eglinton, Egremont, Exeter, Jersey and Uxbridge, Colonel Peel, Greville and a few other gentlemen ran their horses at Goodwood at this time. There was also a different group who could not really be described as Richmond's 'friends'. These included the difficult Mr Gratwicke (in fact a racing confederate of the 5th Duke until they disagreed and parted) and John Gully, the ex-prize fighter, who both won two Derbys. There were also the trainer-owners: the

16 *Sir M. W. Ridley's
Fleur-de-Lis. Mezzotint
after Abraham Cooper*
RA.

17 *The Duke of
Beaufort's Lop.
Stipple engraving
after Ben Marshall.*

[38]

Chifneys and Days. The next ten years saw the apogee of racing at Goodwood, largely at Ascot's expense.

The increasing regularity with which meetings began to produce cards with annual events led to a procedure for entering horses far in advance of the day they were due to run. Although the breeding of a colt or filly counted for much in its expected performance, a real idea of the animal's potential did not become clear until it ran in trials, usually involving older horses whose position in the equine hierarchy was sufficiently closely defined to enable carefully devised weights to show the precise quality of the younger horses. Trainers then told the owners of their hopes or fears for each animal in their charge and decisions were taken on whether or not to enter a horse for classics a year or more later. The general rule was, if in doubt, enter; the horse could always be withdrawn later, albeit after paying the due forfeit. Once nominated, the public wanted to know how good the horse was and compare him or her with others also entered. The trials were kept secret as far as this was possible but touts, known euphemistically as 'gentlemen of observation', hid in ditches and hedges to discover each horse's form. The trainers in turn often resorted to subterfuge to conceal the true quality of a horse so that they could obtain long odds on what might appear to those not in the know to be only a moderate animal. The aim of all these ploys and counter-ploys was to achieve the largest gambling coup possible.

While in the past owners usually arranged wagers directly with each other on a Match or race in which their horses were running, the time had now arrived when it was necessary to back other people's animals to provide sufficient 'income' to maintain a stable. Touts were used to gather information and commission agents were employed to obtain the best odds they could. In time some of these agents started books of their own, quoting odds for anyone who wished to place a bet; others progressed to becoming racehorse owners. These bookmakers and owners were from a very different background to those who made private wagers in earlier days.

Gamblers, among them some of the less scrupulous owners (including even the nobility), a sprinkling of trainers, and jockeys who in those days were allowed to bet on races in which they took part, soon devised ways of 'making the opposition safe'. This was by a variety of corrupt means ranging from coercion and bribery to, most lamentable of all, tampering with horses by physical mutilation or drugs. By the 1830s

such skullduggery was widespread and no-one seemed to know what to do about it. Fortunately Lord George Bentinck, later nicknamed the Dictator of the Turf, whom one could also call poacher turned gamekeeper, exercised his considerable power and standing to bring in measures which attempted to eradicate some of the worst on-course malpractices. He made many enemies in doing so and was only partly successful. The impecunious Charles Greville sums up the situation in an 1837 diary entry: 'my life is spent in the alternatives of excitement from the amusement and speculation of the turf and of remorse and shame at the pursuit itself.'

The first decade of the century saw a lull in the quantity of racing prints published due, perhaps, to the financial difficulties and uncertainties resulting from the war with France. Ben Marshall was portraying racehorses at Newmarket of which a few were published by himself and W. & G. Cooke of Pentonville, London. Others, stipple engraved by John Whessell, were published by J. Harris of Sweetings Alley near the Royal Exchange. These included Lop [*17*], belonging to the Duke of Beaufort, and Oscar, bred by Mr Turner; both are fine examples of the engraver's art. In 1809, John Lawrence brought out *The History and Delineation of the Horse*, with numerous illustrations engraved by John Scott. Among the racehorses depicted are 'Sir Charles Bunbury's Celebrated Mare Eleanor' by Marshall; J. N. Sartorius's Eclipse and Shakespeare, King Herod and Flying Childers; Stubbs's Godolphin Arabian; and Sawrey Gilpin's Jupiter, the property of Lieutenant Colonel Thornton. Each one adds substance to the record of racing in this period.

In a more active vein, the engraver Charles Turner cooperated with the Swiss, Jacques-Laurent Agasse who settled in England in 1800, to publish two sets of racing scenes. The first to appear, in 1803, were 'Preparing to Start' [*32, see page 72*] and 'Coming In', views of Port Meadow, Oxford where Lord Francis Spencer arranged a private meeting in August 1802. The second set, published four years later, may be of a more public meeting at Brighton, and certainly has something in common in their style with aquatints of racing after Thomas Rowlandson, a frequenter of the Regency resort. 'After Running' [*18*] shows an exhausted horse beside the scales on which his jockey is being weighed in. Gentlemen on horseback review their betting books as they wait for the next event. This set of four plates also provides an insight into some of the other activities which took place at race meet-

18 *(above) After Running. Aquatint after Jacques-Laurent Agasse.*

19 *(below) Panoramic View of British Horse Racing, the Race for the St Leger Stakes of 1812 on Doncaster Course. Aquatint after Clifton Tomson.*

ings, including 'Roulette in a Tent'.

One of the first records of a 'classic' is the engraving of 'The Race for the St Leger Stakes, 1812' after the painting by the Nottingham artist, Clifton Tomson. The names of the horses, jockeys and owners taking part are given below this panoramic view of the whole field approaching the finish at Doncaster. The print [*19*], published by Edward Orme of Bond Street,

London in 1815, was followed by a long line of later 'finishes', although usually of a more manageable size than Orme's double copper plate 140 cm wide. In 1818 and 1819 Robert Pollard published three racing scenes: 'Epsom Races', 'Ascot Heath Races' [*20*]; and 'Newmarket Races'; each is painted and engraved by his son James Pollard, known better for his coaching pictures and prints. Pollard Snr was the first to publish a series of uniformly designed portraits of classic winners running sporadically from the Derby in 1819, the Duke of Portland's Tiresias ridden by Clift, to the St Leger, 1827, the Hon. E. Petre's Matilda, J. Robinson up. They too are engraved by James Pollard, after his own oils and watercolours. These aquatints do not compare in their fineness with the mezzotints and stippled plates of earlier engravers but, despite their naivety, still show an advance over the eighteenth century line engravings after Tillemans, Wootton or Seymour.

W. Sheardown, the proprietor of the *Doncaster Gazette*, commissioned J. F. Herring Snr to portray the winners of the St Leger starting from 1815. The Duke of York and other noblemen gave their patronage to this enterprise. The 1815 winner was Filho da Puta [*21*], the name loosely interprets from the Portuguese as Son of a Bitch! Some of the early portraits must have been painted retrospectively and the first eleven plates were published in 1825. The 1826 winner, Tarrare, was taken from a painting by the north country artist David Dalby, when it is possible that Herring parted company with Sheardown. The possibility that the publisher may have been in difficulties is reinforced

by the fact that S. & J. Fuller of London bought the Sheardown plates in 1827 and, again employing Herring, continued the series, including his own painting of Tarrare for 1826. The portraits, showing jockeys up (except for Antonio, St Leger, 1819, shown in a stable yard [*Plate 4*]) with the owners and trainers in some, ran until 1845 with the last five engravings after paintings by Spalding (1841) and Harry Hall (1842–1845). Messrs Fuller also published a companion series of Derby winners from 1827 to 1846 after Herring, except for 1842 when Colonel Anson's Attila was painted by Abraham Cooper, and the winners from 1843 to 1846 by Hall. The 'Sheardown' plates were engraved by Thomas Sutherland, an outstanding aquatint engraver. The Fuller plates were by the almost equally skilful Richard Gilson Reeve until 1831 when Charles Hunt became the publisher's principal engraver. These three craftsmen, particularly the first two, were outstanding exponents of the aquatint method and these series of plates are the finest ever made of racehorse portraits.

When Queen Victoria ascended the throne the old order had changed. Racing ceased to be dominated by the aristocracy (not that they were very effective in its

20 *Ascot Heath Races. Aquatint after James Pollard.*

21 *Sir W. Maxwell's Filho da Puta, with J. Jackson up. St Leger 1815. Aquatint after John Frederick Herring Snr.*

organisation) and the Jockey Club became increasingly loath to concern itself with betting or indeed much more than the Rules of Racing. It is hardly surprising therefore that the young Queen, under the guidance of her first Prime Minister, Lord Melbourne, had little enthusiasm for racing further afield than the obligatory appearances at Ascot; and even these palled quickly.

For prints of this period, see:

AGASSE, Jacques-Laurent, page 72
ALKEN, Samuel, page 75
ALKEN, Henry Snr, page 75
ALKEN, George, page 75
ANON, page 84
BARENGER, James, page 85
BENSTED, Joseph, page 89
BOULTBEE, John, page 90
CHALON, Henry Bernard, page 93
COOPER, Abraham, page 95
DALBY, David, page 97
DAVIS, Richard Barrett, page 98
DAVIS, Thomas R., page 98
DOYLE, John, page 99
DUBOST, Antoine, page 100
EARP, George, page 101
EGERTON, M., page 102
FERNELEY, John, page 102
FRANKLAND, Sir Robert, page 104
GILBERT, Joseph Francis, page 106
GILL, Edward, page 106
GILPIN, Sawrey, page 106
GWYNN, William, page 108
HANCOCK, Charles, page 112
HAZLEHURST, E., Jnr, page 118
HENDERSON, Charles Cooper, page 118

HERRING, John Frederick, page 119
HILTON, T., page 130
HOWARD, Frank, page 132
HOWITT, Samuel, page 132
HUNT, Charles, page 133
LAPORTE, George Henry, page 137
MARSHALL, Benjamin, page 138
MITCHELL, J. A., page 141
NEWMARCH, G. B., page 143
NOYES, Robert, page 143
POLLARD, James, page 145
ROGERS, J., page 154
ROWLANDSON, Thomas, page 155
SARTORIUS, John Nost, page 157
SNOW, John Wray, page 168
STUBBS, George, page 169
TOMSON, Clifton, page 174
TOWNE, Charles, page 175
TURNER, Francis Calcraft, page 175
WARD, James, page 180
WHESSELL, John, page 182
WOLSTENHOLME, Dean, Snr, page 184
WOLSTENHOLME, Dean, Jnr, page 184
WOODWARD, Thomas, page 184
ZIEGLER, Henry Bryan, page 186

5
STEEPLECHASING

Before the enclosure of the land there were few obstacles larger than streams or ditches to contend with when hunting the stag or fox. At first, when hedges became established, gates and gaps were chosen through which riders would follow hounds and enjoy their sport in comparative safety. However, it was not long before the more adventurous horsemen discovered the excitement and challenge of jumping which, if they stayed in the saddle, also meant they usually kept up with the pack during a good run. At the same time that speed became a more important aspect of flat racing, the exhilaration of dashing across country in a similar rivalry among friends seemed far preferable to the slow progress of those who followed the maxim that it was better to arrive late than not arrive at all. In turn, the Matches arranged between racehorses at Newmarket and elsewhere were paralleled by matches and races across hunting country. There are some early references in literature to these 'Hunting Matches' but no records of who wagered what with whom, or when or where. These matches should not be confused with Hunters' Races which were held on a number of 'flat' courses, usually for gentlemen riders, such as those in which the friends of Lord Francis Spencer took part on Port Meadow near Oxford in 1802.

The first documentary evidence of a cross-country match comes from Ireland in 1752 when a Mr O'Callaghan and a Mr Blake rode a race from Buttevant church to St Leger church – both conspicuous landmarks. Thirty-eight years later, Mr Charles Meynell is reported to have beaten Lord Forester and Sir Gilbert Heathcote in a race of eight miles from Barkby Holt to Billesdon Coplow (Leicestershire) and back. These matches were over natural country with each rider deciding his own line, choosing whether to jump a stream, and perhaps fall in, or to pass safely through a hole in a fence entailing a time-consuming detour. There was some dissent expressed at the profanity of using church steeples (hence steeplechase) as markers in a race on which inevitably money was won or lost;

but the excitement of these events soon attracted sizeable crowds and became immensely popular country pursuits.

The first steeplechase to take place in England over made-up obstacles was at Bedford in 1810. The course was a distance of three miles with eight daunting fences described as 4 ft 6 in. high with a stout rail at the top. To prevent 'flat' hunters from taking part, the organisers required a certificate stating that the horses entered had been in at the death of at least three foxes in Leicestershire! There were eleven subscribers to the sweepstake but only two runners came to the post. The race was won by a Mr Spence riding Fugitive who defeated a horse named Cecilia, both finishing without mishap before a crowd said to number 40,000. Notwithstanding the success of this race, steeplechasing across natural country remained more popular since the ingenuity of choosing the best line to take and the tactics of running gave more interest, variety and excitement to this type of event. However, because of the total lack of rules, organising such races successfully was rather easier said than done.

In 1820 Lord Verulam gave Thomas Coleman permission to train horses in Gorhambury Park at St Albans. Coleman bought a nearby farm and later the Chequers Inn which he converted into the Turf Hotel, with its good stabling, in the town itself. Coleman arranged the first steeplechase at St Albans in 1830 over a course between Harlington church and the obelisk in Wrest Park near Silsoe. The stake was ten sovereigns for each entry. The 'course' was in the shape of a gentle bend allowing Coleman to start the race and then gallop across the cord of the arc to judge its finish. The actual line to be taken by the riders was indicated by flagmen who were hidden until the field approached when they suddenly showed themselves, waving their flags at the extremities of the next obstacle to be jumped. Despite this admirable arrangement which preserved the element of surprise of an open course, two of the sixteen runners lost their way. The race was won by Lord Ranelagh's Wonder, ridden by

Captain Macdowell, with Nailer second, Lord Clanricarde up. The riders who went astray disputed the result and challenged Lord Ranelagh to race again. A second steeplechase took place two weeks later near Bushy when Wonder again won convincingly. This first St Albans Steeple Chase aroused great interest and was continued annually for some years. An additional rule instituted in 1831 was that the last to finish should pay the stake of the runner-up, providing some competition at the back of the field as well as the front! James Pollard painted six views of the race in 1832 which were later engraved. The first plate shows 'Preparing to Start. The Turf Hotel', where there is a parade of the runners on similar lines to that being introduced at the same period on flat courses by Lord George Bentinck. However, these races lacked regulation and were haphazard in their organisation which diminished their standing. By 1836 the St Albans Steeple Chase had lost much of its importance and there were only five runners that year. Coleman was on the point of giving up when Prince Paul Esterhazy

provided a 100 Guineas Gold Cup which quickly restored interest in the race.

Matches continued and steeplechasing was taking place on a more formal and regular basis in a number of counties during the 1830s. Some of these meetings were painted by artists such as Pollard, Henry Alken and Francis Calcraft Turner of whom, by their own acclaim, the last two were accomplished riders to hounds, despite the latter having a wooden leg! The earliest prints after Alken's work, entitled simply 'A Steeple Chase' [22], probably records a match between Mr Francis Holyoake's Clinker, ridden by Captain Ross, and Mr Thomas Assheton Smith's Radical (nominated by Lord Kennedy with whom Captain Ross had a wager) ridden by Captain Douglas. Clinker won over much the same ground as that used by Mr Charles Meynell, Lord Forester and Sir Gilbert Heathcote in 1790. Clinker was a remarkably successful horse until being defeated by Mr George Osbaldeston riding his own horse, Clasher, in a match for 1,000 sovereigns over five miles from Great Dalby

22 A Steeple Chase. Plate 2. Aquatint after Henry Alken Snr.

Windmill to near Tilton-on-the-Hill, again in Leicestershire. On this occasion Dick Christian rode Clinker and they fell exhausted at the last hedge in sight of the equally tired Clasher passing the finishing post. Alken's, or perhaps the publisher Ackermann's claim to illustrate 'The First Steeple-Chace on Record' in the 'Night Riders of Nacton' must be taken with a retrospective pinch of salt. The race is said to have arisen from an after dinner challenge among the officers of the 3rd Dragoons stationed at Ipswich in 1803. The four scenes are delightful and justify their popularity, recording a moonlit ride from the barracks to Nacton church. No doubt there must be an element of truth in the story so brilliantly depicted, but this regiment was not at Ipswich at the time! The prints were first published by Ackermann in 1839 and after Ben Brooks bought the copper plates in 1865, on many later occasions. Among the earliest engravings of steeplechasing after Turner's paintings are the four scenes of the Vale of Aylesbury Steeple Chase, Thursday 11 February 1836 (also painted by Pollard). Each plate is described by its location: 1. Blackgrove Farm; 2. Fleet Marston Brook; 3. Mr Simond's Berry Field Farm; and 4. Mr Josh Terry's Long Furlong Farm. Captain Martin Becher won the race riding Vivian.

Just as Coleman's entrepreneurial skills were being practised near St Albans in the early 1830s, a similarly enterprising individual, William Lynn, was providing sport in the north west. Lynn owned the Waterloo Hotel in Ranelagh Street, Liverpool and one of his schemes to attract business to the city and his inn was to organise a coursing event, the Waterloo Cup, still the premier meeting for testing greyhounds. He also promoted flat racing at Aintree where a stand was built for spectators and racing first took place in July 1829. A few years later Lynn introduced hurdle racing on this course and in 1835 Captain Becher won two such races on the same day riding Vivian. Lynn and Coleman were friends, and it was not long before the former was planning steeplechasing at Liverpool. The first steeplechase was held in February 1836, won by the ubiquitous Becher riding The Duke. This horse also won the following year, piloted by Henry Potts, when the race was run at Maghull.

The Earls of Derby, Sefton, Eglinton, Wilton, Lord Robert Grosvenor, Lord Stanley and Lord George Bentinck, names familiar on the flat, gave their enthusiastic support to the introduction of a Grand Liverpool Steeplechase to be run at Aintree on 26 February 1839. Lynn set about promoting the race, a sweepstake of twenty sovereigns each, with 100 added. The conditions were: twelve stone each, gentlemen riders (a few were certainly not, having previously ridden for hire); four miles across country; the second to save his stake and the winner to pay ten sovereigns towards expenses; no rider to open a gate or ride through a gateway, or more than 100 yards along any road, footpath or driftway. The more formidable of the obstacles to be faced by the seventeen starters were two brooks with accompanying fences (to be jumped twice) and a severe 4 ft 8 in stone wall. There had been a considerable amount of rain before the race and much of the country to be crossed was heavy, not least of which was the plough forming the approach to the brooks. The start of races on the flat was often delayed, usually due to the inadequacy of the organisation to ensure that the runners were at the post at the right time or through the prevarication of the jockeys trying to obtain a good position. The situation was no better at Aintree. The vast crowd which had come to Liverpool from all parts of the country waited patiently for two hours after the expected starting time. Once the runners were off, the taxing going, the jockeying to find the lowest part of each fence, the severity of the obstacles and, in one case, the hostility of the crowd to an unfancied horse doing too well, soon took their toll on the field. Captain Childe's Conrad baulked at the rails in front of the first brook flinging his rider, Becher, into the ditch. The Captain submerged himself in the deepest water he could find while Lottery and four other horses jumped over him. Managing to capture Conrad, Becher remounted only to fall within seconds into the next brook. He emerged unscathed but was unable to continue. The first brook is named after the gallant Captain who never rode in this race again. Mr John Elmore's Lottery was the eventual winner, ridden by Jem Mason; Sir George Mostyn's Seventy Four came second with 'Black' Tom Olliver; and Mr Theobald's Paulina was third, Mr Martin up. Seven horses finished the course; of the others, eight fell (Dictator was killed), one refused and one pulled up. From most viewpoints the race was a success, becoming the Liverpool and National Handicap Steeplechase in 1843 and from 1847 to this day The Grand National Steeplechase or, more simply, 'The National'.

The first Grand National was portrayed by F. C. Turner, George Henry Laporte and Charles Hunt. In each case there are four plates of the race. Turner depicted the preparation for the start by the Grand Stand, with portraits of Lord Sefton, who acted as the tardy Starter, and William Lynn; the rail and brook (which became known as Becher's); the wall, with a novel view from the rear of the field [23]; and the run in. These plates were published by Thomas McLean just two months after the race on 1 May 1839. Laporte's four scenes are of 'The Brook, by the Canal', (to be known as Valentine's when in 1840 this Irish horse, owned and ridden by a Mr Power, stopped, reared up, but somehow managed to wriggle over the bank, brook and rail, eventually finishing third); 'The Stone Wall, opposite the Grand Stand'; 'The Ditch'; and 'The Finish, at the Winning Post'. This undated set was published by Messrs Fores. The third group was engraved by Charles Hunt after his own designs, again showing the more difficult obstacles: 'Stone Wall: First Round'; 'Brook 2nd: Second Round'; 'Brook 3rd: Second Round'; and 'Coming In'. These plates were published by J. W. Laird on 1 June 1839. The National was then largely neglected until the beginning of the present century when some of John Beer's many paintings of the race between 1901 and 1913 were reproduced, as were individual scenes from

Aintree by Gilbert Holiday and Snaffles. There are contemporary engravings of Lottery, who was in any case an outstanding horse apart from winning the first National, but again there is a gap until a number of winners were portrayed and reproduced between 1880 and 1910.

There are far fewer prints of steeplechasing than of the flat, and the initial enthusiasm to publish the former, starting in the early 1830s, had all but petered out by 1860. Indeed, steeplechasing was in the doldrums until revived by the foundation of the National Hunt Committee in 1865. There are some delightful scenes recording less familiar meetings by equally unknown contemporary artists. George Earp's 'Brighton Hurdle Race', 1833 after a sketch by W. H. Mason (two plates); J. S. Harland's 'The Scarborough Steeple Chase', 1851; and Charles Denton's 'Abergavenny Steeple Chase', 1853 (four plates) fall into this category. J. F. Herring's 'Steeple Chase Cracks' published by Fores in 1847 shows eleven leading riders of the

23 *The Liverpool Great Steeple-Chase, 1839. Plate III. Aquatint after Francis Calcraft Turner.*

day and their mounts jumping a wall in a 'composite' scene; an idea followed in 'McQueen's Sportings: The Silks and Satins of the Field', after Ben Herring, published in 1868; and in 'McQueen's Racings: Our Gentlemen Steeple Chase Riders' after George Veal, 1885. However these later plates lack the mishaps and spontaneity of the 1830s racing scenes. Support for jumping being limited compared with the flat presumably resulted in disappointing sales of prints, accounting for comparatively few being produced. Those that were published provide a valuable record of nineteenth and early twentieth century steeplechasing in Britain and Ireland.

For prints of steeplechasing, see:

6
LEGISLATORS AND OWNERS
1840–1875

Charles Greville agonised over his attitude to racing since an interest in the turf in the mid-nineteenth century inevitably meant that he was regarded in some people's eyes as an associate of bookmakers and scoundrels, two descriptions then given one and the same meaning. Such men were not in the same social bracket as the Clerk to the Privy Council, although often better off financially! This was not a situation which worried his cousin Lord George Bentinck at all. Lord George was a Member of Parliament for most of his adult life and was fascinated by politics, leading one faction of the Conservatives after the split with Peel over the Corn Laws, but his overriding ambition was to dominate all aspects of the turf. With ample financial backing and a father and brothers to bail him out if need be, Bentinck was quite capable of taking on the bookmakers and beating them at their own game. In betting he rejoiced in the money he won as a general might count his prisoners as a measure of his sucess. Greville and Bentinck were racing confederates for a time but their very different characters led to breaks in their turf relationship and a series of coolnesses between them which lasted for years on end.

By 1838, Bentinck was running his horses in his own name. His father, the 4th Duke of Portland, enjoyed racing but disapproved of betting large sums. To avoid upsetting the Duke, Bentinck had used the rather thin subterfuge in earlier years of entering his horses in the names of his friends, (including those of Greville, Lord Lichfield and the Duke of Richmond). By 1838, Bentinck was a powerful member of the Jockey Club and was set on ridding the turf of the many malpractices then taking place. In this he had the support and friendship, as far as anyone could be friendly with Bentinck, of Lord Chesterfield, Sir Gilbert Heathcote, Colonels Anson and Peel, Captain Rous, the rising turf legislator, and other leading owners of the day. He was not above using like to catch like. Among such were Harry Hill, a bookmaker whom no-one trusted, John

Barham Day, Bentinck's trainer of doubtful probity, and John Gully. The last started his adult life in Fleet Prison, became the champion boxer of England, pub landlord, commission agent, and by determination and cunning equal to that of Lord George, racehorse owner, Member of Parliament, coal magnate and respected north countryman.

As well as introducing measures to reduce on-course tricks and strategems by trainers and jockeys, in 1843 Bentinck expelled from all racecourses under the control of the Jockey Club any person who failed to meet their betting commitments on the due settling day. As a result, two brothers named Russell served writs on Bentinck and many other owners for contravening the Statute of Queen Anne which did not permit winning more than £10 when betting on a race. The Russells claimed that Bentinck had won £3,000 from John Day on the result of the Derby that year. Gully, Bentinck's commissioner, said that he took the bet on his own account and the case failed. Further court appearances were forestalled by Lord George and the Duke of Richmond bringing their 'Manly Sports Bill' before Parliament which virutally repealed the old Statute. To an extent, what was gained by banning defaulters was lost in the often disastrous consequences of allowing unlimited betting.

To appreciate the state of the turf one has only to examine the 2,000 Guineas and the Derby of 1844. The first classic was won by J. B. Day's The Ugly Buck, ridden by John Day Jnr. Because 'The Buck' was only able to beat Bentinck's very moderate The Devil to Pay by a neck in the Guineas, his Lordship thought nothing of Day's horse's chance at Epsom. However, the Buck was made favourite for the Derby, deliberately interfered with during the running and finished nowhere. The second favourite was the bookmaker and gambler William Crockford's Ratan. The colt was nobbled in his loosebox the night before the race and then ridden so badly by Sam Rogers that the

Stewards launched an enquiry. Rogers was discovered to have laid a large bet against his mount winning, and the jockey was warned off the turf for five years as a result. Leander was suspected of being over-age and, fracturing a leg when knocked down a furlong from the start, had to be destroyed. His lower jaw was sawn off by veterinary surgeons and the Stewards found that he was at least a four-year-old. His owners, German brothers named Lichtwald, were banned from the English turf for ever. Such incidents were almost commonplace and of not much significance when compared with the guile employed to ensure that Running Rein was the winner of the 1844 Derby.

In reality Running Rein was a four-year-old colt named Maccabaeus, although it is unlikely that his owner, Mr A. Wood, knew of the switch which had taken place two years before, organised by a gambler named Abraham Goodman Levy. In 1843 Running Rein (Maccabaeus) won a race for two-year-olds in which a horse owned by the Duke of Rutland was second. Rutland, strongly supported by Bentinck, objected on the grounds of suspecting Running Rein's age. At the Stewards' enquiry a stable lad who had been present at the birth of the real Running Rein came down from Yorkshire and testified that the horse he now saw (Maccabaeus) was the Malton foal he had seen born. Goodman Levy pocketed his substantial stake, but failed to realise that once Bentinck's suspicions had been aroused nothing would stop him from discovering the truth. Running Rein was not entered for the 2,000 Guineas but the evidence which Lord George had amassed before the day of the Derby was such that he confidently objected to Running Rein before the race. The Stewards, still smarting from the surprising outcome of the previous investigation, decided that the horse should run and there would only be an enquiry if he won; which he promptly did. Colonel Peel, the owner of the second horse, Orlando, immediately claimed the stakes and the Stewards sent for Wood, who could not be found. Bentinck, ably assisted by Harry Hill, then set about marshalling incontrovertible evidence against Running Rein and the man responsible for the switch, Goodman Levy. When the case came to court, Wood could not respond to repeated demands to 'produce the horse', withdrew his claim to the stakes and Orlando was declared the winner of the 1844 Derby. The role of Goodman Levy came to light during the hearing and he disappeared abroad without the £50,000 which he might have won. Baron Alderson, the Judge who summed up, pointed out that 'if gentlemen condescend to race with black-

guards, they must condescend to expect to be cheated'. These words did little to enhance the name of racing and only made Greville wring his hands in greater distress!

While 1844 may be considered the nadir of the turf's reputation, replete with men motivated by pecuniary greed rather than acclaim for their ability in their professions, there were many owners, trainers and jockeys who raced honestly according to the standards then accepted. The pattern of the important meetings, the Classics, the Chester Cup (first run in 1824), Ascot, Goodwood and Doncaster Cups gave the racing season a firm structure and, in a fashion, provided an element of stability which was previously lacking. This was of particular value to owners or their managers who could plan their strategy for the year ahead making best use of their funds and stables, however large or limited. The Jockey Club was extending its influence, although after 1842 steadfastly refusing to interest itself in betting matters. The rules and regulations were their forte and Captain Rous was the authority of their interpretation.

Henry John Rous was the younger brother of the 2nd Earl of Stradbroke whose family seat, of modest size compared with many of his racing contemporaries, was at Henham Hall not far from Newmarket. In 1808 Rous sailed as a midshipman in the Royal William and was often at sea until 1836. When at home he was in racing partnership with his older brother and they were both made members of the Jockey Club as young men. In 1834 he took command of a 36-gun frigate, the *Pique*, and during the following year she was badly damaged on uncharted rocks off the coast of Labrador. Rous managed to sail the *Pique* back to England, a hazardous and difficult operation requiring both courage and skill. He was acquitted as blameless at the subsequent Court Martial, but received only grudging thanks from the Admiralty for saving his ship. Going on half-pay in 1836, Rous then devoted his life to the turf, becoming a handicapper whom everybody trusted and an expert on the rules of racing to whom everyone turned when a problem arose.

During the years which followed, Bentinck and Rous (later promoted Rear Admiral of the Blue in 1852) improved the conduct of racing and attempted to stamp out the malpractices and cheating, expelling from the turf the blackguards who gave it such a bad name. Bentinck's zeal and energy were phenomenal. Rous was more careful and circumspect in his decisions, except if driven to writing letters to newspapers when for some strange reason all caution was thrown

24 *The Marquis of Westminster's Touchstone, with G. Calloway up. St Leger 1834. Aquatint after John Frederick Herring Snr.*

out of the window.

Thinking that the Days were running his horses more for their own betting convenience than for his, Bentinck removed them from the Danebury stables in Hampshire to John Kent (the Duke of Richmond's trainer) at Goodwood in 1841. The Days were furious. In the mid-1840s the rivalry between Danebury with its confederacy of bookmaking-owners and Goodwood was intense. The size of Bentinck's string was only matched by Danebury and John Scott's yard, Whitewall at Malton. In 1845 Lord George kept sixty thoroughbreds in training of which thirty-six started in 195 races. Stakes and forfeits alone cost him more than £20,000. Despite this large outlay, partly funded by betting, he was not particularly successful in the classic races – 2,000 Guineas 1838 and 1840; 1,000 Guineas 1837, 1840 and 1842; Oaks 1840 and St Leger 1836, the Derby eluding him altogether. To the astonishment of everyone connected with the turf Bentinck suddenly sold all his horses in 1846 for the paltry sum of £10,000. He was then a Senior Steward of the Jockey Club and continued to attend meetings and follow the fortunes of his 'old' horses; otherwise he concentrated on politics with a similar dedication to that which he had devoted to racing. At the time that he

sold his stud to Edward Lloyd-Mostyn, Bentinck asked that Surplice, a colt by Touchstone out of his favourite Crucifix (2,000 Guineas, 1,000 Guineas and Oaks, 1840) should continue to be trained by Kent at Goodwood. On 24 May 1848, Lord George watched Surplice win the Derby ridden by the admirable and honest jockey Sim Templeman. Bentinck had a very heavy bet on Surplice but the financial gain did nothing to lessen the chagrin of not still being the colt's owner. Disraeli, who admired his leader's energy in politics, tried to console him a few days later. 'Dizzy' describes Bentinck making a 'sort of superb groan' before questioning the significance of the race. To this Disraeli suggested that the Derby was the 'Blue Riband of the turf', plunging Lord George into even deeper gloom. Surplice went on to win the St Leger in September, the first horse to complete this double since Christopher Wilson's Champion in 1800. A few days later Bentinck was found lying beside a path on his father's estate at Welbeck having suffered a major heart attack some hours before. He was forty-six years old. Despite their quarrels, Greville wrote generously in his *Memoires* of his cousin's immense contribution to the turf and to politics. While remembered without much affection, Lord George Bentinck's impact as a reformer and scourge of the scoundrels of racing during his short lifetime is indisputable.

In the mid-nineteenth century the number of horses in training exceeded 1,400 and the colours of more than 300 owners were registered. Their success, and that of trainers and jockeys, was measured (apart from the total stakes won) to a large degree by their record in the three-year-old classic races, with performance in the Gold Cups playing a nearly as important part. Another measure of success was an animal's ability as a sire or brood mare, although good horses were kept racing for longer than the best of today, often going to stud at the age of six or seven rather than at the end of their classic season. An example is Touchstone [24] bred by the Marquis of Westminster. He raced for five years (winning the St Leger in 1834; two Ascot Gold Cups, the second in 1837; and two Doncaster Cups) before becoming a highly successful stallion [Plate 7]. Touchstone's immediate progeny won four 2,000 Guineas, three Derbys, a 1,000 Guineas and Oaks, and three St Legers between 1843 and 1855. However, despite stakes won and stud fees few owners could afford

to keep a substantial number of horses in training without the benefit of betting coups.

John Bowes and Sir Joseph Hawley were contemporaries and leading owners of the period who were both heavy betters when they were confident of their chances, otherwise they had little in common. The son of the Earl of Strathmore, Bowes lived at Streatlam Castle, Durham and in later life mostly in Paris. He inherited a considerable estate from his father but not the title, as the Earl only married Bowes's mother shortly before his death, by which time his son was nine years old. Bowes was a quiet yet determined young man who employed the very successful northern trainer John Scott to look after his horses. He won his first Derby in 1835 (Mundig), second in 1843 (Cotherstone [25], who also won the 2,000 Guineas), third in 1852 (Daniel O'Rourke), and the next year with West Australian. In August 1852 John Scott reported to Bowes that West Australian had gone very well in a trial in Yorkshire. Bowes immediately obtained long odds with the London bookmaker William Davies against his colt winning the Derby the following year. He also secured other bets at good prices before it

25 J. B. Bowes Esq's Cotherstone. Derby 1843. Aquatint after John Frederick Herring Snr.

became general knowledge that Scott had another good one in his stables at Malton. 'The West', as the horse became known, won the 1853 2,000 Guineas convincingly, the Derby after a struggle (earning Bowes £30,000 in bets) and, surprisingly, was not then made hot favourite for the St Leger. Scott, suspecting there might be attempts to get at the horse, guarded him day and night, as he did his jockey Frank Butler! In the event, The West won the St Leger easily with Butler riding past the finishing post with 'hands down'. The colt was the first to win the Triple Crown comprising the 2,000 Guineas, Derby and St Leger [*Plate 10*]. John Bowes was a member of the Jockey Club for many years and played a quiet but effective supporting role in reforming the turf and fighting the skulduggery which continued to spoil its name. Using a manager, he continued to breed and keep horses in training until his death in 1885, although after his marriage to Josephine Coffin-Chevalier in 1852 he spent most of his time in France, not attending any race meetings in England after 1855.

Joseph Hawley, born in 1814, was also the recipient of a large estate on the death of his father, the 2nd Baronet. After short service in the Army and a rather longer period living in Italy, Hawley began racing in earnest in 1844. He employed a succession of trainers both public (those who trained for a number of unconnected owners) and private (usually with a single owner or confederacy). The first was Beresford who had an establishment at Newmarket, then Alec Taylor at Fyfield who was followed for a short time by William Day at Danebury, George Manning at Cannon Heath and finally the outstanding John Porter for whom Hawley built his own stables at Kingsclere in Hampshire. While very closely involved in the running of his horses, secretive and quite difficult to know, Hawley was generous with his trainers and jockeys when his horses won (in the view of Admiral Rous, too generous). He won eight classic races, each with a different horse. Like Bowes, there were four Derby winners, of which the first, Teddington in 1851, landed Hawley a betting coup of more than £80,000; the last was Blue Gown in 1868. Hawley saw himself as a reformer, notably in trying to limit the running of two-year-olds. Rous disliked him, and since other members of the Jockey Club found him somewhat too clever, few of his proposals were adopted.

Another contemporary of Bowes and Hawley was the ironmaster, Mr James Merry; an inappropriate name for an extremely suspicious, humourless man who fell out with nearly every trainer and jockey he employed. Among the former were George Dawson, William I'Anson (who owned two Derby winners), Sanders, Prince, William Day, Mathew Dawson, James Waugh and Robert Peck. He never used the same jockey for his seven classic winners between 1855 and 1873. Merry was not elected to the Jockey Club which clearly rankled since he was a most successful owner. The public wisely followed him knowing that his horses were always run honestly.

Other principal owners and personalities of the mid-nineteenth century included Lords Eglinton, Exeter, Glasgow (who had little luck), Zetland, Baron de Rothschild and Messrs Chaplin (later Lord Chaplin), Savile, Johnstone and Crawfurd to name only a few. They formed the small cabal of active members of the Jockey Club among whom the likes of James Merry were not welcome.

Horses from France began to race in England in the 1850s. From time to time there was considerable animosity towards them because of a lack of reciprocity; English horses were allowed to run only in the Grand Prix de Paris. However their presence, and that of horses from Austria and, much later America did much to invigorate the turf with new ideas. One of the most successful of the French owners was Count Frederic de Lagrange. His horses were managed and trained by the Jennings brothers: Harry at Chantilly outside Paris, and Tom at Newmarket, although the latter also spent much of his time in France. Count Frederic was less wise in his choice of jockeys. To start with he used one of a large family of riders and trainers named Edwards; the Edwards he selected was dishonest. Later, he employed the first-class jockey Harry Grimshaw, but he was extremely shortsighted! Notwithstanding these disadvantages, Lagrange owned seven classic winners between 1864 and 1879, the best being Gladiateur who won the Triple Crown in 1865. The horse, nicknamed the 'Avenger of Waterloo', was difficult to train having injured his forelegs in an accident when a foal. However, Grimshaw rode him skilfully in the 2,000 Guineas, winning by a neck. He went on to take the Derby easily from a moderate lot receiving a good cheer from the crowd who always applauded a winning favourite [*Plate 14*]. The press savaged the horse, the jockey and, in particular, the owner but this did not prevent Gladiateur winning the richest St Leger so far by a clear three lengths. The following year the horse won the Ascot Gold Cup and the Grand Prix de L'Empereur in Paris. He was not a success as a stallion.

Despite the successful efforts of Admiral Rous in

reforming the finances of the Jockey Club, racing at Newmarket was at a low ebb in the 1870s. Many people looked upon the Heath as a private course, unchanged over a period of two hundred years, to be enjoyed only by members of the Jockey Club and their friends. They did not want vast stands or an enclosed course but without some facilities Newmarket attracted neither good fields nor the public. As the correspondent of the *Illustrated London News* put it in May 1874:

> we do desire to see some radical reforms, which would make racing at Newmarket more what it should be at a place with a thousand horses in training, and more worthy of such classic ground.

Sadly, the Newmarket improvements were barely thought of before Admiral Rous died. He attended the Prince of Wales's annual Derby night dinner at Marlborough House in 1877 where he appeared to have lost much of his old spirit and fun. His health deteriorated rapidly and he died, aged 82, on 20 June. Mr George Payne, Rous's boon companion and also a friend of Charles Greville who had died in 1865, survived the sailor by one year. Payne was the inheritor of more than one fortune which he quickly and cheerfully dissipated in gambling, mainly at cards. He also hunted, was an owner of racehorses and acted as a discreet diplomat in smoothing away the disputes which often arose between fellow members of the Jockey Club.

There are portrait prints of the majority of the classic winners throughout this period. The jackets worn by the jockeys and in some cases the studies of the owners and trainers provide colour and interest to these otherwise static and repetitive plates. Horses shown alone in their looseboxes are distinctly dull. Rudolph Ackermann stopped publishing his short series of racehorse portraits after paintings by John Ferneley, Charles Hancock and F. C. Turner in 1844, and Messrs Fuller's line of outstandingly decorative St Leger and Derby winners came to a halt in 1846. However, the style of publication was pursued by John Moore of Upper St Martin's Lane until about 1855. He was followed by the Bailys, (A. H. & C. E. Baily, followed by Baily Brothers, and then A. H. Baily after 1863). They published from Cornhill, London until 1882 when their chief artist, Harry Hall, died. Hall painted almost unbroken strings of Derby and St Leger winners published by the Bailys. J., then G. P., and later F. C. McQueen & Sons of Great Marlborough Street published a few portraits after the paintings of Benjamin Herring in the 1870s, and George Rees produced others in the 1880s after Edwin Hunt.

26 *The Start for the Memorable Derby of 1844. Aquatint after J. F. Herring Snr.*

Excluding steeplechases, the number of prints of races in progress published between 1840 and 1875 are few. James Pollard and Henry Alken Snr had stopped painting such scenes, J. F. Herring was turning to the farmyard for his inspiration, and Harry Hall was barely capable of illustrating galloping horses, although he painted one or two pleasing small 'finishes'. However, even when immersed in domestic subjects, Herring painted 'The Start for the Memorable Derby of 1844' [26] which was published by Fores in 1845, later becoming Plate 1 of their 'National Sports'. Four more racing scenes: 'Saddling'; 'A False Start'; 'The Run In' [Plate 12]; and 'Returning to Weigh', representing great winners taken from a number of years of racing (described here as 'composites'), also by Herring, were added to this series in 1856. Herring's picture of the finish of the Emperor's Cup in June 1845 [75, page 127] and another of the last strides of the famous Match between Lord Eglinton's Flying Dutchman and Lord Zetland's Voltigeur [Plate 9] were also published shortly after each event by Fores.

J. Moore published a delightful and rare set of four aquatints of the Cambridgeshire Stakes, 1853 after the watercolours of Seffrien Alken. The McQueens produced composites after Benjamin Herring, 'The Silks and Satins of the Turf' (1867); and 'The Silks and Satins of the Field' (1868), followed by two pairs of prints of the Derby of 1865 (Gladiateur's year) and 1872 (won by Mr Henry Savile's Cremorne, ridden by C. Maidment) after Henry Alken Jnr, published in 1871 and 1873 respectively. Finally, pictures of steeplechasing by John Sturgess are better known than his records of the flat, but Messrs Brall published two prints, 'Rounding the Bend' and 'The Struggle for Victory', after his paintings in 1873. These were, again, composite scenes and not of a particular race.

As the nineteenth century drew to a close the paintbrush and the engraving tool were being replaced by photography and photographic methods. The latter, in particular, destroyed the freshness and originality of prints. It must be admitted however that by 1860 there were few engravers who could still translate a painting into an engraved plate with anything like the brilliance of fifty years before. The next half-century saw their extinction.

7
ROYALTY RETURNS
1875–1940

At the time (1874) that Newmarket was being berated in the press, there were moves afoot elsewhere which were to change the face of most meetings and, in consequence, improve standards of racing: this was the enclosure of courses. The railway companies went out of their way to provide special trains to the towns where race meetings were held. This resulted in far larger crowds attending meetings than before, particularly if there was a programme of famous horses and well known jockeys competing in short, fast and exciting races. Having arrived on the course, only those who watched from the available stands were charged entrance money, apart from a few who paid a fee to have their private coaches by the rails. In 1875 Sandown Park was enclosed and turnstiles installed. Far from deterring the 'working class' element of the crowd it increased their number. They could afford to pay (usually one shilling, though more at Sandown) and knew that by being charged they were entitled to some well organised entertainment, which they received. It also meant that the company which owned Sandown, and those running other courses who followed Sandown's lead, were able to add more money to the prizes, in turn attracting better runners and riders. By the end of the century most courses were enclosed. Those which were not, disappeared; between 1870 and 1899 over ninety meetings came to an end. However, the open meetings at Ascot, Epsom, Goodwood, Doncaster and York did survive, partly due to their standing in the social calendar and partly by the heavy tolls levied for the facilities which were provided. In this way the Jockey Club also slowly improved the position at Newmarket which remained 'open' but where new stands were built and enclosures provided at a cost to those who used them.

Queen Victoria took very little interest in racing and probably disapproved of many aspects of its conduct. On the other hand she and her Consort maintained the Royal Stud at Hampton Court and in 1875 their son Edward, the Prince of Wales, registered his colours. The long period of royal neglect dating from early in the reign of William IV came to an end and the connection was renewed. The Prince was attracted to racing and its society, which in turn embraced him enthusiastically since he gave the turf a certain legitimacy and standing which it had lacked for so long. Edward was a sportsman who everyone admired, not least for his lack of flamboyance in a field about which he as yet had little knowledge, but particularly since he did not succumb to the betting excesses of some of his predecessors.

The Prince witnessed the 1863 Derby but his introduction to racing was under National Hunt Rules. His colours were first carried in a steeplechase of the 10th Hussars, of which Regiment he was Colonel. At a meeting at Southall on 31 March 1871, the Prince of Wales's horse Champion came second in the Regimental Challenge Cup. Five years later, Regal (of whom the Prince was said to be a part owner) won the Grand National in the name and colours of the redoubtable manager and trainer Captain James Machell. The first horse to run in the National in his Royal Highness's name was The Scot in 1884. He was a son of Blair Athol (Derby, 1864) and had been fifth in the race in 1881. The horse ran well but fell at the Canal Turn the second time round to the great disappointment of the crowd which had backed him down to 6 to 1 for no better reason than loyalty to the crown!

The Prince was made a member of the Jockey Club in 1864, but his first success under their Rules was not gained until twenty-two years later when his Counterpane won a race at Sandown Park. At this time, 1886, the Prince's horses were trained by John Porter at Kingsclere; Lord Marcus Beresford was his manager. The stable had little success for the royal owner, perhaps because Prince Edward was unwilling to pay high prices for young horses, being constrained by the views of his mother whom he did not wish to upset by apparent extravagance. However in 1890 John Porter bought a mare named Perdita II at the end of her five-year-old season for £900. In the years which followed she produced a number of outstanding foals, completely changing the Prince's racing fortunes. So that his horses were closer to Sandringham from where he could more easily follow their training, The Prince placed them in the hands of Dick Marsh at Egerton House, Newmarket in 1893. The first of Perdita's foals to run well was Florizel II (by St Simon). After a moderately successful three-year-old season Florizel developed further to take the Ascot Gold Vase, Manchester Cup, Goodwood Cup and Jockey Club Cup a year later. He was also successful at stud. Florizel's full brother, Persimmon, foaled in 1893, gave the Prince his first Derby victory. The horse did not run in the 2,000 Guineas which was won by Leopold de Rothschild's St Frusquin, who became the favourite for the Blue Riband. Persimmon could sometimes be difficult to manage and he chose such a time when being boxed at Newmarket for the rail journey to Epsom. Having failed to move the horse for the best part of the morning, Dick Marsh cried out in desperation to the assembled onlookers: 'A sovereign apiece

for those who help to get him in'. The horse was almost thrown into the van by the volunteers to whom Marsh is said to have paid out 70 sovereigns! In a thrilling race Persimmon, ridden by Jack Watts, beat St Frusquin by a neck. The crowd on the Downs and even more sedate spectators in the stands heartily cheered this long awaited Royal victory. St Frusquin in receipt of 3 lb beat Persimmon by a half-length in the Princess of Wales's Stakes at Newmarket but had broken down before the St Leger which the Prince's colt won easily. Persimmon became the last Epsom Derby winner to take the Gold Cup at Ascot as a four-year-old, and went on to be the champion sire twice before and twice after his early death at the age of fifteen.

Lord Falmouth dominated the turf for more than twenty years and by his quiet manner commanded the loyalty of those who worked for him and the affection of the public who followed his success. He unexpectedly inherited the title of Viscount Falmouth from his cousin in 1852. Living at Tregothnan in Cornwall and using his wife's estate at Mereworth Castle in Kent for breeding, his horses were trained by John Scott at Malton until he gave up shortly before he died. For a year Falmouth's horses went to William Boyce, and

27 *The Duke of Westminster's Bend Or, with F. Archer up. Derby 1880. Aquatint by and after Edwin Hunt.*

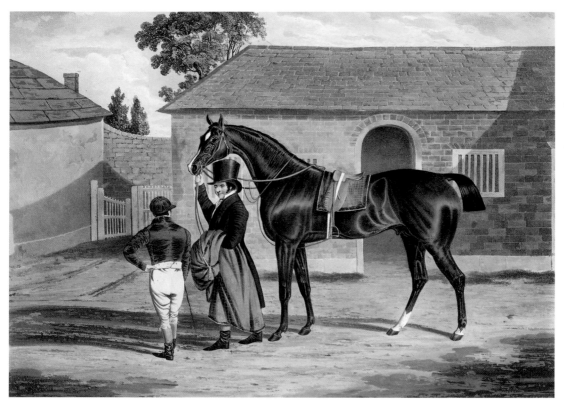

*Thomas Ferguson
Esq's Antonio,
with his trainer
and the jockey,
J. Nicholson.
St Leger 1819.
Aquatint after
John Frederick
Herring Snr.*

PLATE 4

*The Earl of
Jersey's Bay
Middleton, with
J. Robinson up.
Derby 1836.
Aquatint after
John Frederick
Herring Snr.*

The Earl of Chesterfield's Hornsea, with W. Scott up.
Goodwood Gold Cup 1836.
Aquatint after Francis Calcraft Turner.

PLATE 5

Mr W. Ridsdale's Bloomsbury, with S. Templeman up. Derby 1839. Aquatint after John Frederick Herring Snr.

PLATE 6

Charles XII and Euclid. The Decisive Heat for the Great St Leger Stakes at Doncaster, 1839. Aquatint after John Frederick Herring Snr.

*Mr Collins's Isaac,
with Sam Darling up.
Darling's two sons in
attendance.
Aquatint after Thomas
Woodward.*

PLATE 7

*(below)
Touchstone and Emma.
Aquatint after John
Frederick Herring Snr.*

then in 1868 were moved to Mathew Dawson at his Heath House stables at Newmarket. Falmouth started racing in 1857 and between 1862 and 1882 won sixteen classics with twelve different horses. Dawson's first call jockeys, Tom French (who died in 1873) and Fred Archer, served Falmouth well and he was intensely loyal to them. The association of Falmouth, Dawson and Archer was a close one, each knowing his place and the part to be played in the breeding, preparation and the riding of thoroughbreds to ensure success. Due mainly to ill-health, Lord Falmouth broke up his stud in 1884. The regard and friendship of the triumvirate is well demonstrated by the inscription on a piece of silver presented to Falmouth by Dawson and Archer:

Offered for the acceptance of the Right Honourable the Viscount Falmouth by his trainer and jockey, Mathew Dawson and Frederick J. Archer, as a token of gratitude and esteem to the best, kindest, and most generous of masters on his retirement from the turf, January 1884.

Lord Falmouth died five years later, having been deeply shocked by Archer's suicide in 1886.

Among the last of the great owners of the nineteenth century was the Marquis of Westminster, created the 1st Duke in the 1874 dissolution honours. The family had been associated with racing for well over a hundred years, since the time of the birth of Hugh Lupus Grosvenor in 1825. He succeeded his father, the 1st Marquis (who won six classic races between 1810 and 1840), in 1845. One of his early, notably essays in racing was to pay the very large sum of 14,000 guineas to the owner-trainer Robert Peck for his stallion Doncaster (Derby, 1873) in 1876. Bend Or [27] was by Doncaster, trained by Peck, winning the Derby in 1880 to give His Grace his first classic victory. Westminster's horses were trained later by John Porter at Kingsclere from where Ormonde, a son of Bend Or, was sent out to win the Triple Crown in 1886. Others of this line included a son of Ormonde, Orme, who was poisoned either intentionally or by a tooth as a three-year-old but won two Eclipse Stakes; and Flying Fox, a son of Orme, winner of the Triple Crown for the Duke again in 1899. Westminster also won the 2,000 Guineas in 1881 with Peregrine, the 2,000 Guineas and Derby in 1882 with Shotover, and the 1,000 Guineas with Farewell (by Doncaster) in 1885. Fred Archer rode Bend Or, and Ormonde in the Derby and St Leger, the jockey's last classic ride. The Duke was an undemonstrative and reserved man whose considerable knowledge of breeding was put into practice at his Eaton stud near Chester with a surprising lack of care. His Grace's one reported exuberant act was

while watching Flying Fox win the 2,000 Guineas in the year he died. Letting out a hunting holloa heard throughout the Newmarket stand, his lack of self-control quite shocked his fellow members of the Jockey Club.

Born in 1897, and for that reason named Diamond Jubilee, a second full brother to Persimmon was to make 1900 the Prince of Wales's most successful racing season. It opened with his Ambush II [28] winning the Grand National on 30 March. Diamond Jubilee [29] was a difficult horse of uncertain temper. In a good but uneven two-year-old career, the only matter which became clear was that the horse intensely disliked Marsh's stable jockey, Jack Watts. The following spring he savaged Mornington Cannon after a training gallop, and as a last resort the trainer decided to put up the colt's lad, Herbert Jones (whom Persimmon tolerated), for the 2,000 Guineas – they won the race by four lengths. The Derby and St Leger also fell to this combination, but thereafter Diamond Jubilee achieved little else.

The following year the death of the Queen took the royal colours off the turf and the new King's horses were temporarily leased to the Duke of Devonshire so that they could continue racing. After his accession King Edward increased the number of horses he had in training but his luck failed to match the size of the stable. It was not until 1909 that Dick Marsh turned out a leased horse as a worthy successor to Perdita's sons. His name was Minoru. The trainer had little faith in the Irish bred animal until he improved quickly in the spring of his three-year-old season. Minoru won the 2,000 Guineas with Herbert Jones, now an established jockey, on his back. Jones and Minoru went on to win at Epsom by a short head in the presence of the King and the Prince of Wales (King George V). The wildly enthusiastic crowd cheered the horse to victory by the slimmest margin. This was the first occasion on which the reigning monarch had won the Derby.

Among the foremost owners of the period in which the Prince of Wales (later King Edward VII) was racing were the Duke of Westminster, already mentioned, the Duke of Portland, Lord Rosebery, Major Eustace Loder, Mr Leopold de Rothschild and Mr J. B. Joel. Each looked upon racing from a different viewpoint. While the Duke of Westminster and Lord Rosebery (the 5th Earl) were most interested in breeding, the latter rarely attended a meeting. Until the end of the century the Duke of Portland was a patrician figure of the turf, a sport which he enjoyed more than others;

28 *HRH the Prince of Wales's Ambush II, with A. Anthony up. Grand National 1900. Chromolithograph after N. Arthur Loraine.*

29 *HRH the Prince of Wales's Diamond Jubilee, with Herbert Jones up. Triple Crown 1900. Chromolithograph after N. Arthur Loraine.*

his most successful horse was St Simon [*30*]. He was particularly attentive to the well-being of all who worked for him in the racing world as well as the many tenants on his estates in England and Scotland. However, he had little luck after 1900 and his interest in the turf appeared to diminish, culminating in an avoidable disagreement with his fellow members of the Jockey Club at the outbreak of the First World War. Like many soldiers, Major Eustace Loder's interest in racing was aroused through steeplechasing. He was a sensitive man who would quietly explain that: 'You may put all the brains you have into racing but you will be nowhere unless you have luck.' Mr Leopold de Rothschild was an exceptionally generous man, always popular with the public despite a quick but shortlived temper. Mr Jack Joel, who made a fortune early in his life from the diamond fields of South Africa, in part looked upon racing as another of his commercial enterprises. However his keen interest in the turf was rewarded by an intense loyalty from his trainers (only two in a period of forty years racing) and others whom he employed. Although he claimed eleven classic races, he was not blessed with as much good fortune as 'Lucky Loder' who raced on a much smaller scale.

Of the old-established print publishers, Messrs Fores was the most active at the turn of the century. The firm had bought copper plates from others who had gone out of business and continued to print from them, as they still do today. At the same time they employed Alfred Charles Havell to portray winners and John Beer to paint steeplechases and finishes almost before the participants were back in their stables. In print form the portraits give little idea of their subjects' characters and Beer's tubular racehorses lack the excitement which the illustrators who followed captured with such panache. This was achieved by using a closer viewpoint than Beer and, more particularly, from understanding the motion of a galloping horse after studying the photographic research of the American, Eadweard Muybridge. There was also a brief fashion for group portraits on a large scale which, like the horse portraits, suffered from the static pose. An air of informality was attempted by not portraying anyone facing the 'camera'. In print form, the figures are small and due to the fashion for beards, it is even difficult to discover which portrait is of the King or the Prince of Wales without the accompanying key. The photogravures of 'The Royal Stand at Ascot' after J. Vincent Gibson; 'Newmarket, "The Birdcage"' after

30 *The Duke of Portland's St Simon. Ascot and Goodwood Gold Cups 1884. Photogravure after Alfred Charles Havell.*

31 *Newmarket Fin-de-Siecle. 'The Birdcage'. Photogravure after Isaac Cullin.*

Isaac Cullin [*31*]; and 'The Household Brigade Cup' after Adrian Jones and H. Jermyn Brooks fall into this inescapably dull category of print, today lacking even the interest of easily recognizing some of the personalities.

By 1900 racing had, for the most part, rid itself of some of the worst criminals although scandals occasionally surfaced through the veneer of rectitude which has become the apparent hallmark of the late Victorian era. Those who disliked racing were not slow to try to stop it altogether when war broke out in 1914. For some, the morality of a few comparatively wealthy people enjoying themselves at home while so many were suffering in Belgium and France was itself a sufficiently sound reason to close down racing in the atmosphere of the time, even when the soldiers were expected back by Christmas! The Government took the more practical view that the valuable resources of transport and fodder could no longer be used to maintain the turf in pre-war style. With considerable skill Lord Jersey,

the Senior Steward, and other members of the Jockey Club succeeded in keeping the sport alive at Newmarket on the grounds that the employment of the town depended upon it, and the need to maintain the strains of the English thoroughbred for better times. Racing was severely curtailed and the calendar reduced, but summer meetings at the home of racing enabled the running there of the New Derby and New Oaks from 1915 to 1918. The St Leger was also run at Newmarket as the September Stakes.

By enduring common hardships, the Great War brought the young men of means and those with next to nothing apart from love of their country closer together. At home, the enormous gulf which existed between stratas of society before the War was also reduced as the fortitude in adversity of each layer was recognised by the others. After the War there was a realisation that racing could not and should not for ever be an activity and pleasure open only to those with money or position. The Jockey Club, again with the guidance of Lord Jersey and that of Lord Hamilton of Dalzell, examined ways of popularising the sport and making it more accessible to a much wider public.

An immediate and urgent step to be taken was to stamp out the racketeers and gangs of pickpockets who appeared on nearly every racecourse after the War. This was dealt with comparatively quickly and effectively, but other measures took longer. There were too many small meetings providing poor standards of sport, so some were amalgamated with neighbouring courses while others disappeared with their visible remains today no more than a once proud but rickety stand in an open field. Moves to reduce costs for owners, improve the facilities on courses (particularly for women), and to use the press to the turf's advantage soon showed a beneficial effect in reducing the traditional hostility between those organising racing and the public. Rules for the conduct of racing were also more forcefully applied to reduce fraud, not least over the ages of horses; to deter the misuse of inside information; and to bring criminal prosecutions in the courts where these were appropriate rather than rely on the limited authority of the Stewards of the Jockey Club. Horses were required to run on their own merits and the use of assumed names by owners was stopped. Another long overdue change was to allow horses to run even if their owners died between nomination for a race and the event. Similar improvements were introduced by the National Hunt Committee which had made Cheltenham its home in 1911. The one substantial and comparatively new problem which still defies a totally satisfactory solution today, was the question of ultimate responsibility in cases where horses were doped to enhance their performance. Racing was evolving more quickly and, for the time being, voices raised against the turf were subdued. It has to be admitted that English racing, once far in advance of that anywhere abroad, was rapidly being overtaken by the USA, France and, to a lesser extent, by such countries as Italy and Austria. This was true in regard to prize money and the general standard of organisation if not yet in terms of quality of the horse population. It was not until after the Second World War that all this came to be appreciated. Perhaps it would be fair to say that this relative decline mirrored that of the country itself, at least in economic terms.

George V was less interested in racing than his father. The Royal Stud was maintained at Sandringham with a steady flow of moderate foals being sent to Newmarket for training, initially with Marsh. Here the King enjoyed quietly visiting the stables to discuss his animals' performances and potential. The 17th Earl of Derby, Waldorf Astor (later 2nd Viscount Astor) and the Aga Khan were the leading owners between the two World Wars. The first owned fourteen classic winners between 1916 and 1936 (six later); the second, ten from 1910 to 1936 (and one in 1945); and the Aga Khan, nine from 1924 to 1936, with eight more between 1940 and 1952. Such figures might suggest that racing remained dominated by an aristocracy of sorts, but the great majority of owners, few any longer members of the Jockey Club, were self-made men who turned to racing as a colourful recreation. Gambling to meet the costs of keeping strings of horses in training had partly disappeared with new money coming from manufacturing. This broader based and cosmopolitan group of owners made racing a far more healthy 'industry' than in the past.

Between the two World Wars, Cecil Aldin, Lionel Edwards, Gilbert Holiday, Snaffles and Sir Alfred Munnings all painted racing and racehorses, the first four being attracted to steeplechasing in particular from their enjoyment of hunting. The number of colour reproductions of their work made in their lifetimes are few compared with those artists who painted similar scenes a hundred years before them. Many of these prints, usually with the artists' pencil signature below them, suffer from fading and colour distortion despite the up-to-date photographic techniques employed, sadly perpetuating the difficulty of finding racing prints in good, let alone pristine, condition today.

This short story of racing in Britain has many gaps. One which I particularly regret is how little I have written about the jockeys. Many of them, certainly in recent years, graduated from the arduous work of riding, wasting and keeping themselves fit, to become trainers and sometimes owners of successful racehorses. They were colourful characters, usually skilful, often honest although not a few were rogues. Notwithstanding that their personalities and activities add interest to the story, it was for the owners that pictures were painted, and prints were made primarily of horses not of jockeys. Indeed, in many engravings the name of the rider is omitted altogether and sometimes one feels that the sole purpose of including the jockey was to display the owner's colours! The occasions when a serious likeness of the rider was attempted are few. Accordingly I have limited the space devoted to them and, sadly, also to the equally interesting trainers.

I have felt it worthwhile to try to describe how racing was organised to give the layman, like myself, the background to what is depicted in a racing painting or print.

31a *The Downshire Wall, Punchestown. Colour reproduction after Gilbert Holiday.*

By 1830 racing had evolved to a point which is recognisable today; steeplechasing achieved this position more quickly, although some thirty years later with the formation of the National Hunt Committee. With this superficial understanding of the turf the collector will appreciate the very valuable record which prints provide and, I hope, enjoy them all the more for that reason.

Throughout the development of engravings from line to stipple and mezzotint, to aquatint, lithograph, photogravure and colour reproduction, reissues from doctored plates and modern copies of older prints have followed. For the connoisseur of first impressions these often clever facsimiles are anathema; but whether genuinely 'original', reprinted a short time later or, possibly, yesterday, they illustrate the story of racing, how horses were prepared, people dressed and meetings were run. For many, I dare say, the story of racing is far more interesting than the study of prints!

For prints of this period, see:

PRINTS

I

PUBLISHERS AND ENGRAVERS

This short review of publishers and engravers is limited to the narrow field of prints of racing which formed only a small part of their total output. However, the subject of racing is as good a vehicle as any to illustrate the progress and changes which took place generally in print publishing from the early eighteenth to the late nineteenth centuries.

The painters of racehorses had to travel widely to reach their subjects which, in a surprising way, were less mobile than themselves. Once the portrait or scene was completed, the drawing or canvas could quite easily be sent to the publisher and engraver. As with many other aspects of the fine arts, London was where the evolution of decorative English print making took place, not least because it was here that the engravers had the most opportunity for constant employment; also the publishers had access to a number of printers as well as a large proportion of their buying public. A few engravings were produced outside London, but their publishers rarely remained solvent for more than a decade. This was as much due to the comparatively small, interested local population who would buy their prints, as to the difficulties and costs of advertising the plates widely. Modern communications have overcome this problem.

Some of the first (and crudest) racing prints were 'taken from life' providing a simple but not particularly decorative record of the well known racehorses of the day. The majority of early prints are taken from paintings and engraved in line or by the more skilful mezzotinting process. The latter provides a chiaroscuro effect which was far closer to the light and shading of the original than could be achieved by the hatchings of the line engraving. Both types of prints were often produced in book or folio format, and it was not until the 1730s that the 'stand alone' racing print recording some famous Match or incident became common – continuing to the present day. The commissioning of artists by publishers to paint portraits of racehorses specifically for reproduction did not start until the beginning of the nineteenth century.

Carington Bowles (later Bowles and Carver) of St Paul's Churchyard, John Bowles of Cornhill, and Robert Sayer in Fleet Street, London, were among the earliest publishers of racing prints. Occasionally they combined together as in the portraits of Bonny Black and Judgement after Peter Tillemans: 'Printed by John Bowles, 13 Cornhill and sold by Robert Sayer, Opposite Fetter Lane, Fleet Street', c1740. In about 1748, Laurie and Whittle (later R. H. Laurie) succeeded Sayer at 53 Fleet Street and republished a large number of the Sayer mezzotint plates during the following six years before this firm also disappeared from view.

The engravers whom the publishers employed were legion; some far more skilful than others. Among the early line engravers, Remi Parr, who engraved plates after James Seymour, and Joseph Sympson Snr and Jnr, who etched and also sold their engravings after John Wootton and Peter Tillemans from The Dove, Russell Court, Drury Lane, London, stand out. The mezzotinter Robert Houston (plates after Seymour, William Shaw, Thomas Spencer, and Francis and John Nost Sartorius) was pre-eminent among those engraving racing prints in this way.

That most delicate method, stippling, was used by George Townley Stubbs to engrave the plates for his father's short-lived *Turf Review* (1794–1796). A few years later John Whessell was using the same technique in his very fine racehorse portraits after the paintings of J. N. Sartorius, Ben Marshall and his own designs, all published by J. Harris of Sweetings Alley, Cornhill and 8 Old Broad Street, London. Whessell brings us to 1800 when the art of aquatinting – a less laborious process than mezzo – became the principal method of engraving topographical, military and sporting plates in England.

To some the description 'aquatint' suggests an engraving tinted with watercolour. In fact the 'aqua' is aqua fortis or acid which was used to give an overall grain to a specially prepared copper plate. Variations in the strength and consequent darkness of the grain which held the ink was controlled by the length of time the acid was allowed to burn into exposed parts of the copper. The majority of aquatint engravings were hand-coloured (with watercolour) but a few were printed in colour by applying different inks to the major portions of the metal plate; watercolour was then added to give highlights and tint the smaller areas of the paper engraving. This process provided a more robust plate than the mezzotint in terms of the number of engravings which could be drawn from the copper surface before it became too worn to give a good impression. John William Edy was an outstanding aquatint engraver who was employed by Harris to reproduce a number of J. N. Sartorius's paintings between 1788 and 1799. Francis Jukes was equally talented during the same period, but did not engrave many racing plates.

By 1810, mezzotinting was fast disappearing as were some of the more familiar names of the publishers who had flourished in the previous century. In their absence a number of artists employed engravers and published their own plates, among whom were Sawrey Gilpin and George Garrard in the last years of the eighteenth, and Henry Bernard Chalon and Ben Marshall at the start of the nineteenth century. In the 1820s, James Ward drew his own lithographs of famous horses which, at first, he published himself. Publishers with a small list of engravings to their names came and went with a rapidity which suggests that as in other spheres of business, the uncertain times at the turn of the century affected confidence and no doubt the sales of prints.

Robert Pollard (founded in 1764), Rudolph Ackermann (1783), S. W. Fores (1783), Thomas McLean (1800), S. & J. Fuller (1812), John Moore (1820) and lastly Baily Brothers, who first made decorative prints in the 1830s, each published series of aquatint portraits of famous racehorses in the nineteenth century. The design of these plates sprang from those published by Robert Pollard (after watercolours by his son, James) in 1819, and from the retrospective set of St Leger Winners painted by J. F. Herring going back to 1815, published by the Doncaster firm of W. Sheardown & Sons in 1825. The style was a consolidation of the late eighteenth century prints with the jockey at last recognised as worth depicting. Also the earlier very detailed descriptions of performance and pedigree of the horses were considerably shortened since this information was available in periodicals elsewhere. The Sheardown engravings, those published by Fuller (who took over the series in 1826), and some which followed from other publishers could be subscribed to in anticipation of printing, as was the arrangement with the plates of

the *Turf Review*. The names of the painters and the engravers were invariably recorded in the publication line, but the commercial value of the artist's signature on a limited edition or number of prints is a modern occurrence. Had it been employed in the early nineteenth century, the problems for collectors today trying to distinguish between early or late impressions and reissues would be considerably less.

If without money to pay for tuition or not sufficiently talented to gain admittance to the Royal Academy Schools, apprenticeship to a publisher was another way of entering the artists' profession. The aspiring Charles Bentley, Edward Duncan, two Fieldings, two Lewises and William Callow first coloured prints before graduating to engraving plates for the enlightened Rudolph Ackermann Jnr and other publishers. For those who did not take up painting, engraving provided a modest income with the security of knowing that while their eyesight lasted, their work was always in demand. However, despite their undoubted skill, they lacked status since for many years the Royal Academy would not accept their craft as art. With some this rankled, but the majority had few pretensions to this kind of recognition.

John Heaviside Clark (1771–1863); Thomas Sutherland (fl 1809–1838); Richard Reeve (1780–c1835) and his two sons: Richard Gilson Reeve (1803–1889) and Augustus William Reeve (1807–c1880); Henry Pyall (1795–1833); Charles Hunt (1803–1877) and John Harris (1811–1865) were among the more prolific and successful aquatint engravers of the mid-nineteenth century; Thomas Fairland (1804–1852) was a fine lithographer of other painters' work. These names gave way to those of William Summers (fl 1853–1880) and Edward Gilbert Hester (1843–c1910) who engraved rather 'heavy' plates in the detailed style of the period until photogravure became popular (simpler, mechanical and less expensive than manual engraving) in their lifetimes. The various photographic methods of colour reproduction have met the demands of modern print making, but even in 1940 the process failed to prevent colour fading and distortion. This effect produces far more bizarre changes than with the straightforward daylight fading of the watercolour applied to much earlier prints.

Of the old publishing firms, only Ackermann, Fores and McLean remained at the turn of the twentieth century, with the last named disappearing in about 1910. Other publishers such as The Sporting Gallery have come and gone, while Messrs Frost and Reed's reproductions of paintings by Sir Alfred Munnings are among the last to be published within the timeframe of this book. By photography replacing the painter in part and the engraver in full, the colour reproduction changed the relationship which had existed for two centuries between artists, engravers, printers and publishers. To many, a sad day; but the evolution of racing prints, which some will call progress, reflects the changing manners and customs of the turf which must always be dynamic if racing is to survive.

The Work of the Engravers
(References are to the Catalogue of Prints, by Artists)

Alken, Samuel, Snr Garrard **1**; Rowlandson **3**.
Alken, Henry, Snr Alken, Henry, Snr **5, 6, 8, 12, 16**; Gill **1**.

Barlow, Francis Barlow **1**.
Barnard, William S. Marshall **6**.
Baynes, Thomas Mann Noyes **1**.
Beckwith, Henry Hancock **4**.
Bell, Edward Sartorius, J. N. **9**.
Bensted, Joseph Bensted **1**.
Bentley, Charles Alken, Henry, Snr **18–20**; Pollard **33**.
Black, G. B. Martin **1, 2**.
Blanchard, Auguste Thomas Marie Frith **1**.
Bouvier, J. D'Orsay **1**.
Brooks, Vincent Browne **1**; Herring, J. F. **26**.
Brown, G. Lambert **1**.
Burford, Thomas Burford **1, 2**; Seymour **5**.
Burke, Thomas Stubbs **5**.

Cannon, W. Seymour **11**.
Canot, Pierre Charles Seymour **2**.
Chalon, Henry Bernard Chalon **12**; Marshall **12**; Stubbs **18**.
Clarke, John Heaviside Alken, Henry, Snr **4**; Gilbert **1**; Tomson **2**.
Collyer, Joseph Burney **1**.
Cooke, William and George Marshall **4**.

Denton, Charles Denton **1**.
Dodd, Robert Sartorius, J. N. **5**.
Doyle, John Doyle **1, 2**.
Du Bosc, Claude Tillemans **1**.
Dubost, Antoine Dubost **1**.
Dubourg, Matthew Pollard **4**; Tomson **2, 3**.
Duncan, Edward Ferneley **1–3**; Gill **1**; Hancock **1–3**; Henderson **1**; Howard **1**.

Easling, J. C. Chalon **5**.
Edge, J. Pollard **20**.
Edwards, Samuel Arlent Wombill **1**.
Edy, John William Sartorius, J. N. **2–4, 6, 10**.
Elliott, William Smith, T. **1**.
Engleheart, John H. Cooper **3**.
Engleheart, Timothy Stansfield Cooper **3**.

Faber, John Morier **1**.
Fairland, Thomas Cooper **2**; Davis, T. R. **1**; Ferneley **4**.
Fellows, William M. Anon **3**; Howitt **1**.
Fielding, Newton Smith Limbird Lami **1**.
Fisher, Edward Hone **1**.

Gauci, M. Seymour **13**; Stubbs **18**.

Gilpin, Sawrey Gilpin **5**.
Gleadah, Joshua Pollard **19**.
Godby, James Howitt **2**.
Gooch, Thomas Gooch **1**.
Green, Benjamin Stubbs **8**.

Hancock, Robert Sartorius, F. **3**.
Hanhart, Michael and N. Rook **1**.
Harris, John Alexander **1**; Alken, Henry, Snr **13–15, 21, 23, 24**; Barratt **1**; Barraud **1**; Cooper **7**; Hall **4–6, 8, 10**; Hancock **1, 2**; Harland **1**; Herring, J. F. **13, 18–25, 27**; Hubbard **1**; Laporte **1, 2**; Pollard **29, 30, 31, 36**; Sextie **1, 2**; Tattersall **1**; Turner **5**; **13**; Woodward **1**.
Hassell, John Rowlandson **2**.
Havell, Robert Pollard **2, 3**.
Herring, John Frederick, Snr Herring, J. F. **6**.
Hester, Edward Gilbert Hall **4–6, 8, 9**; Hester **1, 2**; Sturgess **3, 5, 6**; Veal **1**.
Hodges, Charles Howard Gilpin **4**; Stubbs **11**.
Houston, Robert Sartorius, F. **1, 7**; Sartorius, J. N. **1, 8**; Seymour **9, 10**; Shaw **2**; Spencer **2, 3**.
How, R. Sartorius, F. **4**.
Howitt, Samuel Howitt **3**.
Hunt, Charles (Charles Hunt & Sons) Alken, Henry, Snr **22**; Alken, Henry, Jnr **3, 4, 5**; Barenger **3, 4**; Cooper **4, 5**; Davis, R. B. **2**; De Prades **1**; Desvignes **1**; Earp **1**; Hall **1–4, 6, 7**; Harrington **1**; Herring, B. **4**; Herring, J. F. **3, 4, 8–12, 14–19**; Hillyard **1**; Hunt, C. **1–16**; Lambert **2**; Mitchell **1**; Pollard **22, 26, 27, 33, 35, 37, 38**; Sartorius, F. **13**; Shayer **1**; Snow **1**; Spalding **1**; Stubbs **19**; Sturgess **4**; Swandale **1**; Towne **1**; Turner **1, 3, 4, 11, 12**; Voss **1**.
Hunt, Edwin Henry & Son Hunt, E. H. **1**; Powell **1**; Wombill **1**.
Hunt, George Barenger **3**; Egerton **1**; Hall **3**; Herring, J. F. **11**; Mitchell **1**; Pollard **9, 33, 35, 37**; Turner **1, 11**; Woodward **2**; Ziegler **1**.
Hunt, George Charles & Son Hunt, G. C. **1**.

Jenkins, J. Mason **1**.
Jukes, Francis Ansell **1**; Boultbee **1**; Gilpin **3**; Mason **1**.
June, John Sartorius, F. **6**.

Killingbeck, Benjamin Killingbeck **1**.
Kingsbury, Henry Sartorius, F. **9**.

Lewis, Charles George Herring, B. **1**.
Lewis, Frederick Christian Hancock **1**.
Lupton, Thomas Cooper **1**.

Mackrell, James R. Cooper **5, 6**; Herring, J. F. **16, 18**; Shayer **1**; Turner **8, 9**.

Merke, Henri   Davis, R. B. **1**; Howitt **2**.
Meyer, Henry   De Prades **1**.
Miller, John   Shaw **3**.

O'Bryan Lomax, J.   O'Bryan Lomax **1**.

Papprill, Henry A.   Laporte **3**.
Parr, Remi   Seymour **2, 3**; Tillemans **4**; Wootton **3, 4**.
Pether, William   Stubbs **1**.
Pollard, James   Pollard **5–7, 10–16, 18, 21**; Tomson **2**.
Pyall, Charlotte   Pollard **24**.
Pyall, Henry   Herring, J. F. **5**; Newmarch **1**; Pollard **23–25, 33, 34**.

Quentery, Charles C.   Cooper **7**; Hall **4, 6**; Herring, J. F. **19**; Sextie **2**.

Ravenet, Simon Francois   Tillemans **5**.
Reeve, Augustus William   Alken, Henry, Jnr **5**; Laporte **4**.
Reeve, Richard   Hazlehurst **1**; Marshall **7**.
Reeve, Richard Gilson   Alken, Henry, Jnr **5**; Herring, J. F. **3, 4, 7**; Laporte **4**; Pollard **17, 28, 38**; Turner **2**.
Roberts, Henry   Roberts **1–3**; Seymour **2**; Spencer **1**.
Rogers, J., Jnr   Rogers **1**.
Rooe, R.   Seymour **1**.
Rosenberg, Charles, Snr   Pollard **1**.
Rosenberg, Charles, Jnr   Pollard **37**.
Rowlandson, Thomas   Rowlandson **1, 4, 5, 7**.

Sargent, Francis James   Boultbee **1**.
Say, William   Chalon **10, 11**.
Scott, John   Gilpin **6**; Marshall **5**; Sartorius J. N. **15, 17**; Stubbs **16**; Tomson **1**.
Simmons, William Henry   Hayes **1**.
Smart, Robert William   Herring, J. F. **3, 4**; Pollard **22, 26**.

Smith, C. N.   Alken, Seffrien **1**; Bretland **1**; Davis, H. T. **1, 2**; De Prades **1**; Hall **3**; Smith, C. N. **1**.
Smith, Thomas   Smith, T. **1**.
Stevens, W.   Hall **11**.
Stock, C. R.   Bird **1–3**; Douglas **1**; Stock **1**; Veal **1**; Walsh **1**.
Stubbs, George Townley   Stubbs **3, 4, 6, 7, 12–14**.
Sturgess, John   Sturgess **2**.
Summers, John   Herring, B. **2, 3**.
Summers, William   Alken, Henry, Jnr **1, 2**; Hall **4–6, 8**; Herring, J. F. **19**; Neville **1**.
Sutherland, Thomas   Alken Samuel, Jnr **1**; Alken, Henry, Snr **2, 3, 5, 7**; Barenger **2**; Dalby **1, 2**; Herring, J. F. **2**.
Sympson, Joseph, Jnr   Anon **1**; Tillemans **2**; Wootton **1, 2**.
Sympson, Joseph, Snr   Tillemans **1, 2**.

Tallberg, Axel   Cullin **3**.
Thompson, James   Seymour **4**.
Tomson   Tillemans **3**.
Townley, Charles   Marshall **1**.
Turner, Charles   Agasse **1, 2, 3**; Chalon **1**; Marshall **11**.
Turner, George Archibald   Turner **6, 7, 10, 14**.

Ward, James   Ward **1**.
Ward, William   Chalon **2–4, 6–9**; Frankland **1**; Gilpin **1, 2**; Herring, J. F. **1**; Marshall **8, 9**; Sartorius, J. N. **18**.
Webb, John   Ferneley **1–3**.
Whessell, John   Hilton **1**; Marshall **2, 3, 10**; Sartorius, J. N. **11, 13**; Whessell **1, 2**.
Wolstenholme, Dean, Jnr   Wolstenholme Snr **1**; Wolstenholme Jnr **1**.
Wood, John   Seymour **7**.
Wright, J. H.   Gwynn **1**.

Ziegler, Henry Bryan   Ziegler **1**.

2
ENGRAVING METHODS

The more common engraving methods met with in the production of racing prints are line engraving, mezzotint, etching, alone or in combination with stipple or aquatint, types of lithography, and soft-ground etching, a rarity employed almost exclusively by Henry Alken Snr. Photographic colour reproduction cannot be described as engraving but there are a number of these prints included in this book. Each method has its attractions and drawbacks. The passage from early line engraving to modern reproduction has not been a progression in terms of skill or interpretation but an expedient toward simpler, mechanical and less costly methods of print publication. To the connoisseur of 'old' prints the modern reproduction is not worth a second glance, notwithstanding the fact that it is sometimes a far better likeness of an original oil or watercolour than the crude results achieved by the early line engravers. Dismissing both ends of the engraving and reproduction spectrum, the period 1780 to 1850 (which includes mezzotint, requiring the greatest skill from the engraver, stipple and the much-used aquatint process) provides both the most admired and the majority of British sporting and, of course, racing prints.

The engraved surface for many prints was a copper plate. Its softness was easily attacked by the engraving tool or acid, but this same characteristic meant that comparatively few good engravings on paper could be drawn from it before the plate deteriorated and the crispness of the ground or line was lost. One way of extending the life of a copper plate was to give it a steel surface and, after about 1860, steel plates became commonplace. However, engravings from steel or steel plating lack the strong texture and some of the warmth of those taken off copper. What is gained by the publisher in being able to make more prints from a plate is lost by the collector who recognises the inferior quality of a steel plate engraving.

At the beginning of the present century the practice of reproducing both copper plate and lithographic engravings by photographic methods became widespread. While deception was not intended, a careful examination of the 'flatness' of these reproductions (since no ground or line was etched into a plate giving a raised ink surface on the print) is necessary to determine how they were made. An outline understanding of the engraving methods employed is essential. This enables the collector to identify the type of engraving being considered and avoid the deepest pitfalls of buying reproductions at prices appropriate only to the first dozen prints taken from a plate.

Line Engraving

Lines are cut into a copper plate using a handheld gravure or burin. The depth and width of the line can be varied and the surplus metal which is turned away at its edges is removed leaving a clean groove to hold the ink. Paper is placed over the plate under pressure (the edge of the plate usually indents the paper) and when lifted provides a reverse image of what is engraved on the plate.

Mezzotinting

A tool, called a rocker, is used to give the surface of a copper plate a rough texture or surface burr. Some parts of this texture are then polished away eradicating the burr which could hold ink, so making the highlights. The remaining engraved surface prints a tone of varying depth according to how far the surface has been honed out. For colour mezzotints, inks were applied by 'painting' appropriate parts of the copper plate with a 'dolly' – a piece of ink-soaked rag at the end of a stick. The majority of early mezzotint racing plates were printed uncoloured but, at some later date, watercolour or gouache was applied to the paper surface by hand.

Etching

A copper plate is covered with a 'skin' of wax which resists the action of acid. The outline or design is then drawn in the wax with a sharp tool exposing the copper which is bitten into when the plate is immersed in a bath of acid. The depth of the 'engraving' depends upon the length of time the plate is attacked and the strength of the acid. When the wax surface is cleaned from the plate it is ready for inking and printing in the same manner as line engraving.

Stipple Engraving

For the general or large areas of a design, the waxed surface of a copper plate was punctured by a roulette (a small wheel with a minutely cogged rim making a line of dots) or by a mattoir or 'macehead' (a flat-headed punch with raised pins) providing an etched ground. Direct engraving on the copper with a tool nicking out small pieces of the metal was employed where a more careful or detailed design was required. The plate or print was coloured in the same manner as described for mezzotints.

Aquatint

In aquatinting a ground or tone was applied to the whole surface of a copper plate in the following manner. Resin was dissolved in spirits of wine and the solution poured over the surface of the plate. When the plate was warmed the spirits evaporated leaving a deposit of resin crystals evenly dispersed over its surface. During subsequent immersions in acid (aqua fortis), minute islands of polished plate remained where the resin protected the surface. Successive stopping out (covering parts of the plate surface with acid-resistant wax or gum) and immersion in acid produced a graduated and deepening tone as the exposed areas became larger and more deeply bitten to subsequently hold more ink. The most difficult part of the process was the timing of the plate's immersion in acid. The 'biting' strength would vary with the air temperature and atmospheric pressure. The relative activity of the acid on a bright, sharp morning could be quite different on the wet, close afternoon of the same day. However, if an area became over-bitten, there was always the safeguard of being able to polish out the grain, as in mezzotinting, to recreate the lighter tone.

In some aquatints colour was applied to the copper plate before printing but usually only to large areas such as the sky or greeny-brown foreground. Small areas were then hand-coloured with watercolour. In many cases the whole paper print was coloured in this way.

Soft-Ground Etching

In this type of etching a copper plate is covered with a soft wax/tallow film. A sheet of thin paper is laid over this and the design drawn on the paper with a pencil. When the paper is lifted it removes with it the tallow where it has been slightly compressed by the pencil through the paper. This exposes parts of the copper to the action of acid, in turn holding ink and reproducing with remarkable similarity the effect of a pencil drawing.

Lithograph

In what may be described as basic lithography, a lithographic chalk or crayon with a faintly oily texture was used to draw a design onto a finely ground stone 'plate'. The substance of the crayon was dragged onto the stone by the roughness of the grain and this waxy line or design subsequently held any ink applied. Paper placed over the stone required very little pressure to pick up the design accounting for the lack of plate marks on a lithographic print. For colour, a number of stones were used with each colour applied to its appropriate area on a single stone. Sometimes these areas coincided to make a combined (third or more) colour. The **chromolithograph** is no more than a coloured lithograph, but the name has been used to describe prints with bold, flat planes of ink usually associated with commercial prints and posters.

Photogravure

A light-sensitive, acid-resisting ground etched on a copper plate is the basis of photogravure reproduction. However, this type of plate lacks the clarity and brilliance of the hand-engraved prints described above.

An early print in brilliant condition is a revelation of the engraver's and colourist's art quite apart from being a rarity; but it sometimes seems that too much emphasis is placed on its condition and quality and too little on the story it tells. Today, without a very long pocket, it would be extremely difficult to build a representative collection of racing prints in good condition. However, by choosing a limited theme such as Gold Cup winners, Jem Mason and Lottery or portraits of, say, Lord Falmouth's horses, a satisfying and comparatively inexpensive collection could be assembled if one is prepared to accept that age, particularly light and often dampness is bound to take a toll on every type of print on paper. Whatever the condition of the print and whatever the engraving method, it will always tell an interesting story of racing.

3
CATALOGUE OF RACING PRINTS, BY ARTISTS

I have not included portraits of 'turf worthies' in this catalogue, delightful as many of these are, because it would be difficult to decide the criteria for who should be in and who out. The lists of prints are of races or racehorse portraits.

The detail of each print is not as comprehensive as that often found on the plate, but provides the essential facts from the viewpoint of illustrating racing history. The title is that which is shown on the plate; this results in the spelling of some of the names of the racehorses, in particular, being different to those recorded in the Calendar. With the racehorse portraits, success in other races than those recorded on the print are added, in parenthesis, only where they took place before the publication date. In a number of instances individual prints in a set of racing or steeplechasing scenes have no title. In such cases I have assumed a title to match the scene and entered these in parenthesis. Similarly for publication dates, unless the print definitely has no date; on these occasions I show 'Not Dated'.

Unless stated otherwise, print measurements are of the image, height before width.

I realise there are a number of gaps, and no doubt some inaccuracies. I welcome any information about omissions or mistakes.

The following abbreviations may be found in the biographical notes on the artists:

ARA	Associate of the Royal Academy
ARCA	Associate of the Royal Canadian Academy
b	Born in the year shown
BI	British Institution
c	Circa (about) the year shown
d	Died in the year shown
fl	Working during the period of the years shown
FSA	Fellow of the Society of Artists (before 1791)
FSA	Fellow of the Society of Antiquaries
Jnr	Junior
KCVO	Knight Commander of the Royal Victorian Order
MVO	Member of the Royal Victorian Order
op	Working in the year shown
PRA	President of the Royal Academy
RA	Royal Academy or Royal Academician
RBA	Royal Society of British Artists
RCA	Royal College of Arts
RHA	Royal Hibernian Academy
RI	Royal Institute of Painters in Watercolours
RNVR	Royal Navy Volunteer Reserve
Snr	Senior

ADAM, Emil, 1843–1924

Emil Adam came from a family of horse and battle painters, the most distinguished of whom was his grandfather, Albrecht Adam. Albrecht was present at battles of the Franco-Austrian War, saw Moscow set in flames by the Russians retreating before Napoleon, and later recorded incidents in the Austro-Italian campaign as well as painting portraits of horses. Emil's was a precocious talent and his portraits of horses in Austria were admired by all Europe. The Prince of Wales, the Dukes of Westminster and Portland, Lord Derby and Baron de Rothschild were among the many racehorse owners in England who wanted their thoroughbreds to be painted by him. This he did to their entire satisfaction, providing detailed pictures of great quality and realism but sometimes with little life. He only visited England, living for the most part in Germany and dying in November 1924 in the house which he had built for himself at Nymphenberg thirty years previously.

1 *Manifesto*. Portrait of a racehorse owned by Mr J. G. Bulteel, Winner of the the Grand National, 1897 (when owned by Mr H. M. Days, ridden by T. Kavanagh) and 1899, ridden by G. Williamson.

Aquatint. Pl. approx. 620 × 750 mm.

AGASSE, Jacques-Laurent, 1767–1849

Jacques-Laurent Agasse studied as a boy in his native Geneva and later under David and Vernet in Paris, as well as at the veterinary school in the city. In 1800 he settled in England at the invitation of the Hon. George Pitt (later 2nd Baron Rivers). He painted a number of very fine equestrian and greyhound portraits for Lord Rivers who had estates at Stratfield Saye and Hare Park near Newmarket. He quickly found other patrons, many of them friends of Lord Rivers, and his ability to portray horses sympathetically and with anatomical accuracy was widely recognised. He hoped that a collaboration in the early 1800s with Charles Turner, the artist and engraver, would be financially rewarding. However, these projects were short-lived and Turner found Agasse unreliable. Later coaching scenes engraved after his paintings proved more successful.

Agasse also portrayed animals at the Exeter Exchange in the Strand and he became friendly with Edward Cross who was responsible for finding wild beasts for the Royal Collection at Windsor. Agasse portrayed a Nubian giraffe and other animals for George IV. By 1830, Agasse was running short of equestrian commissions but continued painting animals as well as London street scenes. Many of the

32 *Preparing to Start. Aquatint after Jacques-Laurent Agasse.*

latter were populated by the children of George Booth, a publisher and bookseller, with whose family he lodged in Newman Street, just off Oxford Street.

He was probably a rather difficult character and, apart from his earlier friendship with Lord Rivers (who died in 1828), Agasse resented not being treated as an equal by the English aristocracy, his potential patrons. Towards the end of his life his studio was filled with paintings which he could not sell. He died virtually penniless just after Christmas, 1849.

1 Racing scenes.

1st Plate   Preparing to Start. [*32*]
2nd Plate   Coming In.

Horses painted by Agasse. The scene of Port Meadow near Oxford, the Hunters Stakes, 4 August 1802, sketched by C. Turner. Dedicated to Lord Francis Spencer on Madcap, (unplaced). G. F. Stratton on Skylight came 1st.

Mezzotints engraved by C. Turner. Published by C. Turner, 56 Warren Street, Fitzroy Square, London. 20 January 1803. Approx. 415 × 615 mm.
Republished by R. Ackermann in 1806.

2 Racing scenes.

No 1   Horses Taking their Gallop.
No 2   After Running. (Weighing). (*18, see page 40*)
No 3   Sketch from a Race Ground. (Roulette in a tent).
No 4   Peasants Coming to the Race.

Aquatints engraved by C. Turner. Published by C. Turner, as above. 19 October 1807. Approx. 215 × 290 mm.
Republished by Hassell & Rickards, 344 Strand, London. 1 June 1814.

3 The Wellesley Arabian. Portrait of a stallion with two attendants in a stable.

Mezzotint engraved by C. Turner. Published by J. L. Agasse, Newman Street, London. 19 August 1810. Approx. 440 × 565 mm.

ALDIN, Cecil Charles Windsor, RBA, 1870–1935

Cecil Aldin was primarily an illustrator but his art education included a time at the Frank Calderon School of Animal Painting. As well as drawing and pen-work, he employed watercolour and pastels; occasionally he painted in oils. Much of his work is plainly designed for reproduction, with large planes of single colour within hard but accurate outlines. However, this does not detract from his skill in creating atmosphere in a scene or character and personality in the humans and animals which he drew. His pictures of hunting were based on his experience as a Master of Harriers, Beagles, Basset Hounds and the South Berks Foxhounds. He is equally, if not better, known for his drawings and etchings of dogs; many of them his boon

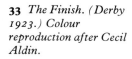

33 *The Finish. (Derby 1923.) Colour reproduction after Cecil Aldin.*

companions for long periods of his life.

The number of his racing paintings which were reproduced is small but those of the 1920 Grand National are extremely fine, particularly in the early, large version. Reproductions of these prints have recently been published. His nearly aerial view (presumably painted from the top of the Epsom stand) of the finish of the 1923 Derby is both novel and effective.

Cecil Aldin with his wife and dogs settled in Majorca in 1930 where the amusing and finally poignant autobiography of his life, *Time I Was Dead*, was written shortly before he died in 1935.

Racing

1 The Derby.

(1) The Start.
(2) The Finish. [*33*]

These prints represent the 1923 Derby, won by Mr B. Irish's Papyrus, ridden by S. Donaghue; 2nd, Lord Derby's Pharos, E. Gardner; 3rd, Mr M. Goculda's Parth, A. Walker.

Colour reproductions. Published by Richard Wyman & Co., 18 Bedford Street, London WC2.

Steeplechasing

2 The Grand National.

1 The First Open Ditch.
2 The Canal Turn.
3 Valentine's. [*Plate 15*]
4 Becher's Brook. [*34*]

These prints represent the Grand National 1920, won by twelve lengths by Major T. G. C. Gerrard's Troytown, ridden by Mr J. R. Anthony; 2nd, Mr C. L. Wilcox's The Turk II, R. Burford; 3rd, Mr H. A. Brown's The Bore, Owner.

1. l to r: 3 Sir J. Buchanan's Silver Ring (White, violet sleeves, red cap), ridden by G. Duller; 19 Captain Willoughby Norrie's Bonnie Charlie, (black, scarlet sleeves and cap), Mr M. D. Blair; 7 Mrs H. M. Hollins's Turkey Buzzard (light blue and brown hoops), W. Payne; 10 Mr M. H. Benson's Sergeant Murphy (amber, two black stripes, red cap), W. Smith, (4th); 2 Troytown (black, Eton blue collar and cuffs, quartered cap); 22 Turk II.

2. 6 Mr O. Toole's Clonree (green, yellow sleeves, pale blue cap), E. Morgan; 9 The Bore (brown, primrose collar and cuffs); 7 Turkey Buzzard; 10 Sergeant Murphy; 22 Turk II; 2 Troytown.

3. 2 Troytown; 10 Sergeant Murphy; 9 The Bore; 7 Turkey Buzzard; Unknown; 3 Silver Ring; 22 Turk II.

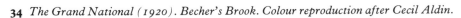

34 *The Grand National (1920). Becher's Brook. Colour reproduction after Cecil Aldin.*

4. Unknown (possibly Neurotic); 6 Clonree; 8 Captain Hanbury's Ardonagh (rose, chocolate cap), Mr P. Whitacker; 7 Turkey Buzzard; 2 Troytown; 10 Sergeant Murphy; 9 The Bore; 22 Turk II; 3 Silver Ring; and the faller: Mr F. C. Romilly's Little Rover (scarlet, green sash, black cap), Captain Doyle. There is a self-portrait of Aldin on the rails, on the left.

Colour reproductions. Published by Richard Wyman & Co. Ltd, 16 Bedford Street, Strand, London WC. c1920. Approx. 330 × 635 mm.

A smaller version was subsequently published by Wyman. Approx. 160 × 305 mm.

There are contemporary reproductions, slightly smaller than the first (large) versions, of this set.

ALEXANDER, Lady, born c1810, op1843

I believe that Lady Alexander (née Eveline Marie Cornwallis Michell) was the wife of Major (later General) Sir James Alexander. Alexander married Eveline Cornwallis Michell in 1837 and was knighted the following year for leading an exploratory expedition in Africa. He served in Canada with the 14th Foot from 1841 to 1846 and was then ADC to two successive commanders of the forces in Canada from 1847 to 1855. Presumably the engraving was 'worked up' from a contemporary sketch by Lady Alexander.

1 Grand Military Steeple Chase at London, Canada West, May 9th, 1843.

Aquatint engraved by J. Harris. Published by R. Ackermann, 191 Strand, London. 21 February 1845. Approx. 375 × 510 mm.

ALKEN, Samuel, Jnr 1784–c 1825
ALKEN, Henry Thomas (Henry Alken Snr), 1785–1851
ALKEN, George d before 1856
ALKEN, Samuel Henry (Henry Alken Jnr or Henry Gordon Alken 1810–94)
ALKEN, Seffrien, 1821–1873

The Alkens, possibly then named Sefferin, came to England from Denmark early in the eighteenth century. A Sefferin Alken and his wife Eleanor were living at 3 Dufours Place, Broad Street, Golden Square, London in 1745. Sefferin was a carver and gilder in partnership with his brother Oliver. Eleanor died in 1752, and Sefferin married again. When he died in 1782 he left five children of whom Samuel Alken (Snr)

was the eldest of three sons. Samuel, born in 1756, was admitted to the Royal Academy Schools at the age of sixteen and was awarded a silver medal in 1773. I do not think he painted, but he became an etcher and engraver in aquatint of the work of Thomas Rowlandson (qv), George Morland, George Garrard (qv) and Francis Wheatley, among many other artists. He married in 1781. His first son, Samuel Jnr, was born in 1784 and Henry Thomas (Henry Alken Snr) a year later. Two more sons of Samuel Snr became artists: George, whose date of birth is not known, and Sefferin John, born in 1796.

Samuel Jnr painted racing and hunting scenes in both watercolour and oils. Their style is simpler than that of his more famous younger brother, Henry. All trace of Samuel Jnr disappears in about 1825 and paintings signed S. Alken and dated after this year may have been painted by Sefferin. Undoubtedly the most pleasing of Samuel Jnr's racing pictures is the portrait of Lap Dog.

At the time of their father's death, Samuel Jnr and Henry Alken Snr were independent artists in their own right and it may be that in acquiring experience of what they painted their lifestyles were not to the liking of Samuel Snr; this thought is suggested by the little regard the father had for these two sons in his Will.

Henry Thomas Alken was born at 3 Dufours Place on 12 October 1785 and three weeks later was baptised at St James's Church, Piccadilly. The artistic atmosphere of his parents' home soon led Henry to drawing and painting. He studied under the miniature painter J. T. Barber. At the age of sixteen and again a year later, Henry Alken exhibited miniature portraits at the Royal Academy and this ability to paint human detail and character in a small compass stood him in good stead and can be seen repeated in all his later work. In 1809 he married a Maria Gordon at St Clement's Church, Ipswich. Both Henry and Maria are shown as living in this Suffolk parish. There was a family of Alkens in the county who may have been related, and it seems likely that Henry's (and Samuel Jnr's) experience of horses, hunting and, to a lesser extent, racing accounts for Henry being able to flatter himself 'that his work [*Beauties and Defects in the Figure of the Horse*, published in 1816] will be found useful; and his remarks are the result of the most attentive observation during many years entirely devoted to the pleasures of the field . . .'. From this date onwards Henry produced an unending stream of paintings, drawings and engravings of every type of field and other sporting activity. He is best remembered for his hunting prints, many of which he engraved himself until the late 1830s. A procession of publishers engaged him and no doubt prospered in the process rather more than the artist himself. Maria died in 1840 and from that date Henry's output fell dramatically. After eleven months of illness and pain, Henry Alken Snr died on 7 April 1851 at Ivy Cottage, Milfield Lane, Kentish Town. He was buried in Highgate Cemetery at the expense of his eldest daughter, Lydia Anne Zeitter, who had nursed him for some time before his final release. To many, sporting art is 'Alken', and to describe his work or ability is quite unnecessary. As a recorder of the racing scene, his paintings and the prints after them give us considerable information on the management and training of racehorses, as well as views of the early steeplechases, so close to his foremost love – hunting.

George Alken was both a painter and engraver. I only have a record of one set of racing plates after his work; and none after his younger brother Sefferin John.

Henry Alken Jnr continued where his father had left off, with less ability and sometimes disingenuously using his father's signature to pass off his mediocre paintings. However, a valuable record of the Derbys of 1865 and 1872 sprang from his brush at a period when few other sporting artists were engaged in painting action pictures of racing. His younger brother, Seffrien, painted in watercolour and he too gives us a vivid impression of a race – the Cambridgeshire, 1853.

Samuel Alken Jnr

1 Races at Newmarket.

  1 Training.
  2 Weighing In.
  3 Racing.
  4 The Winning Post.

Aquatints engraved by T. Sutherland. Published by T. Shepherd, Islington, London. 2 July 1817. Approx. 220 × 290 mm.

35 *Newmarket – Training; and Ascot Heath – Preparing to Start. Aquatints after Henry Alken Snr.*

36 *Epsom Races, with Horses preparing to Start for the Two Mile Heat. Aquatint after Henry Alken Snr.*

2 Delineations of British Field Sports. (25 Plates)

> 13 Race Horses in Training.
> 19 Racing.

Lithographs. Published by J. Hudson, Cheapside, London. 1822. Approx. 285 × 460 mm.

3 Lap Dog. Portrait of a racehorse owned by Lord Egremont. Winner of the Derby, 1826.

Aquatint. Published by S. Knight, Sweeting's Alley, Cornhill, London.

Henry Alken Snr

Racing

1 Racing scenes.

> Plate 1 Training.
> Plate 2 Mounting.
> Plate 3 Starting.
> Plate 4 Racing.

Unknown. *c*1817. Approx. 225 × 275 mm.

2 Racing scenes.

> Plate 1 Newmarket – Training. [*35*]
> Plate 2 Ascot Heath – Preparing to Start. [*35*]
> Plate 3 Epsom – Running. [*Plate 2*]
> Plate 4 Ipswich – Weighing. [*Plate 2*]

Aquatints engraved by T. Sutherland. Published by J.

Hudson, 85 Cheapside, London. 29 May 1818. Approx. 215 × 650 mm.
   Reprinted by R. Ackermann, 191 Regent Street, London. Not dated.

3 Epsom Races.

> Plate I With the Horses Preparing to Start for the Two Mile Heat. [*36*]
> Plate II With Mr Thornhill's Chestnut Colt Sam, Beating Lord Darlington's Grey and Sir John Shelley's Prince Paul for the Derby Stakes May 28th 1818.

The race was won by Mr T. Thornhill's Sam, ridden by Sam Chifney Jnr; 2nd, Lord Darlington's Raby, W. Pierse; 3rd, Sir J. Shelley's Prince Paul, Edwards.

Aquatints engraved by T. Sutherland. Published by S. & J. Fuller, 34 Rathbone Place, London. 9 February 1819. Approx. 315 × 620 mm.   Reprinted at a later date.

4 The National Sports of Great Britain. (50 Plates).

> 3 Racing, from Newmarket Heath. [*37*]
> 4 Racing. [*37*]
> 5 Racing.

Aquatints engraved by J. Clark. Published by Thos. McLean, 26 Haymarket, London. 1 January 1820. Approx. 150 × 215 mm.

5 The High Mettled Racer.

> Plate 1 The Foal. [*38*]

[77]

Plate 2   In Training. [*39*]
Plate 3   The Racer.
Plate 4   The Hunter.
Plate 5   The Post Horse.
Plate 6   The Death.

Aquatints engraved by H. Alken and T. Sutherland. Published by S. & J. Fuller, as above. 1 March 1821. Approx. 275 × 380 mm.

Republished in a smaller version, with verses, by Thos McLean, as above in 1828 and 1830. Approx. 75 × 125 mm.

6 The National Sports of Great Britain. (50 Plates).

2   Race Horse.
3   Pl 1   Racing. Training.
4   Pl 2   Racing. Saddling.
5   Pl 3   Racing. Preparing to Start.
6   Pl 4   Racing. Off.
7   Pl 5   Racing. Doing their Best.
8   Pl 6   Racing. Going to Weigh.

Soft ground etchings drawn by H. Alken. Published by Thos McLean as above. 1824. Approx. 130 × 210 mm.

37 *Racing from Newmarket Heath; and (below) Racing. Aquatints after Henry Alken Snr.*

38 *The High Mettled Racer. The Foal. Aquatint after Henry Alken Snr.*

39 *The High Mettled Racer. In Training. Aquatint after Henry Alken Snr.*

[79]

7 Racing scenes.

   (1)   The Walk.
   (2)   Starting.
   (3)   The Race: Coming In.
   (4)   Weighing and Rubbing Down.

Aquatints engraved by T. Sutherland. Published by Thos McLean, as above. 1824. Approx. 135 × 600 mm.

   Reprinted without the names of the artist and engraver, and without a publication line.

8 The Seven Ages of the Horse.

   (1)   At first, the Foal . . .
   (2)   And then, the Colt . . .
   (3)   And then, the Race-horse . . .
   (4)   Then, the Hunter . . .
   (5)   And then, the Harness-horse . . .
   (6)   . . . the Post-horse . . .
   (7)   . . . and would it were oblivion; . . .

Soft ground etchings drawn by H. Alken. Published by S. & J. Fuller, as above. 1 January 1825. Approx. 190 × 250 mm.

9 Newmarket Races.

   (1)   The Gallop.
   (2)   The Race.

Aquatints. Published by S. & J. Fuller, as above. 1 January 1825. Approx. 230 × 700 mm.

10 Sporting Medallions.

Five sets, of which one is of Racing and one Steeplechasing, see **17** below.

Aquatints. Published by R. Ackermann, 191 Regent Street, London. 1828. Approx. 75 × 125 mm.

11 Racing scenes.

   (1)   Going off for the first heat.
   (2)   Between the heats.
   (3)   Coming in for the last heat.
   (4)   The Winner at the Weighing house.

Aquatints. Published by R. Ackermann Jnr, 191 Regent Street, London. April 1831. Approx. 83 × 120 mm.

12 G. Osbaldeston Esq. performing his wonderful and unprecedented feat of 200 miles against time, November 5th 1831, for One Thousand Guineas.

Aquatint engraved by the artist. Published by G. S. Tregear, 123 Cheapside, London. 15 November 1831. Approx. 320 × 425 mm. Republished by J. Moore, 1 West Street, Upper St Martin's Lane, London.

13 Racing scenes.

   (1)   The Start.
   (2)   Coming In. (*Plate 10*)

Aquatints engraved by J. Harris. Published by R. Ackermann, as above. 5 February 1845. Approx. 420 × 630 mm.

14 'Fores's Sporting Scraps'.

Four racing scenes on one plate.

Aquatints engraved by J. Harris. Published by Messrs Fores, 41 Piccadilly, London. January 1850. Approx. 570 × 700 mm.

15 R. Ackermann's Racing Scraps.

   Plate 1   Training.
   Plate 2   Preparing to Start.
   Plate 3   Started.
   Plate 4   The Race.

Aquatints engraved by J. Harris. Published by R. Ackermann, as above. 27 April 1850. Approx. 215 × 275 mm.

Steeplechasing

16 A Steeple Chase.

   (1)   The Start – off they go with White for choice.
   (2)   Getting over an Old blind-road way and doing it well, even betting.
   (3)   A Slap at a Stone enclosure, – five to four on White.
   (4)   Crossing a Deep ravine dangerous to pass – with 6 to 2 on White.
   (5)   Crossing a Strong Bullock fence, down for a hundred without any odds on White.
   (6)   The Winner, and to such Wondrous doing brought his horse, Hamlet.

These plates may depict the celebrated race in 1826 between Mr Francis Holyoake's Clinker, ridden by Captain Ross, and Thomas Assheton Smith's Radical (nominated by Lord Kennedy) ridden by Captain Douglas. Clinker won easily over the distance of four miles from Barkby Holt to Billesdon Coplow.

Etchings engraved by H. Alken. Published by S. & J. Fuller, as above. 1 January 1827. Approx. 190 × 270 mm.

17 Sporting Medallions.

Four sets, of which one is Steeplechasing and one Racing, see **10** *above.*

Aquatints etc. As **10** above.

18 Grand Leicestershire Steeple Chase, 12th of March 1829. Dedicated to Captain Ross and the Gentlemen of the Quorn Hunt.

   Plate I   The Start. (*With names of horses and riders, and rules of the race*).
   Plate II   Going the Pace, Captain Ross leading – Mr Field Nicholson taking a line of his own.
   Plate III   Symptoms of Distress. The Cocktail Floored. [*40*]
   Plate IV   The field becomes Select. The Captain still leading.

40 *Grand Leicestershire Steeple Chase, on the 12th of March 1829. Plate III. Aquatint after Henry Alken Snr.*

Plate V	A Rich scene; . . .
Plate VI	Dick Christian's last fall; . . .
Plate VII	'The Climax of Disaster'.
Plate VIII	The Winning Post at Billesdon Coplow. (*Description of the finish and the result : 1st, Sir Harry Goodricke's Magic, ridden by Mr Field Nicholson; 2nd, Mr Maxse's King of the Valley, Dick Christian; 3rd, Mr Patrick's Lazy Bet, Bill Wright; 4th, Captain Ross's Clinker, Mr Haycock; the other three No-Where*).

Plates II–VII also have descriptions of their scenes and the names of the horses and riders.

Aquatints engraved by C. Bentley. Published by R. Ackermann Jnr, as above. 1 January 1830. Approx. 260 × 360 mm. Reprinted, with flaw in the 'rails' shown in Plate IV.

19 A Steeple Chase.

Pl 1	Now, my brave youths . . .
Pl 2	See how their coursers . . . [*22, page 44*]
Pl 3	With emulation fired . . .
Pl 4	O'er the deep ditch . . .
Pl 5	and brush the Thorny-twining hedge.
Pl 6	. . . Flourish the Whoop.

The quotations are taken from William Somerville's poem 'The Chase'.

Aquatints engraved by C. Bentley. Published by S. & J. Fuller, as above. March 1832. Approx. 290 × 460 mm. Reprinted by Messrs Fores, as above in *c*1848.

20 Aylesbury Grand Steeple Chase, 9th February 1836.

(1) The Start.

(2) The Brook Scene.
(3) The Lane Scene.
(4) Coming In.

The race was won by Mr Armytage's Saladin, ridden by Mr Powell; 2nd, Captain Lamb's Vivian, Captain Becher; 3rd, Lord Waterford's Yellow Dwarf, Owner.

Aquatints engraved by C. Bentley. Published by S. & J. Fuller, as above. 9 February 1836. Approx. 250 × 425 mm. Reprinted in 1866 with all dates changed to '1866'.

21 Night Riders of Nacton. The First Steeple-Chace on Record.

Plate I	Ipswich, the Watering-place behind the Barracks.
Plate II	The large field near Biles's Corner.
Plate III	The last field near Nacton.
Plate IV	Nacton Church, and Village.

Aquatints engraved by J. Harris. Published by R. Ackermann, as above. 1 March 1839. Approx. 270 × 370 mm.
Reissued by R. Ackermann.
Republished by Ben Brooks, 48 High Street, Oxford in 1865.

In Plate III of the first issue the shadow of a broken gate is engraved intact. This was altered, but the original mistake was later reinstated. Shadows thrown by the moon in wrong directions appear in all issues.

22 Cheltenham Grand Steeple Chase.

(1)
(2)

41 *Fores's Steeple Chase Scenes. The Brook. Aquatint after Henry Alken Snr.*

(3)
(4)

The Cheltenham Grand Steeple Chase run on 4 April 1839 was won by Mr J. Elmore's Lottery, ridden by Jem Mason; 2nd, Mr Vever's Charity, T. Olliver; 3rd, Mr. J. R. Newcombe's Cannon Ball, Powell.

Aquatints engraved by C. Hunt. Published in 1839.

23 'Fores's Steeple Chase Scenes'.

Plate 1 The Starting Field . . .
Plate 2 Wattle Fence with a deep drop . . .
Plate 3 In and Out of the Lane . . .
Plate 4 The Warren Wall . . .
Plate 5 The Brook . . . [*41*]
Plate 6 The Run In . . .

Aquatints engraved by J. Harris. Published by Messrs Fores as above. 24 April 1848. Approx. 270 × 375 mm.

24 'R. Ackermann's Steeple Chase Scraps'.

Plate 1 Getting Away. Now for the Fence.
Plate 2 The Brook. Clearing the Brook – now for the Stone Wall.
Plate 3 The Stone Wall and the double fence.
Plate 4 The Last Struggle.

Aquatints engraved by J. Harris. Published by R. Ackermann, as above. 20 February 1850. Approx. 115 × 195 mm.

George Alken

1 Racing scenes.

(1) Exercising.
(2) Preparing to Start.
(3) Running.
(4) Coming In.

Aquatints. Published by S. W. Fores, 41 Piccadilly, London. February 1827. Approx. 170 × 245 mm.

Henry Alken Jnr

Racing

1 Epsom Races.

(1) Tattenham Corner.
(2) The Winning Post. [*Plate 14*]

'The Winning Post' represents the finish of the Derby, 1865, won by Count Frederic de Lagrange's Gladiateur, ridden by H. Grimshaw; 2nd, Mr Richard Walker's Christmas Carol, T. French; 3rd, Mr W. Robinson's Eltham, S. Adams.

Aquatints engraved by W. Summers. Published by J. McQueen, 37 Great Marlborough Street, Regent Street, London, and 22 Rue de Dunkerque, Paris. 21 April 1871. Approx. 440 × 760 mm. An additional publication line: T. McLean, 7 Haymarket, appears under the titles of some of these plates.

2 'McQueen's Racings'.

(1) The Start.
(2) The Finish.

(2) represents the Derby, 1872, won by Mr Henry Savile's Cremorne, ridden by C. Maidment; 2nd, Mr J. N. Astley's

Pell Mell, T. Chaloner; 3rd, Lord Falmouth's Queen's Messenger, T. French.

Aquatints engraved by W. Summers. Published by G. P. McQueen, 37 Great Marlborough Street, as above. 1 April 1873. Approx. 435 × 765 mm.

Hurdle Racing

3 A Hurdle Race.

Plate 1st	Preparing to start . . .
Plate 2nd	The Third Leap . . .
Plate 3rd	Slashing Work . . .
Plate 4th and Last	Here they come . . .

Aquatints engraved by C. Hunt. Published by G. S. Tregear, Cheapside, London. *c*1835. Approx. 290 × 445 mm. Reprinted by Lewis & Co., 79 Leadenhall Street, London.

Steeplechasing

4 A Steeple Chase.

(1)	1st Mile . . .
(2)	2nd Mile . . .
(3)	3rd Mile . . .
(4)	4th and Last Mile . . .

Aquatints engraved by C. Hunt. Published by G. S. Tregear, 123 Cheapside, London. May 1832. Approx. 220 × 320 mm. Reprinted by Lewis & Co., as above.

5 The Last Grand Steeple Chase. Representing the last Steeplechase which took place at the Hippodrome Race Course Kensington, London W.

Plate 1	The First Hurdle.
Plate 2	The Brook.
Plate 3	In and Out. [*42*]
Plate 4	The Last Fence.

The last race meeting at the Kensington (Notting Hill) Hippodrome, which opened in 1837, took place on 2 and 4 June 1841.

Aquatints engraved by: Plates 1–3, C. Hunt; Plate 4, R. G. and A. W. Reeve. Published by G. S. Tregear, 96 Cheapside, London. Reprinted by G. Lewis & Co., as above, with title 'Steeple Chasing Illustrations'.
Reprinted with title 'Sheldon's National Sports', by James Sheldon, 31 Ely Place, London.

Seffrien Alken

1 The Cambridgeshire Stakes, 1853.

(1)	They're Off.
(2)	Quite Fresh.
(3)	Dead Beat.
(4)	The Finish.

The race was won by Mr W. Smith's Little David, ridden by G. Fordham; 2nd, Mr Drinkald's Nabob, A. Day; 3rd, Sir C. Monck's Hunca-munca, T. Aldcroft.

Aquatints engraved by C. N. Smith. Published by J. Moore, corner of West Street, Upper St Martin's Lane, London. 24 November 1853. Approx. 350 × 530 mm.

42 *The Last Grand Steeple Chase at the Hippodrome Race Course, Kensington. Aquatint after Henry Alken Jnr.*

43 *Mr W. Chifney's Priam. Derby 1830. Lithograph. Anon.*

ANON.

1 Part of a series of portraits of racehorses, with names of their owners. See TILLEMANS **2**; WOOTTON **1**.

(1) Mary-Grey – owned by the Duke of Bolton.
(2) Starling – Duke of Bolton.
(3) Camillus – Duke of Bolton.

Line engravings by J. Sympson Jnr. Sold by J. Sympson at The Dove, Russell Court, Drury Lane, London. *c*1730. Approx. 165 × 205 mm.

2 Bay Malton. Portrait of a racehorse owned by the Marquis of Rockingham.

Line engraving. Printed for and Sold by Carington Bowles, No. 69 in St Paul's Churchyard, London. *c*1770. Approx. 230 × 350 mm.

3 Priam. Winner of the Derby Stakes, May 27th, 1830 (and Goodwood Gold Cups, 1831 and 1832). The Property of Mr W. Chifney. [*43*]

Portrait of the racehorse held by W. Chifney.

Lithograph drawn by Fellows. Published by S. Maunder. *c*1830. Approx. 348 × 420 mm.

4 Iroquois. Portrait of a racehorse owned by Mr P. Lorillard, jockey up. Winner of the Derby (and St Leger), 1881, ridden by Fred Archer.

Colour printed lithograph by Maclure and Macdonald,

Engravers to the Queen, Glasgow. Published by The Turf Fine Art Association, London. 20 July 1881. Approx. 645 × 850 mm.

5 Ladas. Winner of the Derby 1894 (and 2,000 Guineas) with J. Watts up. Owned by Lord Rosebery.

Aquatint, possibly from a photograph. Published by G. Rees, 115 & 116 Strand, London. 21 June 1894. Approx. 480 × 660 mm.

ANSELL, Charles, b1752? fl 1780–1790

He was possibly a student of Vincent in Paris in 1778 where a Charles Ansell is shown as being born in London in 1752. Ansell exhibited portraits at the Royal Academy in 1780 and 1781 from 1 Edward Street, Cavendish Square. He is shown as the author of the plates listed below but they are exactly the same as six paintings exhibited by Thomas Gooch (*qv*) at the Royal Academy in 1783. There are other examples of Ansell's name being given to prints which are plainly after other artists.

1 Life of a Racehorse.

Plate I   As a Foal.
Plate II   As a Colt in Training. Published 2 February 1784.

Plate III   As a Racer after Running. [*7, see page 38*]
              16 April 1784.
Plate IV   As a Hunter going out with Hounds. 20 April
              1784.
Plate V
Plate VI

Aquatints engraved by F. Jukes. Published by John Walker, 148 Strand, near Somerset House, London. Ovals, approx. 235 × 290 mm.
      Republished by R. Pollard, Braynes Row, Spa Fields, London in 1796.

BARENGER, James, 1780–1831

James Barenger was born in London on Christmas Day, 1780. His father was an artist and it may be presumed he was in part his son's tutor. Barenger's mother was a sister of the engraver William Woollet. He first exhibited at the Royal Academy in 1807, and from 1815 until his death paintings were sent to exhibitions from Mr Tattersall's at Hyde Park Corner. He obviously had a satisfactory business arrangement at 'The Corner' where there were good opportunities to meet the patrons of that establishment, who also gave him commissions for paintings. He painted Tattersall's famous horse Highflyer which was engraved by Charles Hunt and published by Thomas McLean in 1823, and later by S. & J. Fuller.

Best known for his pictures of hunters and hunting he also painted dogs and cattle. Barenger's racehorses are carefully drawn and the racing scenes have a frieze-like quality bordering on silhouette.

1 Racing scenes.

Racing No I   (Exercising).
       No II   (Saddling).
       No III   (Racing).
       No IV

Aquatints. Published by C. Random, 65 Pall Mall, London. 25 August 1810. Approx. 190 × 490 mm.

2 Racing scenes.

1
2
3
4

Aquatints engraved by T. Sutherland. Published by C. Random, 5 Hart Street, Bloomsbury Square, London. 1810. Approx. 125 × 420 mm.

3 Portraits of racehorses.

(1)   Rubens – owned by HRH the Prince of Wales.
(2)   Claret – Lord Egremont.
(3)   Highflyer – bred by Lord Bolingbroke. [*8, page 27*]

Aquatints engraved by : (1) G. Hunt; (2) and (3) C. Hunt. Published by Thos McLean, Haymarket, London. 1823.

4 Highflyer. Portrait of a racehorse bred by Lord Bolingbroke.

Aquatint engraved by C. Hunt. Published by S. & J. Fuller, 34 Rathbrone Place, London. September 1843. Approx. 240 × 305 mm.
      Republished: 'Sheldon's Celebrated Racing Sires'.

BARLOW, Francis, c1626–1704

'The Father of British Sporting Painting'. This apt title for Francis Barlow is based on his ability to draw, paint and etch all kinds of animals and sport of his time. Apparently a Lincolnshire man, he spent most of his life in London where his patrons, of whom Denzil Onslow of Clandon Park in Surrey was one of the more important, sought him out to decorate their country houses with sporting scenes (in the Dutch manner). His paintings of hounds, dogs and birds are more realistic than those of horses. Barlow's lightness of touch as a graphic artist and engraver link his name with Wenceslaus Hollar with whom he collaborated in illustrating a number of publications. However, his ability to fill a sheet of paper with all kinds of birds and beasts in an animated scene of sport is his particular trademark. His etchings from his own designs for *Aesop's Fables* published in 1666 are particularly delightful.

Although he received many commissions and, possibly, inherited money on more than one occasion, he is said to have died in straitened circumstances.

1 'The Last Horse Race Run before Charles the Second of Blessed Memory by Dorsett Ferry near Windsor Castle' on August 10th, 1684. [*1, page 14*]

Line engraving 'Drawn from the Place and Design'd by Francis Barlow, 1687'. Published by P. Tempest and S. Baker. 1687. Approx. 560 × 715 mm.

BARRATT, Thomas, fl 1852–1860

Little is known of this artist except for his excellent work, including portraits of racehorses. He derived his affix 'of Stockbridge' from his recorded portraits of

44 *Henry Padwick Esq's Virago, with J. Wells up, accompanied by his trainer John Day and groom William Goater. Aquatint after Thomas Barratt.*

racehorses, all trained by the Days (of Danebury) near Stockbridge in Hampshire where his name appears in a local directory. A Thomas Barratt exhibited portraits of horses at the Royal Academy between 1852 and 1860. There is then a gap in time before a few fishing scenes were exhibited between 1886 and 1888; I suspect these later pictures may be by another Barratt.

1 Virago. Portrait of a racehorse owned by Henry Padwick Esq with her trainer, J. Day and groom, W. Goater. J. Wells up. 'Winner of ten races in 1854' (including the 1,000 Gns). [*44*]

The painting for this print was exhibited at the Royal Academy in 1855.

Aquatint engraved by J. Harris. Published by Ackermann & Co., 96 Strand, London. 1 January 1855. Approx. 480 × 665 mm.

BARRAUD, William, 1810–1850 and Henry, 1811–1874

Although the father of William and Henry Barraud was Prime Clerk in the London Customs House, many members of the family had practised the applied arts since they came to England from France in 1685. William Barraud received some tuition from Abraham Cooper (*qv*) and by the 1830s was exhibiting pictures of horses and dogs at the Royal Academy and British Institution. Henry Barraud became a portrait and figure painter, and the brothers, living first with their father at Camberwell and later sharing a studio in Park Street, Grosvenor Square, London, started working together on commissions in 1836. This proved a fruitful collaboration until William's early death from typhoid in 1850. Many of their paintings were engraved for *The Sporting Magazine* and a few large plates were published by Ackermann, Fores and Graves.

After the death of his brother, Henry continued painting equestrian portraits and scenes from history with moderate success. An engraving after his painting of three choristers, *We Praise Thee O Lord*, was immensely popular, but the print of his tour-de-force of 230 portraits in *The London Season* was less of a hit than was hoped for. At the studio sale after his death in June 1874, the vast canvas of *The London Season*, measuring 4 ft 6 inches by 8 ft 8 inches made only £125 5s. 0d.

The sporting work of the brothers, painted both individually and jointly, comprises mainly equestrian and canine portraits. There is very little excitement to be found among their well groomed horses or neatly brushed hounds, but they are completely honest and by no means totally lifeless.

1 'Fores's Celebrated Winners – Plate 1'.

The Hero. Portrait of a racehorse with his owner and trainer, J. Day and jockey, Alfred Day. Winner of the Emperor's Plate, Ascot, 1847 (and 1848). [45]

'Painted expressly at Danebury by W. & H. Barraud'. Aquatint engraved by J. Harris. Published by Messrs Fores, 41 Piccadilly, London. 15 September 1847. Pl. approx. 550 × 770 mm.

BEER, John Axel Richard, 1883–1916

John Beer spent much of his life working in London for Messrs Fores of Piccadilly. He painted a few portraits of racehorses, but the majority of his work comprises small sets of racing and steeplechasing scenes. His tubular horses run full stretch across the page with their slightly wooden jockeys looking distinctly uncomfortable whether on the flat or jumping a fence. However, he often achieved an overall impression of speed and excitement; this in spite of his taking little note of Eadweard Muybridge's series of photographs showing the exact motions of a galloping horse, evidence which was quickly accepted by Beer's contemporaries.

The Walker Art Gallery at Liverpool has a collection of over one hundred racing watercolours by Beer painted between 1905 and 1915, but the Keeper has no information about the artist's life.

Like the work of many of his predecessors, Beer's pictures may suffer from being painted too quickly to meet the publisher's 'race-result' demands. Those not painted against the clock are often quite pleasing and his painting of weather and light is often very skilful. Beer has a place as a useful recorder of the turf at the beginning of the twentieth century.

Racing

1 Portraits of racehorses. See HAVELL **8**.

   (1) Persimmon, Jack Watts up. (Derby and St Leger, 1896)
   (2) Ormonde, Fred Archer up. (Triple Crown, 1886)

Hand-coloured reproductions. Published by Messrs Fores, 41 Piccadilly, London. Pls approx. 280 × 405 mm.

2 The Life of a Racehorse.

   1 Mother and Son.
   2 The Nursery.
   3 Training.
   4 The Winner.

Hand-coloured reproductions. Published by Messrs Fores, as above. Pls approx. 255 × 355 mm.

3 Racing scenes.

Plate 1   Epsom. The Paddock.
Plate 2   Sandown. The Preliminary Canter.
Plate 3   Doncaster. At the Post.

45 *John Day Snr's The Hero, with portraits of the jockey Alfred Day, and the owner. Aquatint after William and Henry Barraud.*

[87]

Plate 4   Ascot. The Start.
Plate 5   Newmarket. The Race.
Plate 6   Goodwood. The Finish.

Photo-lithographs. Published by Messrs Fores, as above. Pls approx. 370 × 760 mm.

4 The Derby.

1   The Paddock.
2   The Parade.
3   Going to the Post.
4   The Start.
5   Climbing the Hill.
6   Tattenham Corner.
7   The Finish.
8   Returning to Scale.

Hand-coloured reproductions. Published by Messrs Fores, as above. Pls approx. 305 × 530 mm.

5 The Celebrated 'Hardwicke Stakes', Ascot, 1887. Including portraits of the winner Ormonde; 2nd, Minting; and 3rd, Bendigo.

Colour reproduction. Published by Messrs Fores, as above. Pl. approx. 315 × 510 mm.

6 Racing scenes.

(1)   The Liverpool Cup, 1902. Two Dead Heats. (For 1st place and 4th place).
(2)   The Eclipse Stakes, 1903. Ard Patrick and Sceptre.

Colour reproductions. Published by Messrs Fores, as above. Pls approx. 350 × 510 mm.

7 The Finish of the Derby, 1909.

Won by HM King Edward's Minoru, ridden by H. Jones; 2nd, Mr W. Raphael's Louviers, G. Stern; 3rd, Lord Michelham's William the Fourth, W. Higgs.

Colour reproduction. Published by Messrs Fores, as above. Pl. approx. 330 × 535 mm.

8 Ormonde (Triple Crown, 1886), with F. Archer up. Portrait of the racehorse within a wreath, surrounded by his ancestors and descendants, including: Whalebone; Sir Hercules; Irish Birdcatcher; The Baron; Stockwell; Doncaster; Bend Or; Orme; and Flying Fox.

Colour reproduction. Published by Messrs Fores, as above. 1 April 1911. Pl. approx. 460 × 765 mm.

9 The Blacklock Line. Portrait of the racehorse St Simon (Ascot Gold Cup, 1884) in a loosebox, surrounded by his ancestors and descendants, including: Blacklock; Voltaire; Voltigeur; Vedette; Galopin; Donovan; Persimmon; Diamond Jubilee; St Frusquin; William III; Memoire; and La Fleche.

Colour reproduction. Published by Messrs Fores, as above. 1 April 1911. Pl. approx. 460 × 750 mm.

10 Sceptre, in a loosebox. Portrait of the racehorse surrounded by racing scenes of her successes, including: 2,000 Gns; 1,000 Gns; Oaks; and St Leger, 1902; Hardwicke Stakes; The Jockey Club Stakes; and Duke of York Stakes.

Colour reproduction. Published by Messrs Fores, as above. Pl. approx. 360 × 610 mm.

11 Pretty Polly, outside her stable. Portrait of the racehorse surrounded by racing scenes, including: 1,000 Gns; Oaks; and St Leger, 1904; Middle Park Plate; Coronation Stakes; The Jockey Club Cup, 1905; and Ascot Gold Cup, 1906.

Colour reproduction. Published by Messrs Fores, as above. Pl. approx. 360 × 610 mm.

Steeplechasing

12 The Grand National Steeplechase, 1901. (Snowstorm).

1   At the Post.
2   The First Fence.
3   The Water Jump.
4   The Canal Side.

The race was won by Mrs B. Bletsoe's Grudon, ridden by A. Nightingall; 2nd, Mr O. J. Williams's Drumcree, Mr H. Nugent; 3rd, Mr J. E. Rogerson's Buffalo Bill, H. Taylor.

Colour reproductions. Published by Messrs Fores, as above. Pls approx. 270 × 290 mm.

13 The Grand National Steeplechase, 1903.

1   The Open Ditch.
2   The Water Jump.
3   Beecher's Brook.
4   The Last Fence.

Each with the horses' names shown. The race was won by Mr J. S. Morrison's Drumcree, ridden by P. Woodland; 2nd, Mr White-Heather's Detail, A. Nightingall; 3rd, Mr J. G. Bulteel's Manifesto, G. Williamson. (Manifesto won the Grand National in 1897 and 1899, and was 3rd in 1900 and 1902.)

Colour reproductions. Published by Messrs Fores, as above. Pls approx. 330 × 460 mm.

14 Steeplechasing scenes.

(1)   Sandown. The Grand Military, 1906.
(2)   Sandown. The Ripley Steeplechase.
(3)   Plumpton. The Hurstpierpoint Hurdle Race.
(4)   Hurst Park. The Molesey Steeplechase.
(5)   Newbury. The First Steeplechase.

Colour reproductions. Published by Messrs Fores, as above. Pls approx. 305 × 480 mm.

15 Steeplechasing scenes.

1   The Preliminary.
2   The First Fence.

Colonel the Hon.
Anson's Attila,
with W. Scott up.
Derby 1842.
Aquatint after
Charles Hancock.

PLATE 8

The Earl of
Eglinton's Blue
Bonnet, with
T. Lye up.
St Leger 1842.
Aquatint after
Charles Hancock.

The Flying Dutchman and Voltigeur Running the Great Match at York on the 13th May 1851, for 1000 Sovereigns a Side. Aquatint after John Frederick Herring Snr.

PLATE 9

Coming In. Aquatint after Henry Alken Snr.

John Bowes Esq's West Australian, with F. Butler up. Triple Crown 1853.
Aquatint after Alfred F. de Prades.

PLATE 10

3 The Water Jump.
4 The Last Hurdle.

Colour reproductions. Published by Messrs Fores, as above, Pls approx. 330 × 585 mm.

16 The Grand National, 1908.

    (1) The Second Fence.
    (2) The Canal Turn.
    (3) The Water Jump.
    (4) Beecher's Brook.

The race was won by Major F. Douglas-Pennant's Rubio, ridden by H. Bletsoe; 2nd, Mr W. Cooper's Mattie MacGregor, W. Bissell; 3rd, Mr P. Whitaker's The Lawyer III, Owner.

Colour reproductions. Published by Messrs Fores, as above. Pls approx. 245 × 425 mm.

17 Grand National Horses. Portrait of Lottery with Mr Jem Mason up (Grand National, 1839) surrounded by scenes, including: Tom Olliver on Peter Simple (1849, ridden by T. Cunningham and 1853); Mr Thomas on The Lamb (1868, ridden by Mr Edwards and 1871); T. Abbott on Abd-el-Kadar (1850, ridden by Green and 1851); George Stevens on The Colonel (1869 and 1870); W. Dollery on Cloister (1893); and G. Williamson on Manifesto (1897, ridden by T. Kavanagh and 1899).

Colour reproduction. Published by Messrs Fores, as above. Pl. approx. 375 × 610 mm.

BENSTED, Joseph, fl 1828–1847

Little is known of Bensted except from his Royal Academy exhibits between 1828 and 1847 which were sent in from Maidstone in Kent. His subjects were dead game and one picture called *The Dispute*. As well as the picture of the Maidstone Grand Steeple Chase, which he lithographed himself, Bensted painted a few equestrian hunting portraits and scenes, one of which was also engraved.

1 Maidstone Grand Steeple Chase, Friday March 15th, 1839. With dedication to Thomas Franklyn Esq.

Mr 'Jem' Mason on Lottery shown clearing a brook.

Lithograph drawn by the artist, Maidstone. *c*1839. Approx. 265 × 355 mm.

BIRD, John Alexander Harington, ARCA, 1846–1936

Harington Bird was born in London and attended the Royal Academy Schools as a young man. After spending some years in Canada, where he became an Associate of the Royal Canadian Academy, he returned to

46 Newmarket Scenes. Waiting for the Trainer. Aquatint after John Alexander Harington Bird.

47 *Newmarket Scenes. The Trial. Aquatint after John Alexander Harington Bird.*

England in 1885. He very quickly obtained commissions for portraits of racehorses and painted hunting scenes in both oils and watercolours. He was also an illustrator for periodicals of the time. He died in London in January 1936.

1 'McQueen's Derby Winners'.

  (1) Merry Hampton. Portrait of a racehorse owned by Mr Abington. Winner of the Derby 1887, ridden by Jack Watts, with details of pedigree.

  (2) Ayrshire. Portrait of a racehorse owned by the Duke of Portland. Winner of the Derby (and 2,000 Gns), 1888, ridden by F. Barrett. Published 7 June 1888.

  (3) Donovan. Portrait of a racehorse owned by the Duke of Portland. Winner of the Derby 1889, ridden by T. Loates (and St Leger 1889, ridden by F. Barrett). 7 August 1889.

Aquatints engraved by C. R. Stock. Published by F. C. McQueen & Sons, 181 Tottenham Court Road, London. Approx. 500 × 600 mm. See CULLIN **3**.

2 'McQueen's Racings'.

  Turf favourites, 1887.

  A group portrait of thirteen racehorses with jockeys up.

Aquatint engraved by C. R. Stock. Published by F. C. McQueen & Sons, as above; and S. Stiefbold & Co., Berlin; and Knoedler & Co., New York. 31 May 1889. Approx. 505 × 920 mm.

3 Newmarket Scenes.

  1 Waiting for the Trainer. [*46*]

  2 The Morning Gallop.
  3 The Trial. [*47*]
  4 Returning Home. Published 1 June 1892.

Aquatints engraved by C. R. Stock. Published by F. C. McQueen & Sons, as above. 21 December 1891. Approx. 295 × 625 mm.

BOULTBEE, John, 1753–1812

John Boultbee and his twin brother Thomas (also an artist) were born in Leicestershire, the county to which their greatgrandfather had come from Bolteby in Yorkshire some fifty years before, changing his name on the way. The twins moved to London shortly before 1775 when Thomas was admitted to the Royal Academy Schools. No doubt they received tuition elsewhere and Sawrey Gilpin (*qv*) is said to have taught John at some stage in his career. In about 1785 the twins split up with John moving first to Loughborough, then to work at Chester and finally at Liverpool where, just prior to his death, twelve of his pictures were exhibited at the Liverpool Academy. John Boultbee's paintings, of which six were exhibited at the Royal Academy, were all static portraits of hunters and racehorses. His style is reminiscent of George Stubbs (*qv*), some of whose paintings he copied. All his work is extremely pleasing and well painted.

1 Gohanna. Portrait of a stallion, owned by Lord Egremont, with Mr Thomas Bird, with a view of Gohanna Farm and Lodge.

Gohanna is the name of a hill near Petworth, Lord Egremont's seat.

Aquatint engraved by F. Jukes & Sarjent. Probably published privately by Boultbee. 1808. Approx. 475 × 620 mm.

BRETLAND, Thomas Walker, 1802–1874

Thomas Bretland, the older son of the owner of a coach and carriage painting business, was born in Nottingham. From boyhood he was determined to be an animal painter, but dutifully worked for his father. In 1828 he became a partner in the family firm. He continued in this way until three years after his father's death in 1837. Although he had been painting sporting pictures for some years, and it could be said he was the successor to Clifton Tomson of Nottingham (*qv*) who died in 1828, it was not until the 1840s that his work attracted a number of patrons. As well as the local

aristocracy, J. S. Drinkald, the racehorse owner, commissioned Bretland to paint a number of his winners. Bretland's comparatively rare but distinguished paintings include hunting and shooting scenes, fat cattle, the mounted chargers of locally stationed cavalry regiments, as well as portraits of racehorses, hunters and hacks. Thomas Bretland died at his home in Shakespeare Street, Nottingham on 3 May 1874.

1 Portrait of a racehorse with details of pedigree and performance, titled 'Moore's Celebrated Winners'. See COOPER **5**; DAVIS H. T. **1**; DE PRADES **1**; HALL **3**; HERRING J. F. **11**; HILLYARD **1**; SHAYER **1**; SMITH C. N. **1**.

St Lawrence – owned by J. S. Drinkald Esq. Ridden by W. Ford. Chester Cup, 1847. With details of pedigree and performance.

Aquatint engraved by C. N. Smith. Published by J. Moore, 1 & 2, corner of West Street, St Martin's Lane, London. 8 March 1848. Approx. 380 × 500 mm.

BROOKS, Henry Jermyn, fl 1884–1910

Henry Jermyn Brooks was essentially a painter of

48 *Ascot. The Royal Enclosure on Cup Day. Photogravure after Henry Jermyn Brooks.*

human portraits. Those which were exhibited at the Royal Academy between 1884 and 1910 include one of the sculptor Sir J. E. Boehm RA and another of the sculptor and artist Adrian Jones (*qv*).

1 A Yearling Sale at Doncaster. A large scale group portrait.

Photogravure. Published by Messrs Dickinson & Foster, 114 New Bond Street, London. 1 July 1889. Approx. 480 × 905 mm.

2 Ascot, The Royal Enclosure on Cup Day. A large scale group portrait. [48]

Photogravure. Published by Dickinson & Foster, as above. 1 June 1894. Approx. 485 × 875 mm.

3 The Household Brigade Cup. A large scale group portrait.

Painted with Adrian Jones, see JONES 1. Photogravure. Published by The Leadenhall Press Ltd. February 1901. Approx. 410 × 900 mm.

BROWNE, Hablot Knight ('Phiz'), 1815–1882

After the early death of his father, Browne was brought up by his mother in Suffolk where he was apprenticed to an engraver. He then studied at the St Martin's Lane School, London and became an illustrator for the author Charles Dickens until they quarrelled in 1864. He had moved with his family to Thornton Heath in Surrey in 1846 where he continued to contribute illustrations to periodicals until partial paralysis and blindness in one eye reduced him to penury. In 1879 he was granted a small annuity by the Royal Academy and retired to Brighton where he died three years later.

1 The Derby Day.

Pl 1 Down the Road. 'Fresh as the Blush of Early Morning'.
Pl 2 The Plot Thickens. 'The Cry is Still they Come'.
Pl 3 Before the Race. 'Mixing together Profit and Delight'.
Pl 4 The Starting Post. 'A Race of Running Steeds'.
Pl 5 The Race. 'To Be or Not to Be'.
Pl 6 Leaving the Course. 'The Favourite has Won'.
Pl 7 The Return. 'Tickets Gents! Tickets!'.
Pl 8 Nearing Home. 'Curious Effects of Lobster Salad and Fresh Air'.

Chromolithographs by Vincent Brooks. Published by Messrs Fores, 41 Piccadilly. 31 May 1866. Approx. 310 × 760 mm.

BURFORD, Thomas, fl 1730–1775

A member of the Incorporated Society of Artists, Burford exhibited sketches and engravings at their exhibitions between 1762 and 1774; his address was Chapel Street, Westminster, London. He engraved a number of paintings by James Seymour (*qv*) in mezzotint as well as after his own work. His paintings are rare and it is difficult to be certain whether these few in oils are original work or copies after Seymour and Francis Sartorius (*qv*).

1 Gimcrack. Portrait of a racehorse owned by Earl Grosvenor.

Mezzotint engraved by the artist. Published by Thos Burford. 25 May 1769. Approx. 240 × 355 mm.

2 Aaron. Portrait of a racehorse owned by Mr Benjamin Rogers.

Mezzotint engraved from life by the artist.

BURNEY, Edward Francis, 1760–1848

Burney was born at Worcester in 1760. He was sent to London to study art and was admitted to the Royal Academy Schools in 1776. He became friendly with Sir Joshua Reynolds, and painted portraits and domestic scenes which were exhibited at the Royal Academy from 1730 until 1793. He then turned to book illustration, dying in London on 16 December 1848.

1 A View of the Noblemen's and Gentlemen's Trains of Running Horses taking Their Exercise up Warren Hill, east of Newmarket. [10, on page 29]

The Prince of Wales stands in his phaeton, making a bet with the mounted Duke of Orleans. The Duke of York with (possibly) Mrs Fitzherbert stands by the phaeton's team of greys. On the left the Countess of Barrymore stands in a second phaeton beside her husband who is in conversation with Charles James Fox. Between the two carriages there are the mounted and dismounted figures of the Duke of Bedford, Messrs Haggerston, Hanger and Wyndham, Captain Grosvenor, Mr Bullock and Colonel Thornton.

Figures only painted by Burney. Line, stipple and aquatint engraved by Joseph Collyer. Published and sold by John Bodger, Land Surveyor, at Stilton, Huntingdonshire. Or: Sold by the proprietor J. Bodger, Land Surveyor, Stilton, Hunts and at 53 High Holborn; Mr Weatherby, Racing Calendar Office, 7 Oxendon Street; Messrs Molteno & Co., Pall Mall; Messrs Tattersall's, London; and at the Coffee Room, Newmarket. 4 June 1791. Approx. 390 × 660 mm.

CHALON, Henry Bernard, 1770–1849

Henry Bernard Chalon, born in London, was the son of a Dutch etcher and musician. He was admitted to the Royal Academy Schools in 1788, but the reason for his taking up sporting painting (often equestrian portraits) is unknown. He exhibited over 190 works at the Royal Academy between 1792 (when twenty-one years old) and 1845, and also exhibited pictures at the British Institution until the date of his death. In 1796 he married Sarah Ward, the youngest sister of James (qv) and William Ward. The latter engraved some of Chalon's early paintings including many of the racehorses listed below. Unfortunately Chalon and Sarah quickly parted and James Ward, if not his brother, was said to be so bitter about the separation that he did his best to impede Chalon's career. However, Chalon continued to attract Royal patronage throughout his life, although the fact that he was not made even an Associate of the Royal Academy is somewhat surprising.

On occasions Chalon found it difficult to give the correct proportions to the owners, trainers and jockeys who accompanied or rode the racehorses he painted. He portrayed all types of animals and some birds, and his pictures of horses in wide, open landscapes are invariably attractive falling, in style, somewhere between George Stubbs (qv) and his contemporary Ben Marshall (qv). The engravings of the Prince of Wales's racehorses in the early years of the nineteenth century are invaluable records in themselves and illustrate the second surge of royal interest in racing since the death of the Duke of Cumberland.

1 The Bibury Welter Stakes, 16th June 1801. With the Prince of Wales's Feathers crest and dedication to HRH and Members of the Bibury Club. The names of the riders are shown on some states. [49]

Mezzotint engraved by C. Turner. Published by H. B. Chalon, Winchester Row; also to be had at Mr Weatherby, Oxendon Street; Mr Colnaghi, 23 Cockspur Street, Charing Cross, London. 5 August 1802. Approx. 530 × 865 mm.

2 Pavilion. Portrait of a racehorse owned by the Earl of Darlington, Sam Chifney up, with details of pedigree and performance.

Mezzotint engraved by W. Ward. Published by Boydell & Co., 90 Cheapside, London. 1 March 1803. Approx. 400 × 555 mm.

3 Thornton Castle and Thorntonia. Portraits of thoroughbreds owned by Colonel Thornton.

Possibly not racehorses.

Mezzotint engraved by W. Ward. Published by Random & Sneath, 5 Hart Street, Bloomsbury Square, London. 12 February 1808. Approx. 510 × 695 mm.

49 The Bibury Welter Stakes, 16th June 1801. Mezzotint after Henry Bernard Chalon.

50 *Mr G. Crompton's and the late Lord Rous's Quiz. Mezzotint after Henry Bernard Chalon.*

51 *Barbarossa, bred by Lord Spencer Chichester in 1802. Mezzotint after Henry Bernard Chalon.*

4 Violante. Portrait of a racehorse owned by Earl Grosvenor, with Frank Buckle up. With details of pedigree and performance.

Mezzotint engraved by W. Ward. Published by Boydell & Co., as above. 1 March 1808. Approx. 325 × 450 mm.

5 Brainworm. Portrait of a racehorse owned by Arthur Shakespear Esq., with details of pedigree and performance.

The painting was exhibited at the Royal Academy in 1807.

Mezzotint engraved by J. C. Easling. Published by R. Ackermann, 101 Strand, London. 1 March 1808. Approx. 400 × 560 mm.

6 Quiz. Portrait of a racehorse owned by Mr G. Crompton & later Lord Rous, with jockey and lad, and details of pedigree and performance. Winner of the St Leger, 1801. [*50*]

Mezzotint engraved by W. Ward. Published by R. Ackermann, as above. 1 September 1808. Approx. 405 × 550 mm.

7 Orville. Portrait of a racehorse owned by HRH the Prince of Wales, with his groom, Francis Smallman, with details of pedigree and performance. Winner of the St Leger, 1802.

The painting was exhibited at the Royal Academy in 1808.

Mezzotint engraved by W. Ward. Published by Colnaghi & Co., as above. 25 March 1809. Approx. 405 × 545 mm.

8 Sir David. Portrait of a racehorse owned by HRH the Prince of Wales, with Sam Chifney up, and details of pedigree and performance.

The painting was exhibited at the Royal Academy in 1808.

Mezzotint engraved by W. Ward. Published by Colnaghi & Co., as above. 12 August 1809. Approx. 405 × 550 mm.

9 Portraits of racehorses, with details of pedigrees and performances.

(1) Selim – owned by HRH the Prince of Wales, with William Edwards up near the Starting Post at Newmarket. Mr Perren on his hack, Moonshine.
(2) Barbarossa (Foaled in 1802) – HRH the Prince of Wales. [*51*]

The painting of (2) was exhibited at the Royal Academy in 1808.

Mezzotints engraved by W. Ward. Published by C. Random, 5 Hart Street, Bloomsbury Square, London. 2 December 1809. Approx. 405 × 555 mm.

10 Morel. Portrait of a racehorse bred by the Duke of Grafton, with his jockey and trainer, and with details of pedigree. Winner of the Oaks, 1808.

Mezzotint engraved by W. Say. Published by E. Orme, Bond Street, corner of Brook Street, London. 1 January 1811. Approx. 475 × 595 mm.

11 Vandyke. Portrait of a racehorse owned by the Duke of Grafton.

Mezzotint engraved by W. Say. Published E. Orme, as above. 1 January 1814. Approx. 460 × 580 mm.

12 A Comparative View of English Racers and Saddle-Horses. (See MARSHALL **12**; SEYMOUR **13**; STUBBS **18**).

Pl 12   Selim.

Lithograph drawn by H. B. Chalon. Printed by C. Hulmandell. Published by Thos Hookham, 15 Old Bond Street, London. 1836. Approx. 200 × 250 mm.

COOPER, Abraham, RA, 1787–1868

Abraham Cooper was the son of a Holborn tobacconist and later unsuccessful innkeeper. His uncle, William Davis, found employment for the young Cooper at Astley's Amphitheatre (Circus) where he used all his spare moments in sketching the performing horses and other animals. He left Astley's in 1809 when Davis arranged for him to work under Ben Marshall (*qv*), then a successful horse-painter. While not a formal apprentice, he learnt a great deal from the benevolent Marshall and the latter's influence can clearly be seen in Cooper's paintings. He maintained a long association with *The Sporting Magazine* for whom he provided 190 paintings and drawings which were engraved, mainly of shooting, fishing and gun dogs. He also attracted the patronage of the racing aristocracy of the period, as well as that of George IV, Queen Adelaide and Queen Victoria. Cooper exhibited 332 pictures at the Royal Academy over a period of fifty-eight consecutive years, many of which were historical paintings. He was made an Academician in 1820. He also took pupils among whom were William Barraud (*qv*), Thomas Woodward (*qv*) and John Frederick Herring (*qv*), whose style is a compound of that of his tutor and Marshall. One of Abraham Cooper's most delightful paintings was a family group of the Days of Danebury which was exhibited at the Royal Academy in 1838, but sadly not engraved.

Cooper continued painting until the day he died, on Christmas Eve 1868. His obituary described him as 'a guileless and pleasant gentleman with little or no jealousy in him'.

1 Fleur-de-Lis. Portrait of a racehorse owned by Sir M. W. Ridley, MP, jockey and trainer in attendance, with details of pedigree and performance. [*16, page 38*]

Mezzotint engraved by Thomas Lupton. Published by

James Bulcock, 163 Strand, and also to be had of the Engraver, 7 Leigh Street, Burton Crescent, London. 1 July 1828. Approx. 380 × 480 mm.

2 Plenipotentiary. Portrait of the head of a racehorse owned by Stanlake Batson Esq. Winner of the Derby Stakes, 1834, ridden by P. Conolly. [52]

Lithograph drawn by Thomas Fairland. Published by J. McCormick, 147 Strand, London. c1834. Approx. 250 × 300 mm.

3 British Field Sports (22 plates)

    16 Bay Middleton. Portrait of a racehorse owned by Lord Jersey. Winner of the Derby (and 2,000 Gns), 1836.

    21 Harriet. Portrait of a racehorse.

    22 Plenipotentiary. Portrait of a racehorse owned by Mr S. Batson. Winner of the Derby, 1834.

Line engravings by: 16, 22, T. S. Engleheart; 21, J. H. Engleheart. Published by A. H. Baily & Co., Cornhill, London. 21: 1 October 1837; 16, 22: 1 November 1837. Approx. 140 × 190 mm.

4 A series of winners of the Derby Stakes at Epsom. See HERRING 4.

    (16) 1842. Attilla – owned by Colonel Anson. W. Scott up.

Aquatint engraved by C. Hunt. Published by S. & J. Fuller, 34 Rathbone Place, London. July 1842. Approx. 315 × 430 mm.

5 Portraits of racehorses, mainly with jockeys up, winners of Classic races and Gold Cups, with details of pedigrees and performances. Some titled: 'Moore's Celebrated Winners'. See BRETLAND I; DAVIS, H. T. I; DE PRADES I; HALL 3; HERRING, J. F. II; HILLYARD I; SHAYER I; SMITH, C. N. I.

    (1) Our Nell – owned by Mr Dawson. T. Lye up. Oaks, 1842. Published 1 July 1842.

    (2) Refraction – Duke of Richmond. H. Bell up. Oaks, 1845. 29 June 1845.

    (3) Miss Elis – Lord George Bentinck. Abdale up. Goodwood Cup, 1845. 1 October 1845.

Aquatints engraved by: (1), (3) C. Hunt; (2) J. R. Mackrell. Published by J. Moore, 1 & 2 West Street, Upper St Martin's Lane, London. Approx. 370 × 500 mm.

6 A series of winners of the Derby Stakes at Epsom. See HERRING, J. F. 16.

    (1) 1847. Cossack – owned by T. Pedley Esq. S. Templeman up.

Aquatint engraved by J. R. Mackrell. Published by Baily Brothers, 3 Royal Exchange Buildings, Cornhill, London. (1847). Approx. 380 × 505 mm.

52 Stanlake Batson Esq's Plenipotentiary. Derby 1834. Lithograph after Abraham Cooper RA.

7 Virago. Portrait of a racehorse owned by Henry Padwick Esq. Trained by J. Day Snr. J. Wells up. (1,000 Gns, 1854).

Aquatint engraved by J. Harris and C. Quentery. Published by Baily Brothers, Cornhill, London. 1 January 1855. Approx. 480 × 610 mm.

CULLIN, Isaac J., fl 1881–1920

Isaac Cullin was predominantly a painter of human portraits as the subjects of his pictures at the Royal Academy between 1881 and 1887 show. His exhibited work was sent in from a number of different London addresses. From about 1883 he started to paint racing portraits including a few classic winners of the day. His action pictures are similar to those of John Beer (*qv*) – barrelly racehorses at full stretch! He also contributed sketches to the *Illustrated London News* in 1893 and 1894.

Racing

1 The Saddling Room at Epsom.

A group portrait.

Chromolithograph. Published by S. Hildesheimer & Co., Ltd., London, Manchester & New York. 11 July 1887. Approx. 555 × 865 mm.

2 Racing at Epsom Downs.

Photogravure. Published by The Berlin Photographic Co., 133 New Bond Street, London & 14 East 23rd Street, New York. *c*1890. Approx. 430 × 740 mm.

3 'McQueen's Derby Winners'.

Isinglass. Portrait of a racehorse owned by Mr H. M. McCalmont. Winner of the 2,000 Gns, Derby and St Leger, 1893, ridden by T. Loates.

Aquatint engraved by A. Tallberg. Published by F. C. McQueen & Sons, 181 Tottenham Court Road, London. November 1893. Approx. 500 × 600 mm. See BIRD 1.

4 Newmarket Fin-de-Siecle. 'The Birdcage'. A large scale group portrait of three horses, one with jockey up, and gentlemen of the turf, including the Prince of Wales. [*31, page 60*]

Photogravure. Published by I. P. Mendoza Ltd., St James's Gallery, 4A, King Street, St James's, London. 1 February 1900. Approx. 505 × 740 mm.

Steeplechasing

5 Zoedone. Portrait of a racehorse with his owner Count

Kinsky up. Winner of the Grand National, 1883.

Count Charles Kinsky served in the Austrian Embassy in London. There were only 10 starters in the Grand National in 1883.

Painted with J. A. Wheeler Snr. Chromolithograph. Approx. 680 × 520 mm.

DALBY, David, 1794–1836

It is difficult to discover the relationship of the artist members of the Dalby family, of which there were at least four. What is certain is that the work of David Dalby is superior to the others. He was born in 1794 and is noted as an animal painter in a York directory in 1815. Within five years he was busy with commissions from the Yorkshire hunting and racing fraternity. The racehorse owner Richard Watt of Bishop Burton was an important patron. Dalby painted primarily in York but also at Leeds and Doncaster where he may have lived from time to time during his comparatively short life. His portraits of horses are very fine and it is sad that so few were engraved.

1 Portraits of racehorses.
  (1) Jack Spigot – owned by the Hon. T. O. Powlett. Winner of the St Leger, 1821, ridden by W. Scott.
  (2) Barefoot – Richard Watt & Gilbert Crompton Esqs. Winner of the St Leger, 1823, T. Goodisson.

Aquatints engraved by T. Sutherland. Published by T. Sotheran, Bookseller, and Clerk of the Course, York. (1821 and 1823). Approx. 320 × 425 mm.

2 Tarrare. Portrait of a racehorse owned by the Earl of Scarbrough. Winner of the Great St Leger at Doncaster, 1826, ridden by G. Nelson.

Painted by D. Dolby [*sic*] for the Earl of Scarbrough. Aquatint engraved by T. Sutherland. Published by W. Sheardown & Sons. (1826). Approx. 305 × 410 mm. See HERRING 2, (12).

DAVIS, H. T., op 1850

Nothing more is known of this artist than can be gleaned from the entries below. Although his picture of Voltigeur is slightly stiff, his ability as an equestrian artist must have been of some standing for Moore and Ackermann to have used his work.

1 Portrait of a racehorse with details of pedigree and per-

formance, titled: 'Moore's Celebrated Winners'. See: BRET-
LAND I; COOPER 5; DE PRADES I; HALL 3; HERRING, J. F. II;
HILLYARD I; SHAYER I; SMITH, C. N. I.

> Voltigeur. Portrait of a racehorse owned by the Earl of Zet-
> land. Ridden by C. Marlow. Winner of the Derby and St
> Leger (and Doncaster Cup), 1850.

Aquatint engraved by C. N. Smith. Published by J. Moore,
corner of West Street, Upper St Martin's Lane, London.
31 September 1850. Approx. 440 × 690 mm.

2 The St Leger, 1850 between Voltigeur and Russborough.

Lord Zetland's Voltigeur won the run-off after a dead heat.

Aquatint engraved by C. N. Smith. Published by R. Ackermann, 191 Regent Street, London. December 1850. Approx.
450 × 720 mm.

DAVIS, Richard Barrett, RBA, 1782–1854

Richard Barrett Davis was the son of Richard Davis,
huntsman to George III's private harriers. Initially
self-taught, his ability came to the notice of the King
who arranged for him to be given proper training
including attendance at the Royal Academy Schools
but he was not formally admitted as a student. He
exhibited paintings at the Royal Academy for over fifty
years, his first exhibit being in 1802. In 1831 he was
appointed animal painter to George IV and later
Queen Victoria. The majority of his paintings are of
hunts and hunters. In 1836 he introduced a short-lived
Hunter's Annual comprising a group of four paintings
and prints of various hunts each year; a total of twelve
plates were published.

  Although successful in terms of patronage, he died
poor in Kensington, Middlesex on 13 March 1854.

1 Race Horses Exercising.

Aquatint engraved by H. Merke. Published by C. Random.
2 June 1810. Approx. 190 × 490 mm.

2 Raby. Portrait of a racehorse owned by Mr Meiklam, winner of the Cambridgeshire, 1849, ridden by Arnold.

Aquatint engraved by C. Hunt. Published by J. Moore, 1
West Street, Upper St Martin's Lane, London. 1850.
Approx. 510 × 760 mm.

DAVIS, Thomas R., fl 1826–1840

There was a student of this name at the Royal Academy

Schools in 1826 whose painting of Philip Payne,
Huntsman to His Grace the Duke of Beaufort was
engraved by Charles Turner and published by Ackermann in December 1826. However, there is also a
Tyddesley R. T. Davis who exhibited *Hounds running
into a fox, in stone wall country* at the Royal Academy
in 1831 and other equestrian subjects at the British
Institution between 1831 and 1857. The latter's
address is Friars Street, St Ebbes, Oxford. Whether
they are one and the same person is not known, but
it can be said that the portrait below of Passport and
General Gilbert up is not very exciting!

1 Passport. Portrait of a racehorse with General Gilbert up.

Lithograph drawn by T. Fairland. *c*1840. Approx.
335 × 435 mm.

DENTON, Charles, op 1853

1 Abergavenny Steeple Chase, 1853.

  1 'The Start'.
  2 'Taking the Wall'.
  3 'Taking the Brook'.
  4 'The Finish'.

*1–3 give names of the runners; 4 shows 1st, General; 2nd,
Dearest Mae; 3rd, Ploughboy.*

Lithographs drawn and published by Charles Denton,
Abergavenny. Not Dated. Approx. 405 × 520 mm.

De PRADES, Alfred Frank, fl 1844–1883

Suprisingly little is known of this prolific and good
sporting artist. He exhibited landscapes (sometimes in
collaboration with E. J. Niemann) and a painting of
Horses Going to a Fair (1867) at the British Institution
between 1858 and 1867; and, at the Royal Academy
in 1879, *April Shower* and *La Petite Porte*. These pictures were sent in from Southampton Street, Fitzroy
Square, London. A Frank de Prades exhibited at the
Royal Academy in 1857 (a military portrait group) and
1861 (*A Thirsty Dog*), from Newman Street. Whether
these two entries refer to the same de Prades is possible
but doubtful. Alfred de Prades' watercolours of coaching subjects are lively, and his racing scenes in oils are
accurate if slightly stiff, much in the style of his contemporary Harry Hall.

1 Portraits of racehorses, mostly with jockeys up, winners of Classic races and Gold Cups, with details of pedigrees and performances. Some titled 'Moore's Celebrated Winners'. See BRETLAND 1; COOPER 5; DAVIS, H. T. 1; HALL 3; HERRING, J. F. 11; HILLYARD 1; SHAYER 1; and SMITH, C. N. 1.

(1) Nancy – owned by Mr Martinson. Ridden by F. Marson. Chester and Goodwood Cups, 1851.
(2) Newminster – Mr A. Nichol. S. Templeman. St Leger, 1851. 1 December 1851.
(3) West Australian – J. Bowes Esq. F. Butler. Triple Crown, 1853. 6 November 1853. [Plate 10]
(4) Andover and Mincemeat. Andover – J. Gully Esq. A. Day. Derby, 1854. Mincemeat – Mr W. Cookson. J. Charlton. Oaks, 1854. 1 July, 1854.

Aquatints engraved by: (1) C. N. Smith; (2) C. Hunt; (3), (4) C. N. Smith and H. Meyer. Published by J. Moore, corner of West Street, Upper St Martin's Lane, London. Approx. 440 × 670 mm. (3) republished by Barnett, Moss & Co., as a lithograph drawn by Stannard & Dixon.

DESVIGNES, Herbert Clayton, fl 1833–1861

A very competent artist who painted hunting and coaching scenes, dogs, landscapes with cattle and racehorse portraits. He exhibited at the Royal Academy and British Institution between 1833 and 1861 from Newman Street, an artists' colony in London at that period. It is said that his daughter Emily (also an artist) supported him in later life when he became blind.

1 Portraits of racehorses, with names of owners and details of pedigrees and performances.

(1) The Baron – owned by G. Watts Esq. Ridden by F. Butler. St Leger, 1845.
(2) Sweetmeat – Mr A. W. Hill. Whitehouse. Doncaster Cup and HM Gold Vase, Ascot, 1845.

Aquatints engraved by C. Hunt. 1845. Approx. 550 × 660 mm.

D'ORSAY, Count Alfred Guillaume Gabriole, 1801–1852

The son of a Napoleonic General, Count D'Orsay married and was almost immediately separated from the daughter of the Earl and Countess of Blessington. He came to England in 1831 with the recently widowed Lady Blessington, entering into a 'fast' social life with her in London. He was a sculptor of some skills and painted portraits of humans and horses with moderate success. He exhibited mainly bronzes at the Royal Academy between 1843 and 1848. In debt, he left Eng-

land in 1849 and was appointed Director of Fine Arts in Paris by Louis-Napoleon.

1 Portrait of Gipsy, Winner of the Melton Steeple Chase 1840, ridden by the Hon. Augustus Villiers.

Gipsy was owned by Mr J. W. Melville.

Lithograph drawn by J. Bouvier. Published by Thos McLean, 26 Haymarket, London. c1840. Approx. 535 × 605 mm.

2 Portrait of the Celebrated Steeple Chase Horse, Lady Langford, Winner of the Irish Military Steeple Chase 1841, ridden by the Hon. Charles Forester.

Lady Langford was owned by the Hon. Charles Forester.

Lithograph. Published by Thos McLean, as above. c1841. Approx. 530 × 600 mm.

DOUGLAS, Edward Algernon Stuart, op 1860, d 1915

Douglas is one of a small handful of good sporting painters practicing at the end of the nineteenth century. He exhibited hunting scenes at the Royal Academy from an address in Barnes on the outskirts of London from 1882 to 1892. While his pictures are detailed (in the fashion of the time) they are also full of movement and life. Douglas must have had a considerable knowledge of field sports to paint them with such confidence and accuracy.

1 Steeplechasing scenes.

Saddling.
A Close Finish.
Going to Weigh.

Here They Come.
The Half Distance.
There They Go.

Aquatints engraved by C. R. Stock. Published by Arthur Ackermann, 191 Regent Street, London. 19 February 1881. Two sheets, each with three scenes; each approx. 255 × 580 mm.

DOYLE, John, 1797–1868

John Doyle was born in Ireland and after studying under portrait and miniature painters and at the Dublin Society Drawing Academy, he came to England in about 1822. At first a portrait painter, he later became a caricaturist of note signing such work 'H.B.'

53 *Life of the Race Horse. Backing the Colt. Lithograph by and after John Doyle.*

(two conjoined JDs). He exhibited at the Royal Academy between 1825 and 1835 from London addresses. Doyle painted several sporting scenes. Those of horses have a powerful impact both in the subject and his ability to use light to great advantage. Most of all, the portraits of owners and trainers are particularly fine.

1 'Life of the Racehorse'.

Eight lithographs, of which (3) is Backing the Colt. [53]

Lithographs, probably drawn by the artist. Printed by C. Hulmandell. Published by Rodwell and Martin, New Bond Street, London. 1822. Approx. 260 × 370 mm.

2 Barefoot. Portrait of a racehorse owned by Richard Watt Esq. Winner of the St Leger, 1823, ridden by T. Goodisson.

Lithograph probably drawn by the artist. Printed by C. Hulmandell.

DUBOST, Antoine, 1769–1825

The Frenchman Antoine Dubost was taught by Vincent and Vernet in Paris. He travelled widely and came to England in about 1800. He exhibited at the Royal Academy between 1806 and 1808; a painting in 1806 was titled *Preparations for a Horse Race*. Living in London for only a few years he returned to France in 1810. Fifteen years later he was killed in a duel in Paris.

1 Newmarket. The Life of a Racehorse.

1. Title page.
2. Colts; the race horse in the Stud.
3. Colt; the race horse taken in Hand.
4. Plover by Sir Peter; the race horse in the stable.
5. Eaton by Sir Peter; the race horse in the dressing stable.
6. Vandyke by Sir Peter; the race horse at the Starting post.
7. Pope by Waxy; the race horse running at Epsom.
8. Juniper, by Whiskey; the race horse at the Weighing house.
9. Sir David, by Trumpator; the race horse at the Ending post.
10. Morel, by Sorcerer; the race horse rubbing.
11. Marmion, by Whiskey; the race horse put up to Auction.

With titles in French.

Lithographs drawn by the artist from studies made at Newmarket, 1809. Published by Dubost, Paris. 1818. Approx. 495 × 675 mm.

EARP, George, fl 1833–1874

George Earp was a member of a very large family of watercolour artists of that name living principally at Brighton. Possibly brothers, none of them were particularly successful, but there are examples of George Earp's work in the Carlton Museum, Nottingham. Nothing is known of W. H. Mason.

1 Brighton Hurdle Race, Decr. 20th, 1833.

   (1)   The Start.
   (2)   Coming In.

Each with names of horses and riders. The race was won by Cheltenham; 2nd, Souvenir.

Drawn by G. Earp from a sketch by W. H. Mason. Aquatints engraved by C. Hunt. Published by W. H. Mason, 1 Ship Street, Brighton. *c*1833. Approx. 160 × 435 mm.

EDWARDS, Lionel Dalhousie Robertson, RI, RCA, 1878–1966

The son of a doctor, Lionel Edwards was born at Clifton, Bristol but his most vivid impressions of his youth were of the Welsh hills near Conway. After an unusual upbringing and sporadic periods at school, his art training comprised a time under Sir A. S. Cope, RA, at Heatherleys, and at the Calderon School of Animal Painting. Passionately fond of riding and hunting, these activities quickly provided the subjects of his sketches and paintings. He was an illustrator for *The Graphic, Country Life* and a number of other periodicals, providing him with his 'bread and butter' before he started to receive commissions for pictures. He also illustrated many of his own and other authors' books.

Edwards is best known for his paintings of the chase and it is believed that he hunted with more than ninety packs of hounds during his lifetime. His mastery of the countryside in all weathers is exceptional; his huntsmen, followers, horses, hounds and their quarry naturally populate these scenes. His paintings of racing were few, and a smaller number reproduced in colour by The Sporting Gallery and privately. Like many prints of the period, they are liable to fade and for the colour to distort resulting in their bearing very little resemblance to the original painting.

Lionel Edwards lived for his work, hunted until very late in life and was painting on the day that he died at his Wiltshire home in 1966.

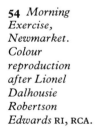

54 *Morning Exercise, Newmarket. Colour reproduction after Lionel Dalhousie Robertson Edwards* RI, RCA.

Racing

1 Racing scenes.

  (1) Morning Exercise: Newmarket. [54]
  (2) The Ditch: Newmarket.
  (3) A Training Gallop: Newmarket.
  (4) Warren Hill: Newmarket.

Limited edition (150) colour reproduction. Published by The Sporting Gallery, 7 Grafton Street, Bond Street, London W1. *c*1937. Approx. 255 × 380 mm.

2 Racing scenes.

  (1) The Two Year Old.
  (2) Half Speed Gallop.

Colour reproductions. Probably printed privately. *c*1937. Approx. 240 × 410 mm.

These titles have been seen below signed prints; (2) also inscribed: Fulke Walwyn on Golden Miller.

Steeplechasing

3 Cheltenham Races.

Colour reproduction. Published by The Tryon Gallery.

EGERTON, M., fl 1821–1828

Egerton's delightful prints, made I suspect from drawings and watercolours, have elements of both caricature and Henry Alken Snr (*qv*) in their manner of composition and painting. Nothing is known of his personal life.

1 Racing scenes.

  I   Preparing to Start.
  II   At Speed.
  III Winning.
  IV Weighing and Rubbing Down.

Aquatints engraved by G. Hunt. Published by J. Brooker, 5 Southampton Row, Russell Square, London. Not Dated. Approx. 190 × 540 mm.
    Reprinted without names of artist or engraver, and without a publication line.

FERNELEY, John, 1782–1860

John Ferneley was born at Thrussington in Leicestershire, the youngest son of a wheelwright. It is said that his talent was first recognised by the Duke of Rutland who saw his paintings of horses on the side of a cart his father was mending. In 1810 the Duke arranged for young Ferneley to study under Benjamin Marshall (*qv*) in London. He remained with Marshall for three years before travelling and painting in England and Ireland. He finally settled at Melton Mowbray in 1814. He built himself a studio and later a house, Elgin Lodge, on the edge of the town. Ferneley portrayed the Leicester hunting fraternity and their activities for nearly fifty years with great success and popularity. He hunted himself and his panoramic views of a hunt in full cry epitomise a supremely important aspect of life in Leicestershire in the early nineteenth century. He also painted thoroughbreds, many of which were engraved by Edward Duncan (1803–1882, a fine watercolourist) and published in Ackermann's short-lived series of racehorse portraits.

His fees for painting were always moderate and, most useful to students of his life and work, he kept a meticulous record of all the pictures he painted. Marrying in 1809, three of his six children followed him as artists: Sarah (1812–1903), who looked after her father in his old age after the death of his second wife in 1854; John Jnr (1815–1862); and Claude Loraine Ferneley (1822–1891). The last two were equestrian artists. John Snr died at Elgin Lodge on 7 June 1860 as a result of a chill caught some weeks before while painting out-of-doors. He was buried at Thrussington.

In the hierarchy of horse painters Ferneley's work lies well below that of George Stubbs (*qv*); on a par, but less sinewy, with that of Marshall and more consistently excellent than portraits by J. F. Herring Snr (*qv*). Engravings of his pictures of racehorses are highly prized.

1 A series of Winners of the Derby Stakes at Epsom.

  (1) 1828. Cadland – owned by the Duke of Rutland. Ridden by J. Robinson. Published 1 April 1831.
  (2) 1830. Priam – Mr W. Chifney. S. Day. 1 October 1830.
  (3) 1831. Spaniel – Viscount Lowther. W. Wheatley. 1 November 1831.
  (4) 1832. St Giles – R. Ridsdale Esq. W. Scott. 1 November 1832.
  (5) 1833. Dangerous – Mr I. Sadler. J. Chapple. October 1833.
       1835 & 1836. See HANCOCK I
  (6) 1837. Phosphorus – Lord Berners. G. Edwards. (1837)
       1838–1843. See HANCOCK I.

Aquatints engraved by: (1)–(4) E. Duncan & J. Webb; (5), (6) E. Duncan. Published by R. Ackermann Jnr, 191 Regent Street (between Conduit St & New Burlington St), London. Approx. 320 × 420 mm.

55 *The Earl of
Jersey's
Riddlesworth, with
J. Robinson up.
2,000 Guineas
1831. Aquatint
after John
Ferneley.*

56 *The Celebrated
Mare 'Beeswing' with
her First Foal 'Old
Port' by Sir Hercules.
Lithograph after John
Ferneley.*

2 A series of Winners of the Great St Leger Stakes at Doncaster.

(1) 1829. Rowton – Hon. E. Petre. W. Scott. Not Dated.
(2) 1831. Chorister – Marquis of Cleveland. J. B. Day. 1 April 1832.
1835–1844. See HANCOCK **2**.

Aquatints engraved by: (1) E. Duncan & J. Webb; (2) C. Turner. Published by R. Ackermann Jnr, as above. Approx. 320 × 420 mm.

3 Portraits of racehorses with jockeys up, winners of Classic races and Gold Cups, with details of pedigrees and performances.

(1) Zinganee – owned by Lord Chesterfield. Ridden by S. Chifney. Ascot Gold Cup, 1829. Published (1829).
(2) Velocipede – Mr Armytage. W. Scott. 1 February 1831.
(3) Riddlesworth – Earl of Jersey. J. Robinson. 2,000 Gns and Newmarket Stakes, 1831. [55] March 1832.
(4) Sultan – Lord Foley. Newmarket Whip, 1832. 1 October 1832.
(5) Harkaway – Thos Ferguson Esq. Goodwood Cup, 1838, Wakefield; 1839, G. Calloway. 1 June 1840.

Aquatints engraved by: (1)–(3) E. Duncan and J. Webb; (4), (5) E. Duncan. Published by R. Ackermann Jnr, as above. Approx. 320 × 420 mm.

4 The Celebrated Mare 'Beeswing' with her first foal 'Old Port' by Sir Hercules. Portrait of a racehorse and her foal, a country house in the background. [56]

Lithograph drawn by T. Fairland. Printed by Day & Haghe. Published by Ackermann & Co., 96 Strand, London. 6 September 1844.

FRANKLAND, Sir Robert, Bart, 1784–1849

An amateur artist with a charming style and humour, Sir Robert Frankland was High Sheriff of Yorkshire in 1838 and had represented Thirsk as Member of Parliament between 1815 and 1834. His hunting and shooting scenes show that he knew all about these sports as a practitioner. He sometimes etched his own plates, mainly after watercolours. The portrait below is unusual and out of the general line of his slightly naive, Alkenesque manner of drawing.

1 Rosette. Portrait of a racehorse owned by Henry Peirse Esq., with John Shepherd up, on the Knavesmire, York, 1809.

Mezzotint engraved by W. Ward. Published by J. Masham, Bedale, York. 1 August 1811. Approx. 405 × 550 mm. The artist is shown as *Amicus R.F. pinxit*.

FRITH, William Powell, RA, 1819–1909

William Powell Frith is better known for his historical genre scenes and extensive canvases of Victorian life

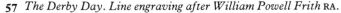

57 *The Derby Day. Line engraving after William Powell Frith* RA.

depicting busy panoramas of *Ramsgate Sands*, or *The Railway Station*, and later moralistic pictures such as *The Road to Ruin*. He painted the large picture of *The Derby Day* (with advice from J. F. Herring (*qv*)) in 1858. The scene is more concerned with the 'sideshows' than the race, but the print warrants inclusion here since it gives a contemporary view of Epsom some years after James Pollard (*qv*) and Henry Alken Snr (*qv*) painted the Downs on similar occasions.

1 The Derby Day. [*57*]

A large scale scene of racecourse spectators and activities. Paintings of horses based on sketches provided by J. F. Herring.

Line engraving by Auguste T. M. Blanchard. Published by E. Gambart & Co., 120 Pall Mall, London. 2 March 1863. Approx. 505 × 1110 mm.

GARRARD, George ARA, 1760–1826

George Garrard was an outstandingly able and versatile artist. He was a pupil of Sawrey Gilpin (*qv*) whose daughter he later married. Garrard was also admitted to the Royal Academy Schools and exhibited his first picture at the Royal Academy in 1781, sent in from his future father-in-law's house. He continued to exhibit a large number of paintings of horses and dogs at the Academy until the late 1790s when he turned to modelling. Among such work his best known commission came from the Board of Agriculture for a series of the various breeds of cattle. He was elected an ARA in 1800. After 1801, his exhibits at the Royal Academy were often portrait busts, although there were occasional paintings until shortly before his death in October 1826.

His paintings of horses have as much in common with those by George Stubbs (*qv*) as Gilpin; all are extremely fine and one wishes that more had been engraved.

1 Soldier. Portrait of a racehorse owned by Dennis O'Kelly Esq., with details of pedigree and performance. [*58*]

Aquatint engraved by S. Alken Snr. Published by G. Garrard, Knightsbridge and 43 Little Britain, London. January 1793. Approx. 370 × 480 mm.

GIBSON, Joseph Vincent, fl 1857–1896

J. V. Gibson worked in Manchester before moving south to London. He exhibited paintings of domestic subjects and some portraits at the Royal Academy and

British Institution between 1862 and 1888. His daughter was the prolific miniature painter Mary Josephine Gibson, and one is tempted to suggest that she may have helped her father in the tour-de-force of small portraits in 'The Royal Stand at Ascot'.

1 The Royal Stand at Ascot.

Photogravure. Published by Thomas McLean, 7 Haymarket, London. 1 July 1896. Approx. 435 × 900 mm.

GILBERT, Joseph Francis, 1792–1855

Joseph Gilbert exhibited paintings at the Royal Academy between 1813 and 1846, and at the British Institution from 1823 to 1853. They were predominantly landscapes with figures. His portraits of horses and dogs are rare, the animals being somewhat stiff in their handling compared with the finely painted backgrounds. However, these paintings (submitted for exhibition from Portsmouth, then Chichester and finally London) accurately record the animals portrayed in the painstaking manner associated with slightly primitive work.

1 Priam. Portrait of a racehorse owned by William Chifney winning the Gold Cup in 1831, on Goodwood Race Course, with a dedication to Charles, Duke of Richmond.

Aquatint engraved by J. Clark. Published by J. F. Gilbert, Chichester. Not dated. Approx. 415 × 680 mm.

GILES, Major Godfrey Douglas, 1857–1941

Godfrey Giles, the son of an officer in the Indian Navy, served in the Army in Afghanistan and Egypt before leaving in the rank of Major in 1884. He had always sketched during his service career and took up painting seriously on resigning his commission. He studied under Carolus Duran in Paris. Giles worked in London, Newmarket and Edinburgh, where he died in February 1941. He provided illustrations for books and periodicals particularly on racing and polo. His paintings are often on a large scale with plenty of action, however his colouring sometimes lacks sparkle.

1 Racing scene.

Persimmon winning the Derby, 1896.

The finish of the race showing HRH the Prince of Wales's Persimmon with J. Watts up beating Mr Leopold de Rothschild's

St Frusquin, T. Loates; 3rd, Mr H. E. Beddington's Earwig, F. Allsopp.

Chromolithograph. c1896. Approx. 635 × 760 mm.

GILL, Edward (of Northampton), fl 1810–1835

All that can be discovered about Edward Gill comes from the engraving below and other prints, usually of hunting scenes. He exhibited one work at the Royal Academy in 1810, *Evening, Wearied Sportsman*, which one may imagine was of a Meltonian at the end of a long but satisfying day!

1 Extraordinary Steeple-Chase For One Thousand Sovereigns between Mr Osbaldeston's 'Clasher' and Captain Ross's 'Clinker', with details of the race (in 1826). [59]

George Osbaldeston rode his own horse; Dick Christian rode Clinker. The race, won by Clasher, was over five miles from Great Dalby Windmill to near Tilton-on-the-Hill, Leicestershire.

Aquatint engraved by H. Alken and E. Duncan. Published by R. Ackermann, 96 Strand and R. Ackermann Jnr, 191 Regent Street, London. 1830. Approx. 395 × 720 mm.

GILPIN, Sawrey, RA, FSA, 1733–1807

After a hazardous upbringing which entailed his mother and seven brothers and sisters being caught up in the Scottish Rebellion and temporary eviction from their home, Scaleby Castle, Cumberland, Sawrey Gilpin came to London in 1794. He was apprenticed to the artist Samuel Scott, and was soon drawing horses, carts, the people and the hubbub of Covent Garden where he worked. In the light of his childhood experiences, it seems singularly appropriate that his first patron should have been the Duke of Cumberland. Within ten years Gilpin became a fully fledged 'horse painter'.

Exhibiting pictures at the Society of Artists from 1762 and the Royal Academy from 1786, Gilpin was elected an FSA and an RA in 1771 and 1796 respectively. He lived mainly in London where Thomas Gooch (*qv*) and George Garrard (*qv*) were among his pupils; the latter married Gilpin's daughter, Matilda.

Sawrey Gilpin often collaborated with other artists, usually to paint animals into their compositions. No doubt he was sometimes assisted in his landscapes, but he was also quite capable of painting his own often romantic settings in which the horses take their natural place. A few are painted in a state of excitement, but the majority are placid animals populating arcadian woods and fields. Some critics attempt to compare his portraits of horses with those by George Stubbs (*qv*), but to my eye Gilpin's overall effect is much softer, taken, it seems, from a more distant viewpoint which makes comparison inappropriate. However, he painted with less consistency than Stubbs with a few rank bad pictures spoiling his undoubted reputation even when he was alive.

That redoubtable Yorkshire sportsman Colonel Thomas Thornton was another of Gilpin's patrons. In 1786 the artist and Garrard accompanied Thornton on his sporting tour of the Highlands which they recorded in a number of paintings. When his wife died, Gilpin stayed for some time at Southill in Bedfordshire, the home of the brewer Samuel Whitbread, the patron and friend of many sporting artists. Later he lived with his daughters at Brompton, going each day to paint in the studio of his son-in-law, Garrard, in Hanover Square. Gilpin died at Brompton in March 1807.

1 Sir Peter Teazle. Portrait of a racehorse owned by the Earl of Derby. Winner of the Derby, 1787, ridden by Sam. Arnull. In a stable with a groom, with pedigree and performance.

Mezzotint by W. Ward. Published by G. Garrard at Mr Gilpin's, Knightsbridge, and at Little Britain, London. 1 January 1788. Approx. 355 × 470 mm.

2 Jupiter. Portrait of a stallion owned by Colonel Thornton. By Eclipse, with pedigree and performance to 1788.

Mezzotint by W. Ward. Published by G. Garrard, as above. Approx. 360 × 490 mm.

3 Highflyer. Portrait of a racehorse owned by Mr Tattersall.

Aquatint by F. Jukes. Published by S. Gilpin, Knightsbridge, London. 1 March 1788. Approx. 360 × 475 mm.

Republished by G. Garrard, as above. 1792.

4 Pot8os. Portrait of a racehorse owned by Lord Grosvenor.

Mezzotint engraved by C. H. Hodges. Published by J. Boydell, 90 Cheapside, London. 25 March 1790. Approx. 360 × 475 mm. See STUBBS 11 for similar prints.

5 Set of eight 'Characters of Horses'.

   2   The Race Horse.

Etchings by S. Gilpin (etched in 1760, inscribed 1786). Published by G. Garrard, Knightsbridge, London. 1 August 1793. Approx. 255 × 325 mm.

59 Extraordinary Steeple-Chase. Aquatint after Edward Gill.

6 *The History and Delineation of the Horse*, by John Lawrence.

    1   Stallion. Jupiter, the Property of Lieut Col Thomas Thornton.

Line engraving by John Scott. Published by James Cundee & John Scott, London. 1 January 1809. Approx. 140 × 200 mm. For other engravings of racehorses from this book, see MARSHALL **5**; SARTORIUS, J.N. **17**; and STUBBS **16**.

GOOCH, Thomas H., *c*1750–1802

Thomas Gooch, for a time a pupil of Sawrey Gilpin (*qv*), was an animal painter who exhibited seventy-six pictures at the Royal Academy between 1781 and 1802. His subjects included hunters, carriage horses and dogs, with some equestrian portraits. His paintings of *The Life and Death of a Racehorse* (engraved and published in 1790) were exhibited at the Academy in 1783. In 1784 a set of six aquatints, engraved by Francis Jukes, of exactly the same subjects were published by a John Walker of 148 Strand, London, allegedly after designs by Charles Ansell (*qv*) who appears to have pirated Gooch's work. Gooch retired to Hampshire where he continued painting any animal subject which caught his imagination until his death in 1802.

    1   The Life and Death of a Race-horse.

        Plate 1   The Foal with it's Dam.
        Plate 2   The Colt in Breaking.
        Plate 3   The Race Horse after Running.
        Plate 4   As a Hunter Going Out.
        Plate 5   As a Post Horse.
        Plate 6   His Dissolution.

Aquatints engraved by (?) T. Gooch, printed in sepia. Published by Thos Gooch, 4 Half Moon Street, London. 30 July 1790. Ovals, approx. 265 × 305 mm.
    Reissued with slightly different titles by T. Gooch in 1792.

GWYNN, William, 1782–*c*1860

William Gwynn was born at Ludlow, Shropshire, one of the twin sons of John and and Ann Gwynn. His father was a labourer and it is probable that he was self-taught as an artist. He worked in London from about 1807 until returning to his native town in 1830, although he also completed commissions in Shropshire during this period. He painted portraits, animals and views. He was still working in Ludlow in July 1860, and is thought to have died shortly after this date.

    1   Portrait of Mr Thomas George of Henley, near Ludlow and his mare 'Little Thought of', with groom & boy on Ludlow Race Course, November 1820.

'The above mare, 14 hands high, in a match against time, performed the distance of 19 miles in 58 minutes over Ludlow Race Course, Rode by Mr George, 70 years of age & weighing 10 stone.'

Aquatint engraved by J. H. Wright. Published privately. Approx. 320 × 525 mm.

HALL, Henry (Harry), 1815–1882

Harry Hall was born at Cambridge in 1815. Coming from a humble background and with very little education, it was found that he could draw. He must have obtained some tuition for by the age of eighteen he was advertising his ability to take likenesses, I suspect in pencil, for subsequent engraving. His natural talent also made him an adequate painter of animals and he was soon depicting racehorses at nearby Newmarket, somewhat in the style of Abraham Cooper (*qv*) who may have given Hall some brief instruction in London.

Hall lived at Newmarket throughout his life having a small stable-studio off the High Street. As well as portraying almost countless racehorses, often with an even better painted jockey up, he provided line illustrations for *The Field* and *Illustrated London News*. He also painted a very large number of small panel sketches, approximately 250 × 320 mm (10 × 13 inches), which were engraved and published in *The Sporting Magazine*. He is probably best known for the engravings of Derby, St Leger and Gold Cup winners published by a succession of London print publishers. The first was Fuller, followed by Moore and then, until his death, by Baily. He also painted a few canvases for Messrs Fores.

Because many of his paintings were required for publication shortly after the subject had won a classic race, they are repetitive in style and over-inclined to exaggerate those points of animal conformation, good and bad, which made the portrait immediately recognisable to the public for just those reasons. However, given time to portray a stallion or group of mares, his pictures are far better, as are those of animals other than horses. The portraits of owners, trainers and jockeys within his paintings are invariably excellent, and one cannot help suspecting that there may be many pictures of East Anglian worthies by his hand hanging unrecognised in that part of the country. He painted a few 'finishes' in the full-stretch manner, but none were engraved in aquatint.

Harry Hall was familiar with every level of the eccentric strata of the turf during his lifetime – some he admired, others he did not; but all made their pilgrimage to his Newmarket studio to discover his views on the racehorses of the day. In his own behaviour he was a quiet man, devoted to his wife and children whom he was determined to give a far better education than he had received. The artist, Sidney Prior Hall, was the most talented of his sons, among the others were a doctor, a solicitor, surveyor and another artist.

At the end of his life, photography was beginning to take the place of the portrait artist, but as a recorder of horses and the turf betwen 1840 and his death at Newmarket in 1882, Harry Hall had no equal.

Racing.

1 Winners of the Great St Leger at Doncaster. See HERRING **3**.

   (29)   1842. Blue Bonnet – owned by the Earl of Eglinton. Ridden by T. Lye. Published 1 November 1842.
   (30)   1843. Nutwith – S. Wrather Esq. J. Marson. 1 November 1843.
   (31)   1844. Foig-a-Ballagh – E. H. Irwen Esq. H. Bell. November 1844.
   (32)   1845. The Baron – George Watts Esq. F. Butler. 20 October 1845.

Aquatints engraved by C. Hunt. Published by S. & J. Fuller, 34 Rathbone Place, London. Approx. 310 × 420 mm.

2 A series of Winners of the Derby Stakes at Epsom. See HERRING **4**.

   (17)   1843. Cotherstone – owned by J. Bowes Esq. Ridden by W. Scott. Published July 1843.
   (18)   1844. Orlando – Colonel Peel. N. Flatman. August 1844.
   (19)   1845. The Merry Monarch – Mr Gratwicke. F. Bell. July 1845.
   (20)   1846. Pyrrhus the First – John Gully Esq. S. Day. 10 July 1846.

Aquatints engraved by C. Hunt. Published by S. & J. Fuller, 34 Rathbone Place, London. Approx. 320 × 435 mm.

3 Portraits of racehorses, mainly with jockeys up, winners of Classic races and Gold Cups, with details of pedigrees and performances. Some titled: 'Moore's Celebrated Winners'. See BRETLAND **1**; COOPER **5**; DAVIS, H. T. **1**; DE PRADES **1**; HERRING **11**; HILLYARD **1**; SHAYER **1**; and SMITH, C. N. **1**.

   (1)   Meteor – owned by J. Bowes Esq. Ridden by W. Scott. 2,000 Gns, 1842. Published 20 June 1842.
   (2)   Mendicant – John Gulley Esq. S. Day. Oaks, 1846. 20 July 1846.

   (3)   Sir Tatton Sykes – Wm. Scott. W. Scott. (2,000 Gns) and St Leger, 1846. [*60*] 13 November 1846.
   (4)   Cossack – Thos Pedley Esq. S. Templeman. Derby, 1847. 1847.
   (5)   The Hero – Mr John Powney of Lansdown, near Bath and Mr John Day of Danebury. Goodwood Cup, 1847 (and Emperor's Plate, Ascot, 1847 and 1848). 31 August 1847.
   (6)   Van Tromp – Earl of Eglinton. J. Marson. St Leger, 1847. 20 October 1847.
   (7)   The Widow – Lord Westminster. R. Pettitt. Cambridgeshire, 1847. 13 January 1848.
   (8)   Chanticleer – James Merry Esq. Goodwood Stakes and Doncaster Cup, 1848.

Aquatints engraved by: (1) G. Hunt; (2)–(5) C. Hunt; (6)–(8) C. N. Smith. Published by J. Moore, 1 & 2 corner of West Street, Upper St Martin's Lane, London. Approx. 380 × 500 mm. (6) reissued to record Van Tromp winning the Goodwood Gold Cup, 1848 and Emperor's Plate, Ascot, 1849.

4 A series of Winners of the Derby Stakes at Epsom.

   (1)   1848. Surplice – owned by Lord Clifden. Ridden by S. Templeman. Published 15 June 1848.
   (2)   1849. The Flying Dutchman – Earl of Eglinton. C. Marlow. Not Dated.
   (3)   1850. Voltigeur – Earl of Zetland. J. Marson. Not Dated.
   (4)   1851. Teddington – Sir Joseph Hawley, Bart. J. Marson. Not Dated.
   (5)   1852. Daniel O'Rourke – J. Bowes Esq. F. Butler. Not Dated.
   (6)   1852. Daniel O'Rourke – J. Bowes Esq. F. Butler. 20 July 1852.
   (7)   1853. West Australian – J. Bowes Esq. F. Butler.
   (8)   1854. Andover – John Gully & Henry Padwick Esqs. A. Day. 15 August 1854.
   (9)   1855. Wild Dayrell – F. L. Popham Esq. Rickaby. 1 July 1855.
   (10)   1856. Ellington – Admiral Harcourt. T. Aldcroft. 1 September 1856.
   (11)   1857. Blink Bonny – Mr William I'Anson. J. Charlton. Derby and Oaks, 1857. 6 July 1857.
   (12)   1858. Beadsman – Sir Joseph Hawley, Bart. J. Wells. 1 August 1858.
   (13)   1859. Musjid – Sir Joseph Hawley, Bart. J. Wells.
   (14)   1860. Thormanby – James Merry Esq, MP. H. Custance. 20 June 1860.
   (15)   1861. Kettledrum – Colonel Towneley. R. Bullock.
   (16)   1862. Caractus – Mr C. Snewing. J. Parsons.
   (17)   1863. Macaroni – R. C. Naylor Esq. T. Chaloner. 1863.
   (18)   1864. Blair Athol – William I'Anson Esq. J. Snowden. 12 July 1864.
   (19)   1865. Gladiateur – Count F. de Lagrange. H. Grimshaw.
   (20)   1866. Lord Lyon – Richard Sutton Esq. H. Custance. 10 July 1866.

60 *William Scott's Sir Tatton Sykes, with the owner up, led by Sir Tatton Sykes. St Leger 1846. Aquatint after Harry Hall.*

(21) 1867. Hermit – Henry Chaplin Esq. J. Daley.

(22) 1868. Blue Gown – Sir Joseph Hawley Bart. J. Wells. 15 August 1868.

(23) 1869. Pretender – J. Johnstone Esq. J. Osborne.

(24) 1871. Favonius – Baron Mayer de Rothschild. T. French. 31 July 1871.

(25) 1872. Cremorne – Henry Savile Esq. C. Maidment. 4 October 1872.

(26) 1873. Doncaster – James Merry Esq. F. Webb. 25 August 1873.

(27) 1875. Galopin – Prince Batthyany. J. Morris.

(28) 1876. Kisber – Mr A. Baltazzi. C. Maidment.

(29) 1877. Silvio – Lord Falmouth. F. Archer. 25 August 1877.

(30) 1879. Sir Bevys – Mr Acton. George Fordham. 1 August 1879.

(31) 1880. Bend Or – Duke of Westminster. F. Archer.

(32) 1881. Iroquois – Mr Pierre Lorillard. F. Archer.

While (5) and (6) both show jockeys up, the scenes are different; the reasons for publishing two plates are not known. (1)–(3), (14)–(31): horses shown in looseboxes or stables; (4)–(13): shown with jockeys up.

Aquatints engraved by: (1)–(5) C. Hunt; (6)–(8), (12)–(18) J. Harris; (9), (10) J. Harris & C. Quentery; (11) J. Harris & W. Summers; (19)–(23) W. Summers; (24)–(32) E. G. Hester. Published by: (1), (2), (4)–(7), (9), (10), (12)–(16) Baily Bros, 3 Royal Exchange Buildings, Cornhill, London; (3), (8), (11) Baily Bros, Cornhill, London; (17)–(19), (21)–(31) A. H. Baily & Co., Cornhill, London; (20) A. H. Baily & Co., 3 Royal Exchange Buildings, as above; (32) A. H.

Baily & Co., 15 Nicholas Lane, London; Goupil & Co., Paris; M. Knoedler & Co., New York. Horses in looseboxes: approx. 395 × 515 mm.; horses with jockeys up: approx. 480 × 665 mm. (23) republished by J. Brall & Son, 6 Great Prescott Street, Goodman's Field, London.

5 A series of Winners of the St Leger Stakes at Doncaster.

(1) 1848. Surplice. Reissue of **4** (1) above.

(2) 1849. The Flying Dutchman. Reissue of **4** (2) above.

(3) 1850. Voltigeur. Reissue of **4** (3) above.

(4) 1850. Voltigeur – owned by the Earl of Zetland. Derby, St Leger and Doncaster Cup, 1850. Not Dated.

(5) 1851. Newminster – Mr A. Nichol. Ridden by S. Templeman. Published 1 November 1851.

(6) 1852. Stockwell – Marquis of Exeter. J. Norman. 1 November 1852.

(7) 1853. West Australian. Reissue of **4** (7) above with new details of performance: 2,000 Gns, Derby and St Leger. 21 September 1853.

(8) 1854. Knight of St George – Mr J. Morris. R. Basham.

(9) 1860. St Albans – Marquis of Ailesbury. L. Snowden. 1 December 1860.

(10) 1863. Lord Clifden. Viscount St Vincent. John Osborne. 1 March 1864.

(11) 1864. Blair Athol. Reissue of **4** (18) above.

(12) 1866. Lord Lyon. Reissue of **4** (20) above with new details of performance: 2,000 Gns, Derby and St Leger.

(13) 1867. Achievement – Colonel Pearson. T. Chaloner. 1 November 1867.

(14) 1868. Formosa – W. Graham Esq. T. Chaloner.

(15) 1869. Pero Gomez – Sir Jospeh Hawley Bart. J. Wells.

(16) 1871. Hannah – Baron Mayer de Rothschild. C. Maidment 1,000 Gns, Oaks and St Leger.

(17) 1874. Apology – Mr Launde. J. Osborne.

(18) 1877. Silvio. Reissue of **4** (29) above.

(19) 1881. Iroquois. Reissue of **4** (32) above.

(4), Voltigeur, is shown unsaddled in the open with trainer R. Hill and jockey, J. Marson, (Nat Flatman rode the horse in the Doncaster Cup). (5), (6), (8) shown with jockeys up; (10), (14)–(17) horses shown in looseboxes; (13) shown held by a groom on a training ground.

Aquatints engraved by: (4)–(6), (8)–(10) J. Harris; (13)–(15) W. Summers; (16), (17) E. G. Hester. Published by: (4)–(6), (8) Baily Bros, 3 Royal Exchange Buildings, as above; (9) Baily Bros, Cornhill; (10), (13)–(17) A. H. Baily & Co., Cornhill, London. Horses in looseboxes: approx. 395 × 515 mm.; horses with jockeys up: approx. 480 × 665 mm. (16) republished by J. Brall, 6 Great Prescott Street, Goodmans Field, London.

6 Portraits of racehorses, some with jockeys up, winners of Gold Cups and other races, with details of pedigrees and performances.

(1) Canezou – owned by Lord Stanley. Ridden by F. Butler. 1,000 Gns, 1848; Goodwood Cup 1849 and 1850; Doncaster Cup, 1849. Not Dated.

(2) Nancy – Mr Martinson of Hull. J. Charlton. Goodwood Cup, 1851. Published 1 October 1851.

(3) Irish Birdcatcher. 1 July 1853.

(4) Rataplan – Seymour Thellusson Esq. 1 March 1856.

(5) Melbourne by Humphrey Clinker. Bred in 1843. 1 March 1856.

(6) Mortemer – Mr T. Lombard. G. Fordham. Ascot Gold Cup, 1871.

(7) Prince Charlie – Henry Jones Esq. Middle Park Plate and 2,000 Gns (1872). [61] 1 May 1874.

(1), (2) shown with jockeys up; (3) shown walking with a groom by a ruin; (4) shown held by a trainer; (5)–(7) horses in looseboxes.

Aquatints engraved by: (1), (2) C. Hunt; (3) J. Harris; (4) J. Harris & C. Quentery; (5) J. Harris & W. Summers; (6), (7) E. G. Hester. Published by: (1), (2), (4), (5) Baily Bros, Cornhill, London; (3) Baily Bros, 3 Royal Exchange Buildings, as above; (6), (7) A. H. Baily & Co., Cornhill, London. Up to approx. 500 × 670 mm.

7 The Great Match. Between The Flying Dutchman, owned by the Earl of Eglinton and Voltigeur, owned by the Earl of Zetland. Run at York, the 13th of May 1851; Distance 2 Miles for One Thousand Pounds.

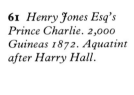

61 Henry Jones Esq's Prince Charlie. 2,000 Guineas 1872. Aquatint after Harry Hall.

Shows portraits, from left to right, of Lord Zetland; Nat Flatman on Voltigeur; the trainer Robert Hill; Admiral Rous; Mr George Payne; The Flying Dutchman with Charles Marlow; Earl of Eglinton; and his trainer John Fobert.

Aquatint engraved by C. Hunt. Published by Baily Bros, Cornhill, London. 1 May 1854. Approx. 535 × 1085 mm. Also published as by Baily Bros, Royal Exchange Buildings, Cornhill.

Republished as 'Sheldon's National Sports', from 31 Ely Place, London E.C.

8 Portraits of racehorses, with names of their owners and details of pedigrees and performances.

(1) Mademoiselle de Chantilly – owned by Count Frederic de Lagrange. Ridden by Spreoty. Winner of races in France and the City and Suburban Handicap, Epsom, 1858.

(2) Ventre-Saint-Gris – Count F. de Lagrange. Kendall. Won the French Derby, 1858. [*Plate 11*]

(3) Etoile du Nord – Count F. de Lagrange. Won the Prix de Diane, Chantilly, 1858.

(4) Black Prince – Count F. de Lagrange. Quinton. Winner of races in France in 1858 and 1859.

(5) La Toucques – Marquis de Montgomerie. (1863).

(6) Fille de L'Air – Count F. de Lagrange. A. Edwards. Winner of races in France 1863–1865, the Oaks, 1864 and the Claret Stakes, 1865.

(7) Gladiateur – Count F. de Lagrange. H. Grimshaw. Triple Crown, 1865.

(8) Gladiateur – Count F. de Lagrange. H. Grimshaw. Triple Crown, 1865 and Grand Prix de Paris, 1866.

(9) Montargis. Trained by Tom Jennings. J. Carratt. Cambridgeshire, 1873.

(10) Jongleur – Count de Juigne and Prince Auguste d'Arenberg. French Derby and St Leger, and Cambridgeshire, 1877.

(11) Rayon D'Or – Count F. de Lagrange. J. Goater. St Leger, 1879.

(1)–(6), (8), (11) shown with jockeys up; (7), (9), (10) horse in a loosebox.

Aquatints engraved by: (1)–(7) J. Harris; (8), (10), (11) W. Summers; (9) E. G. Hester. Published by Goupil & Cie., Paris, Maison a Londres, 17 Southampton Street, Strand; La Haye; Verlag von Goupil & Co., Berlin; M. Knoedler, New York. Not Dated. Approx. 480 × 670 mm.

9 Isonomy. Portrait of a racehorse owned by Mr F. Gretton, in a loosebox. Cambridgeshire, 1878; Ascot, (and 1880), Goodwood and Doncaster Cups, 1879.

Aquatint engraved by E. G. Hester. Published by Thomas McLean, 7 Haymarket, London. 1 October 1880.

Steeplechasing

10 Winners of the Grand National Steeple Chase.

(1) 1863. Emblem – owned by Lord Coventry, ridden by George Stevens. Published 1863.

(2) 1864. Emblematic – Lord Coventry. George Stevens. 1864.

Aquatints engraved by J. Harris. Published by A. H. Baily & Co., Cornhill, London. Approx. 480 × 670 mm.

11 The Colonel. Winner of the Liverpool Grand National Steeple-Chase in 1869 and 1870. Portrait of a racehorse owned by Mr M. Evans, with George Stevens up.

George Stevens died after a fall from his cob on 2 June 1871. He rode five Grand National winners: Free Trader (1856); Emblem (1863); Emblematic (1864); and The Colonel.

Aquatint engraved by W. Stevens. Published at Cheltenham by W. Stevens. 1870. Approx. 480 × 670 mm.

HANCOCK, Charles, 1802–1877

It is a pity that Charles Hancock spent so little time painting and so much being diverted by potentially exciting inventions on which he did not have the business acumen to capitalise.

After leaving the family home in Marlborough where his father was a cabinet maker, Hancock learnt to draw and paint under James Stark in London and Norfolk. However, within a few years of mastering technique, colour and composition, Charles joined two of his brothers in setting up a factory in Essex to process rubber suitable for waterproofing ships' hulls. Disagreements with their financial backers led the brothers to ruin and Hancock was thrown back onto his trade of 'Animal, subject, portrait and miniature painter' which he practised in Reading.

In the 1830s and early 1840s his paintings of horses came to the attention of the proprietor of *The Sporting Magazine* (later combined with *The Sporting Review*) and, more importantly, to Rudolph Ackermann in Regent Street. Hancock succeeded John Ferneley (*qv*) in supplying paintings of Derby and St Leger winners to Ackermann who was publishing prints of these classics racehorses in competition with S. & J. Fuller at the time. He became a well established animal and portrait painter until his discovery of a way of making artificial corks and, by a different method, insulating cables led him again along the path of litigation and loss, from which he only recovered a few years before his death in 1877.

His paintings of racehorses, which bear comparison with those by his contemporary J. F. Herring (*qv*), are

62 *The Marquis of Westminster's Satirist, with W. Scott up. St Leger 1841. Aquatint after Charles Hancock.*

63 *Mr Irwin's Foig-a-Ballagh, with F. Bell up. St Leger 1844. Aquatint after Charles Hancock.*

excellent. The prints made from such pictures, engraved mainly by Edward Duncan, are extremely fine.

1 A series of Winners of the Derby Stakes at Epsom. See FERNELEY **1**.

(1) 1835. Mundig – owned by J. Bowes Esq. Ridden by W. Scott. Published 20 July 1835.
(2) 1836. Bay Middleton – Earl of Jersey. J. Robinson. 1 July 1836.
(3) 1837. Phosphorus. See FERNELEY **1** (6).
(4) 1838. Amato – Sir Gilbert Heathcote, Bart, MP. J. Chapple. 1 August 1839.
(5) 1839. Bloomsbury – Mr William Ridsdale. S. Templeman. 18 June 1839.
(6) 1840. Little Wonder – D. Marjoribanks Robertson Esq. W. Macdonald. 21 August 1840.
(7) 1841. Coronation – A. T. Rawlinson Esq. P. Conolly. 5 July 1841.
(8) 1842. Attila – Hon. Col. Anson. W. Scott. [*Plate 8*] 12 July 1842.
(9) 1843. Cotherstone – J. Bowes Esq. W. Scott. 1843.

Aquatints engraved by: (1) F. C. Lewis; (2), (4)–(6), (9) E. Duncan; (7), (8) J. Harris. Published by R. Ackermann, 191 Regent Street, London. Approx. 320 × 420 mm.

2 A series of Winners of the Great St Leger Stakes at Doncaster. See FERNELEY **2**.

(1) 1835. Queen of Trumps – owned by E. Mostyn Esq. Ridden by T. Lye. Published 1 November 1835.
(2) 1836. Elis – Lord Lichfield. J. B. Day. 1 November 1836.
(3) 1837. Mango – C. C. Greville Esq. S. Day Jnr. 1 November 1837.
(4) 1838. Don John – Earl of Chesterfield. W. Scott. 1 November 1838.
(5) 1839. Charles the Twelth – Major Yarburgh. W. Scott. 15 November 1839.
(6) 1840. Launcelot – Marquis of Westminster. W. Scott. 1 November 1840.
(7) 1841. Satirist – Marquis of Westminster. W. Scott. [*62*] 1 November 1841.
(8) 1842. Blue Bonnet – Earl of Eglinton. T. Lye. [*Plate 8*] 21 October 1842.
(9) 1843. Nutwith – Mr S. Wrather. J. Marson. 1 November 1843.
(10) 1844. Foig-a-Ballagh – E. H. Irwin Esq. F. Bell. [*63*] 1 November 1844.

Aquatints engraved by: (1)–(4), (6) E. Duncan; (5), (7)–(10) J. Harris. Published by R. Ackermann, as above. Approx. 320 × 420 mm.

3 Portraits of racehorses, with jockeys up, winners of Classic races and Gold Cups, with details of pedigrees and performances.

(1) Glencoe – owned by the Earl of Jersey. Ridden by J. Robinson. 2,000 Gns and Goodwood Gold Cup, 1834; Ascot Gold Cup, 1835. [*64*] Published 2 May 1836.
(2) Deception – Fulwar Craven Esq. J. B. Day. Oaks, 1839. 15 July 1839.

Aquatints engraved by E. Duncan. Published by R. Ackermann, as above. Approx. 320 × 420 mm.

4 British Field Sports.

Plate 5 Thorngrave and Sir Hercules. Portraits of racehorses.

Line engraving by H. Beckwith. Published by A. H. Baily & Co., Cornhill, London. 1 November 1839. Approx. 140 × 190 mm.

HARDY, M. Dorothy, fl 1908–1925

Dorothy Hardy illustrated children's books and painted a few hunting and racing scenes which were published. Her style is similar to the early work of Cecil Aldin (*qv*) with bold outlines and flat surfaces of colour. *The Grey Leads* is a lively and colourful chromolithograph, perhaps part of a set of four. In 1925 Dorothy Hardy was living at Long Eaton, Derbyshire, but little else is known of her life.

1 Steeplechasing scene.

The Grey Leads.

Chromolithograph. Published by Richard Wyman & Co. Ltd. J. L. Goffart, Printer, Brussels. Approx. 310 × 520 mm.

HARLAND, John Sawdon, born c1829, op 1853

J. S. Harland was a farmer, the son of Dr William Harland of Scarborough, Yorkshire. Apart from this print his only other recorded work is an oil of a hunter in a landscape by the sea, (presumably near Scarborough). The Scarborough Steeplechase was for 'Farmers or Farmer's Sons'. Harland rode Mr Crowe's Arab Chief in the race and was placed seventh. The Clerk of the Course describes in the *Scarboro' Gazette* (13 November 1851) how: 'Arab Chief ran a very game horse, having carried two stone overweight, but on getting out of the brook the snaffle rein broke, and the horse got away with the snaffle reins dangling about his legs, the other horses obtaining a lead of three fields; Mr Harland ran after him across a field, mounted again, and caught his horse within a mile from home, and by dint of perseverance came in seventh.'

64 *The Earl of Jersey's Glencoe. 2,000 Guineas 1834. Aquatint after Charles Hancock.*

1 The Scarborough Steeple Chase, run November 4th, 1851, with dedication by Lord Londesborough.

The race was won by Mr Hopper's Agitation, ridden by G. Hopper; 2nd, Mr Stewart's Flower Girl, Danby; 3rd, Mr Johnson's Charley, W. Ford. Lord Londesborough presented a Silver Cup.

Aquatint engraved by J. Harris. Probably published privately. 1853. Approx. 320 × 495 mm.

HARRINGTON, Robert, 1800–1882

Robert Harrington is believed to have been a pupil of Abraham Cooper (*qv*). He painted a variety of sporting scenes, cattle and poultry, a few of which were engraved and some published by him at Carlisle. His paintings of horses are well observed and his use of light is clever.

1 The Celebrated Mare, Bee's Wing. (Winner of 51 Prizes). Portrait of a racehorse owned by William Orde Esq.

Winner of the Ascot Gold Cup, 1842. ridden by Cartwright, and four Doncaster Cups, 1837, 1840, 1841 and 1842.

Aquatint engraved by C. Hunt. Published by S. Brown, 407 Oxford Street, London. 30 November 1842. Approx. 305 × 405 mm.

HAVELL, Alfred Charles, 1855–1928

Alfred Charles was a member of the Havell family of artists living in Reading throughout the eighteenth and nineteenth centuries. His best known forbears were Robert Havell Snr (1769–1832) and Jnr (1793–1878), both engravers (the latter engraved the plates of J. J. Audubon's *Birds of America*), and Robert Snr's cousin, the painter William Havell (1782–1857). A. C. Havell, born at 41 Sloane Square, London in March 1855, was the son of Edmund Havell Jnr (1819–1894), a nephew of William. A.C.H. lived nearly all his life in London and it may be safely assumed learnt his art from his father who also painted equestrian portraits. Alfred first exhibited at the Royal Academy in 1878, and soon afterwards was employed by Messrs Fores of Piccadilly to record the important racehorses of the day for subsequent publication. A.C.H. worked for Fores until his death from pneumonia in 1928 – his Will, made in 1924, is witnessed by Mr George Poole Fores, then head of the firm.

His paintings are very carefully executed and, as a result, sometimes appear a little wooden; but when not working under pressure from his publisher some of his portraits are quite fine. All his pictures provide a valuable record and link in racehorse portraiture between the death of Harry Hall in 1882 and the work of James

Lynwood Palmer (*qv*), Alfred Grenfall Haig, F. Mabel Hollams and Nina Colmore, all of whose main output came at the beginning of this century.

Racing

1 Portraits of racehorses, some with jockeys up, winners of Classic and other races, with details of pedigree and performances. Some titled 'Fores's Celebrated Winners'. See LUCAS-LUCAS I; WHEELER, A. I; WHEELER, J. I.

(1) Minting – owned by Mr Robert Vyner. Winner of the Grand Prix de Paris, 1886.
(2) Merry Hampton – 'Mr Abington' (Mr George Baird). Ridden by J. Watts. Derby, 1887.
(3) Ayrshire – Duke of Portland. F. Barrett. 2,000 Gns and Derby, 1888.
(4) Donovan – Duke of Portland. T. Loates. Derby (and St Leger, 1889, ridden by F. Barrett).
(5) Sainfoin – Sir James Miller. J. Watts. Derby, 1890. [*65*] Published 10 July 1890.
(6) Sheen. Cesarawitch, 1890, ridden by F. Webb. 16 March 1891.
(7) Alicante. Cambridgeshire, 1890. 1 June 1891.
(8) Common – Lord Alington and Sir Frederick Johnstone. G. Barrett. Triple Crown, 1891.
(9) Sir Hugo – Lord Bradford. F. Allsopp. Derby, 1892. 10 July 1892.

(10) Isinglass – Mr H. M. McCalmont. T. Loates. Triple Crown, 1893 and Ascot Gold Cup, 1895.
(11) Sir Visto – Lord Rosebery. S. Loates. Derby (and St Leger), 1895. 13 July 1895.

Photogravures. Published by Messrs Fores, 41 Piccadilly, London, Approx. 425 × 570 mm.

2 Portraits of racehorses, in or outside looseboxes and stables, winners of Classic and other races, with details of pedigrees and performances.

(1) Hampton – owned by Lord Ellesmere, Goodwood Gold Cup, 1877.
(2) Bend Or – Duke of Westminster. Ridden by F. Archer. Winner of the Derby, 1880.
(3) St Simon – Duke of Portland. Ascot and Goodwood Gold Cup, 1884. An outstanding stallion. [*30, page 59*] Published 1 January 1903.
(4) Melton – Lord Hastings. F. Archer. Derby and St Leger, 1885.
(5) Gallinule – Captain Greer. An outstanding stallion.
(6) Carbine – Duke of Portland. An outstanding stallion. (Melbourne Cup, Australia, 1890).
(7) Persimmon – HRH the Prince of Wales. J. Watts. Derby (and St Leger), 1896. 13 July 1896.
(8) Cyllene – Mr C. D. Rose. Ascot Gold Cup, 1899. A successful stallion.
(9) Sceptre – Mr Robert Sievier. H. Randall. 2,000 and

65 *Sir James Miller's Sainfoin. Derby 1890. Photogravure after Alfred Charles Havell.*

1,000 Gns, Oaks and St Leger, 1902. In the St Leger ridden by F. W. Hardy.

(10) Pretty Polly – Major Eustace Loder. W. Lane. 1,000 Gns, Oaks and St Leger, 1904.

(11) Dark Ronald – Sir Abe Baily. W. Williams. Royal Hunt Cup, Ascot, 1909. An outstanding stallion.

(12) Tracery – Mr A. Belmond. G. Bellhouse. St Leger, 1912.

(13) Desmond – Lord Dunraven. Champion Sire, 1913.

Photogravures. Published by Messrs Fores, as above. Approx. 380 × 510 mm.

3 Portraits of racehorses, some with jockeys up, winners of Classic and other races, with details of pedigrees and performances.

(1) Ormonde – owned by the Duke of Westminster. Triple Crown, 1886. F. G. Barret up for 2,000 Gns, and F. Archer up for Derby and St Leger.

(2) Flying Fox – Duke of Westminster. Ridden by M. Cannon. Winner of the Triple Crown, 1899.

(3) Diamond Jubilee – HRH the Prince of Wales. H. Jones. Triple Crown. 1900.

(4) Volodyovski – Mr W. C. Whitney. Lester Reiff. Derby, 1901.

(5) Ard Patrick – Mr John Gubbins. J. H. Martin. Derby, 1902.

(6) Sceptre – Mr Robert Sievier. H. Randall. 2,000 and 1,000 Gns. Oaks and St Leger, 1902. In the St Leger ridden by F. W. Hardy. Published 16 February 1903.

(7) Rock Sand – Sir James Miller. D. Maher. Triple Crown, 1903. In the 2,000 Gns, ridden by J. H. Martin. 15 July 1903.

(8) St Amant – Mr Leopold de Rothschild. K. Cannon. 2,000 Gns and Derby, 1904. 15 July 1904.

(9) Pretty Polly – Major Eustace Loder. W. Lane. 1,000 Gns, Oaks and St Leger, 1904. 24 October 1904.

(10) Cicero – Earl of Rosebery. D. Maher. Derby, 1905.

(11) Spearmint – Major Eustace Loder. D. Maher. Derby, 1906.

(12) Orby – Mr Richard Croker. Jonny Reiff. Derby, 1907. 15 July 1907.

(13) Velocity. Cambridgeshire, 1905. 1 November 1907.

(14) Signorinetta – Chevalier Ginistrelli. W. Bullock. Derby and Oaks, 1908.

(15) The White Knight – Colonel Kirkwood. W. Halsey. Ascot Gold Cup, 1907 and 1908, Goodwood Cup, 1907. 30 November 1908.

(16) Bayardo – 'Mr Fairie' (Mr A. W. Cox). D. Maher. St Leger, 1909. 23 May 1910.

(17) Neil Gow – Earl of Rosebery. D. Maher. 2,000 Gns, 1910.

(18) Sunstar – Mr J. B. Joel. G. Stern. 2,000 Gns, and Derby, 1911.

(19) Tagalie – Mr W. Raphael. L. Hewitt. 1,000 Gns, and Derby, 1912.

(20) The Tetrarch – Major D. McCalmont. Champion sire, 1919.

Photogravures. Published by Messrs Fores as above. Approx. 305 × 380 mm.

4 Minoru. Portrait of a racehorse owned by HM King Edward VII. Winner of the 2,000 Gns and Derby, 1909, ridden by H. Jones. A group portrait of the horse with jockey up, HM the King, the Prince of Wales, the trainer, Mr Richard Marsh, and other gentlemen of the turf in front of the Stand at Epsom.

Photogravure. Published by Messrs Fores, as above. Approx. 380 × 510 mm.

5 Racing scenes.

1 A False Start.
2 They're Off.
3 Coming into the Straight.
4 A Close Finish.

Colour reproduction. Published by Messrs Fores, as above. Pls approx. 280 × 375 mm.

6 Racing scenes.

Plate 1 Epsom. Inspecting the Competitors.
Plate 2 Kempton. The Parade.
Plate 3 Sandown. Preparing to Start.
Plate 4 Newmarket. Waiting for the Verdict.

Hand-coloured reproductions. Published by Messrs Fores, as above. Pls approx. 360 × 585 mm.

Steeplechasing

7 Steeplechasing scenes.

Plate 1 Warwick. At the Bend.
Plate 2 Sandown. The First Time Round.
Plate 3 Manchester. A Refusal.
Plate 4 Liverpool. The Water Jump.

Hand-coloured reproductions. Published by Messrs Fores, as above. Pls approx. 360 × 585 mm.

8 Portraits of steeplechasers. See BEER 1.

(1) Cloister. Grand National, 1983.
(2) Manifesto. Grand National, 1897 and 1899.

Hand-coloured reproductions. Published by Messrs Fores, as above. Pls approx. 280 × 405 mm.

HAYES, Michael Angelo, RHA, 1820–1877

The son of the artist Edward Hayes RHA, he was born at Waterford in Ireland in July 1820. M. A. Hayes first exhibited at the Royal Hibernian Academy in 1840,

66 *Corinthean Cup. Punchestown, 1854. Mixed method engraving after Michael Angelo Hayes.*

and subsequently became known for his watercolours of military subjects. He was elected a Member of the RHA in 1854, and an Associate of the Institute of Painters in Watercolour in London. He also painted in oils. Hayes died after an accident on 31 December 1877.

1 Corinthean Cup, Punchestown, 1854. A large scale group portrait of mounted gentlemen and racehorses with jockeys up. [66]

This plate shows, left to right: Earl of Clonmell; Lord Cloncurry; John J. Preston on 'Auburn'; Lord St Lawrence on 'Mushroom'; Captain Barclay, 16th Lancers on 'Merlin'; Marquis of Drogheda; F. Rynd Esq.; Captain, the Hon. J. W. Hely Hutchinson ADC on 'Torrent' (Corinthean Cup, 1854); Lieut-Colonel Campbell on 'Free Trade'; W. Kennedy Esq., Master of the Kildare Hounds; Marquis of Waterford; J. G. Price Esq., 2nd Dragoon Guards; Earl of Howth on 'Flavelle'; Major Dickson, 16th Lancers; H. J. Wilkin Esq., 11th Hussars on 'Squire'; Sir Philip Crampton, Bart on 'Potteen'; Marquis of Conyngham; Samuel Reynell Esq., Master of the Meath Hounds; R. W. Reynard Esq. on 'Beware'; E. Warburton Esq.; Captain Severne, 16th Lancers; Captain Wombwell ADC; Captain Chichester, 7th Dragoon Guards; Thomas Boyse Esq., 4th Lancashire Militia.

Mixed method engraving by W. H. Simmons. Published by Thos Cranfield, Grafton Street, Dublin. c1854. Approx. 535 × 915 mm.

HAZLEHURST, E., Jnr, op 1815

Nothing is known of Hazlehurst, but this slightly naive and busy scene of Knutsford Racecourse in Cheshire is delightful. H. B. Ziegler's (*qv*) picture of Worcester Racecourse, published eight years later, has some similarities with Knutsford in showing the various non-racing activities enjoyed at such meetings.

1 The Adventures of Knutsford Race Course. Taken on the Spot. With dedication to the 'Nobility and Gentry of Lancashire'. [67]

Aquatint engraved by R. Reeve. Published by C. Richards. November 1815. Approx. 605 × 720 mm.

HENDERSON, Charles Cooper, 1803–1877

Cooper Henderson was the younger son of the amateur artists John and Georgiana Henderson. His mother was the daughter of George Keate, FSA, an antiquarian and artist; she also painted. This background of the arts manifested itself in Cooper as a child in drawing what he saw from the tall windows of his parents' house in

Montague Street, near the British Museum. He was educated at Brighton and then Winchester before studying rather idly for the Bar and enjoying a European tour with his father and elder brother, John. While his father and brother sketched panoramas in France, Spain, Austria and Italy, Cooper Henderson found, to him, more interesting subjects among the coaches, carriages and postilions 'on the road'.

On Christmas Eve, 1829, he was married secretly to Charlotte Bye (then aged sixteen), the daughter of a Thames lighterman. Disapproving of the marriage, his father gave him a small allowance and told him to leave London. Thrown mainly onto his own resources, Cooper Henderson moved to Bracknell in Berkshire and started to paint for his living. He was quickly successful and his pictures of coaches and coaching are well known, being more accurate and lively than those of his near contemporary, James Pollard (*qv*). He soon received sufficient commissions to afford to return to London where he was reconciled with his parents. His father died in 1843 and at the death of his mother in 1851 Cooper Henderson was left sufficient money to be able to give up painting seriously. He then lived a leisurely and gentlemanly life by the river at Halliford-on-Thames, dying there in 1877.

1 Returning from Ascot Races.

Aquatint engraved by E. Duncan. Published by R. Ackermann, 191 Regent Street, London. 16 September 1839. Approx. 380 × 825 mm.

Reissued by Messrs Fores, 41 Piccadilly, London. Not dated.

HERRING, John Frederick (Snr), 1795–1865
HERRING, Benjamin (Jnr), 1830–1871

John Frederick Herring, the son of a fringe-maker of Dutch origin, was born in London in 1795. When still a young man he moved to Doncaster where he embellished coaches and later became a coach driver. In time he graduated from driving local stages to taking the ribbons of the High Flyer which ran daily between Doncaster and London. At the same time he was attracting Yorkshire patrons whose horses he painted. In about 1816 he gave up driving, settling to painting as his profession. He was soon receiving as many commissions as he could handle to paint portraits of racehorses and hunters. However, his first exhibit at the Royal Academy in 1818 was a painting of a dog. This was followed by pictures of racehorses and, from 1840 to 1865, by farm subjects. His twenty-seven paintings

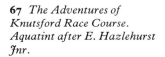

67 *The Adventures of Knutsford Race Course. Aquatint after E. Hazlehurst Jnr.*

which were shown at the Royal Academy during his lifetime comprised a minute fraction of his prolific output between 1818 and his death in 1865.

His first portrait of a famous racehorse to be published (engraved by William Ward) was of Dr Syntax, owned by Ralph Riddell Esq. This was in September 1824. Another portrait of this horse was painted and engraved by James Pollard (qv) in 1817. In 1825 *The Doncaster Gazette* commissioned Herring to paint a series of pictures of the winners of the St Leger starting from 1815. Many of these must have been portrayed retrospectively and some not from life. W. Sheardown and Sons of Doncaster published these brilliantly engraved prints (by Thomas Sutherland) in 1825 with the 1826 winner, Tarrare, contributed by David Dalby (qv). Messrs Fuller of London bought the plates and continued the series until the mid-1840s. Fullers also published a similar series of Derby winners after Herring's paintings between 1827 and 1841, at which latter date the artist seems to have parted company with this publisher. These prints provide a 'benchmark' in their quality of painting, engraving and printing which subsequent publishers attempted to emulate, but rarely with such success.

In 1831 J. F. Herring moved to Newmarket and then on to London in 1834. He visited France to paint some of the Duc d'Orlean's horses in 1840 and 1841 soon after making yet another move, this time to Essex, where he stayed for only a few years before returning to London. Finally, in 1853, Herring took his family to Meopham Park near Tonbridge in Kent. Here he turned to domestic, farmyard and narrative subjects, but still painted a few of the more interesting incidents and events of the turf.

The list of prints which follows demonstrates Herring's phenomenal output of both racehorse portraits and racing scenes which were used by all the principal publishers of the mid-nineteenth century. They do not, of course, include the many other subjects that he painted, particularly hunting, many of which were also engraved. After an uncertain start when first in London, Herring was well paid for his efforts and this financial stability, so unusual for an artist, enabled him to live more comfortably than his contemporaries among horse painters. However, this does not seem to have bred complacency since he was working to the end of his life despite infirmities which latterly confined him to a chair.

In most references to sporting paintings it is necessary to describe J. F. Herring as 'Senior' to avoid con-

68 *The Hon. E. M. L. Mostyn's The Queen of Trumps, with T. Lye up. St Leger 1835. Aquatint after John Frederick Herring Snr.*

Count Frederic de Lagrange's Ventre-Saint-Gris, with Kendall up,
at Chantilly. French Derby 1858.
Aquatint after Harry Hall.

PLATE 11

PLATE 12

Racing. The Run In. Aquatint after John Frederick Herring Snr.

Mr William Day's The Promised Land, with Alfred Day up.
2,000 Guineas and Goodwood Cup 1859.
Aquatint by and after Charles Hunt.

PLATE 13

fusing his work with that of a son of the same name who painted in a similar manner to his father, but not half so well. As far as I can discover, there are no racing prints after the paintings of J. F. Herring Jnr. Nor are there any after another son, Charles, of whom Herring Snr was particularly fond, and who helped his father in some of his later paintings. However, there are a few quite important prints after the work of the youngest son, Benjamin. For the purist, 'Junior' should perhaps be added to his name since J. F. Herring Snr had an artist brother of that name who died in the year that his nephew was born (1830). Ben Herring (Jnr), for whom his father had little regard, was an accomplished artist. As well as supplying portraits of racehorses and pictures of racing to a number of periodicals and for books, aquatint plates after his work were published by J. and later G. P. McQueen. These 'composite' scenes of racing provide a valuable and no doubt accurate portrayal of the leading horses and jockeys of the years between 1860 and 1875.

John Frederick Herring

1 Dr. Syntax. Portrait of a racehorse – owned by Ralph Ridell Esq. Winner of twenty Gold Cups.

Mezzotint engraved by William Ward Jnr. Published Doncaster. September 1824. Approx. 405 × 510 mm.

2 A series of Winners of the Great St Leger at Doncaster.

(1) 1815. Filho da Puta – owned by Sir W. Maxwell, Bart. Ridden by J. Jackson. [21, page 42]
(2) 1816. The Duchess – Sir B. R. Graham, Bart. B. Smith.
(3) 1817. Ebor – Henry Peirce Esq. R. Johnson.
(4) 1818. Reveller – Henry Peirce Esq. R. Johnson.
(5) 1819. Antonio – Thos Ferguson Esq. J. Nicholson. [Plate 4]
(6) 1820. St Patrick – Sir E. Smith, Bart. J. Johnson.
(7) 1821. Jack Spigot – Hon. T. O. Powlett. W. Scott.
(8) 1822. Theodore – Hon. E. Petre. J. Jackson.
(9) 1823. Barefoot – Richard Watt and Gilbert Crompton Esqs. T. Goodisson.
(10) 1824. Jerry – R. O. Gascoigne Esq. B. Smith.
(11) 1825. Memnon – Richard Watt Esq. W. Scott.
(12) 1826. Tarrare. See DALBY 2.

Aquatints engraved by T. Sutherland. Published by W. Sheardown & Sons (Doncaster). (1)–(11): (1825); (12): (1826). Approx. 310 × 420 mm. (5) in a stable yard with jockey and trainer in attendance; remainder with jockeys up at Doncaster or on a training ground.

Some of the paintings and prints were made retrospectively when Sheardown announced his short-lived enterprise in 1825. In 1827 the plates were bought by Messrs. Fuller. This publisher

continued the series in the same style, see 3 below; and also started a series of Derby Winners, see 4 below.

3 Winners of the Great St Leger at Doncaster.

(13) 1826. Tarrare – Earl of Scarbrough. G. Nelson. Published 20 November 1826.
(14) 1827. Matilda – Hon. E. Petre. J. Robinson. 1 January 1928.
(15) 1828. The Colonel – Hon. E. Petre. W. Scott. 15 January 1829.
(16) 1829. Rowton – Hon. E. Petre. W. Scott. 21 December 1829.
(17) 1830. Birmingham – Mr Beardsworth. P. Conolly. 21 March 1831.
(18) 1831. Chorister – Marquis of Cleveland. J. B. Day. 14 February 1832.
(19) 1832. Margrave – J. Gully Esq. J. Robinson. 21 February 1833.
(20) 1833. Rockingham – Richard Watt Esq. S. Darling. 2 December 1833.
(21) 1834. Touchstone – Marquis of Westminster. G. Calloway. 15 December 1834. [24, see page 50]
(22) 1835. The Queen of Trumps – Hon. E. M. L. Mostyn, MP. T. Lye. Also won the Oaks. [68]. 20 November 1835.
(23) 1836. Elis – Earl of Lichfield. J. B. Day. November 1836.
(24) 1837. Mango – C. C. Greville Esq. S. Day Jnr. November 1837.
(25) 1838. Don John – Earl of Chesterfield. W. Scott. November 1838.
(26) 1839. Charles XIIth – Major Yarburgh. W. Scott. Also won the Gold Cup at Doncaster, 1839. November 1839.
(27) 1840. Launcelot – Marquis of Westminster. W. Scott. 1 November 1840.
(28) 1841. Satirist. See SPALDING 1.
(29) 1842. Blue Bonnet. See HALL 1.
(30) 1843. Nutwith. See HALL 1.
(31) 1844. Foig-a-Ballagh. See HALL 1.
(32) 1845. The Baron. See HALL 1.

Aquatints engraved by: (13)–(17) R. G. Reeve; (18)–(20) and (22)–(27) C. Hunt; (21) R. W. Smart and C. Hunt. Published by S. & J. Fuller, 34 Rathbone Place, London (13); and at Messrs White's, Doncaster; (14)–(18) and at J. F. Herring, Doncaster; (19), (20) and at J. F. Herring, Six Mile Bottom, near Newmarket. (13) approx. 335 × 445 mm; (14)–(27) approx. 310 × 420 mm. All with jockeys up; (16) also shows Voltaire; and (26) shows Euclid.

The painting of Sheardown's St Leger winner (Tarrare) by David Dalby suggests that Herring parted company with this publisher in 1826. He was then engaged by Messrs Fuller to paint their contemporary series of St Leger Winners, initially perhaps in competition with Sheardown. The engraving of Tarrare after Herring is larger than the Sheardown or subsequent Fuller plates. Fuller then acquired Sheardown's plates and adopted the format and size of the latter's prints providing a uniform series from 1815 to 1845.

69 *Thomas Thornhill Esq's Emilius at stud. (Derby 1823.) Aquatint after John Frederick Herring Snr.*

4 A series of Winners of the Derby Stakes at Epsom.

(1) 1827. Mameluke – owned by the Earl of Jersey. Ridden by J. Robinson. Published 18 September 1827.

(2) 1828. Cadland – Duke of Rutland. J. Robinson. 15 July 1828.

(3) 1829. Frederick – Mr Gratwicke. J. Forth. 14 September 1829.

(4) 1830. Priam – Mr William Chifney. S. Day. 20 September 1830.

(5) 1831. Spaniel – Lord Lowther. W. Wheatley. 15 August 1831.

(6) 1832. St Giles – Mr Ridsdale. W. Scott. 12 August 1832.

(7) 1833. Dangerous – Mr Sadler. J. Chapple. 25 August 1833.

(8) 1834. Plenipotentiary – S. Batson Esq. P. Conolly. 12 August 1834.

(9) 1835. Mundig – J. Bowes Esq., MP. W. Scott. 18 July 1835.

(10) 1836. Bay Middleton – Earl of Jersey. J. Robinson. [*Plate 4*] 1 July 1836.

(11) 1837. Phosphorous – Lord Berners. G. Edwards. July 1837.

(12) 1838. Amato – Sir Gilbert Heathcote, Bart. J. Chapple. July 1838.

(13) 1839. Bloomsbury – Mr W. Ridsdale. S. Templeman up. June 1839. [*Plate 6*]

(14) 1840. Little Wonder – D. Robertson Esq. W. Macdonald. 1840.

(15) 1841. Coronation – A. T. Rawlinson Esq. P. Conolly. July 1841.

(16) 1842. Attila. See COOPER **4**.

(17) 1843. Cotherstone. See HALL **2**.

(18) 1844. Orlando. See HALL **2**.

(19) 1845. The Merry Monarch. See HALL **2**.

(20) 1846. Pyrrhus the First. See HALL **2**.

Aquatints engraved by: (1)–(4) R. G. Reeve; (5)–(7) and (9)–(15) C. Hunt; (8) Messrs Smart and Hunt. Published by S. & J. Fuller, as above, (1), (2), (4) and by J. F. Herring, Doncaster; (6), (7) and by J. F. Herring, Six Mile Bottom, near Newmarket; (8) and at J. F. Herring, Newmarket. Approx. 320 × 435 mm. (1) held by his trainer; remainder with jockeys up.

5 Bessy Bedlam. Portrait of a racehorse bred by Colonel King of Ashby House, Lincoln, with dedication to Colonel Neville King.

Aquatint engraved by H. Pyall. Published by S. Knights, Sweetings Alley, Cornhill, London and J. Noble. Also by Moon, Boys & Graves, 6 Pall Mall, London and Rees Davis, Hull. 1 July 1828. Approx. 315 × 440 mm.

6 Dunsinane. Portrait of a racehorse owned by His Majesty, in a loosebox.

Lithograph drawn by J. F. Herring. Published by S. & J. Fuller, as above. 1828. Approx. 300 × 400 mm.

7 Bessie Bedlam. Portrait of a racehorse, as in **5** above.

Aquatint engraved by R. G. Reeve. Published by S. & J. Fuller as above. 15 September 1828. Approx. 305 × 420 mm. Reissued by Fuller in 1845.

8 Grey Momus. Portrait of a racehorse owned by Lord George Bentinck, J. Day up, with details of pedigree and performance.

Aquatint engraved by C. Hunt. Published by S. & J. Fuller as above. July 1838. Approx. 310 × 424 mm.

9 Euclid. Portrait of a racehorse owned by Thomas Thornhill Esq., with his jockey, and details of pedigree and performance.

Aquatint engraved by C. Hunt. Published by S. & J. Fuller as above. 6 April 1840. Approx. 315 × 425 mm.

10 A series of stallions successful at stud, in or outside their looseboxes, with details of pedigrees and performances. See SARTORIUS, F. **13**.

(1) Tramp – owned by Mr Ridsdale. Published 20 May 1834.
(2) Emilius – Thos Thornhill Esq. Derby, 1823. [*69*] 26 May 1834.
(3) Orville – His late Majesty, George the Fourth. St Leger, 1802. 25 June 1834.
(4) Velocipede – Mr W. Armytage. 1 February 1836.
(5) Whisker – bred by the Duke of Grafton. Derby, 1815. 1 February 1836.
(6) Blacklock – Richard Watt Esq. 1836.
(7) Zinganee – bred by the Marquis of Exeter. Ascot Gold Cup, 1829. 1836.
(8) Camel – Mr Theobald. 1836.
(9) Catton – bred by Lord Scarbrough. 1836.
(10) Partisan – Duke of Grafton. 1836.
(11) Sultan – bred by Mr Crockford. 1836.
(12) Gohanna. 1838.
(13) Whalebone – Duke of Grafton. Derby, 1810. 1838.
(14) Walton – bred by Sir H. Williamson, 1799. 1838.
(15) Actaeon – bred by Mr Newton, 1822. 1840.
(16) Glaucus – Earl of Chesterfield. 1840.
(17) Comus – Mr Christopher Wilson. 1840.
(18) Langar – Lord Sligo. 1840.
(19) Muley – Alexander Nowell Esq. 1843.
(20) Defence – Mr Isaac Sadler. September 1843.
(21) Venison – Mr J. Day.
(22) Sheet Anchor – J. Golden Esq.

Aquatints engraved by C. Hunt. Published by S. & J. Fuller as above. (1)–(3) approx. 275 × 370 mm; remainder approx. 240 × 300 mm.

All were republished under the title 'Sheldon's Celebrated Racing Sires' by James Sheldon, 31 Ely Place, London.

11 Portraits of racehorses, mainly with jockeys up, winners of Classic races and Gold Cups, with details of pedigrees and performances. Some titled 'Moore's Celebrated Winners'. See BRETLAND **1**; COOPER **5**; DAVIS, H. T. **1**; DE PRADES **1**; HALL **3**; HILLYARD **1**; SHAYER **1**; and SMITH, C. N. **1**.

(1) Miss Letty – owned by Hon. T. O. Powlett. Ridden

71 *Fulwar Craven Esq's Deception, with J. Day up. Oaks 1839. Aquatint after John Frederick Herring Snr.*

72 *Caravan, with his owner Mr Isaac Day, and jockey J. Robinson. Ascot Gold Cup 1839. Aquatint after John Frederick Herring Snr.*

73 *Grand Stand, Ascot (1839) showing l to r: St Francis; Ion; Caravan; and the Dey of Algiers, in the presence of HM Queen Victoria. Aquatint after John Frederick Herring Snr.*

by J. Holmes. Oaks, 1837. [70] Published July 1837.

(2) Industry – Earl of Chesterfield. W. Scott. Oaks, 1838. July 1838.

(3) Deception – Fulwar Craven Esq. J. Day. Oaks, 1839. [71] June 1839.

(4) Harkaway – bred by Mr. Ferguson. Wakefield. Goodwood Cup, 1838 & Goodwood Gold Cup 1839 (ridden by G. Calloway). 1839. July 1839.

(5) Bee's Wing – bred by W. Orde Esq. Jockey up. Various Gold Cups. 25 November 1839.

(6) Caravan – Mr Isaac Day. J. Robinson. Ascot Gold Cup, 1839. [72] 13 April 1840.

(7) Doncaster Great St Leger, 1839. The Dead Heat between Charles XIIth and Euclid, and the eleven others that contested the race. 6 May 1840.

(8) Charles XIIth & Euclid, The Decisive Heat for the Great St Leger Stakes at Doncaster, 1839. W. Scott and P. Conolly. 19 May 1840. [*Plate 6*]

(9) Crucifix – Lord George Bentinck. J. Day. Oaks, 1840. 18 July 1840.

(10) Beggarman – Duke of Orleans. J. Robinson. Goodwood Cup, 1840. 21 September 1840.

(11) Anatole – Baron A. de Rothschild. E. Flatman. Chantilly St. Leger, 1840. 6 January 1841.

(12) Ghuznee – Marquis of Westminster. W. Scott. Oaks, 1841. 1 July 1841.

(13) Poetess – Lord Henry Seymour. W. Boyce. Chantilly Derby, 1841. 1 August 1841.

(14) Bee's Wing – bred by W. Orde Esq. Jockey up. Ascot Gold Cup, 1842. 20 June 1842.

(14) is a reprint of (5) with titles changed.

Aquatints engraved by: (1), (2) C. & G. Hunt; remainder by C. Hunt. Published by J. Moore, 1 & 2, corner of West Street, Upper St Martin's Lane, London, (10), (12) and by Rittner & Goupil, Boulevard Montmartre, No.15, Paris. (7)

approx. 510 × 750 mm; remainder approx. 315 × 425 mm.

(7) reprinted by Barnett, Moss & Co., Leman Street, Goodmans's Field, London in 1852; and by L. Brall, 6 Great Prescott Street, London on 1 August 1870.

12 The Grand Stand, Ascot. (Caravan, Gold Cup Day, 1839). [73]

Shows the starters, l. to r: St Francis, Ion, Caravan, Dey of Algiers. The race was won by Captain Berkeley's Caravan, ridden by J. Robinson; 2nd, Mr Thornhill's St Francis; 3rd Colonel Peel's Ion.

The background and spectators painted by James Pollard. Aquatint engraved by C. Hunt. Published by J. Watson, 7 Vere Street, London. June 1839. Approx. 620 × 825 mm. Reprinted by J. Moore, as above, in September 1839; and by Barnett, Moss & Co., as above, in September 1852.

13 Charles the Twelfth. Portrait of a racehorse owned by Major Yarburgh. Winner of the St Leger, 1839. With details of pedigree and performance.

Aquatint engraved by J. Harris. Published by Messrs Fores, 41 Piccadilly, London.

14 Chantilly Races. Special Prize of 5,000 francs. Run May 1841.

(1) The Running.
(2) The Finish.

Won in three heats by HRH Duke of Orlean's Roquencourt, ridden by C. Edwards; 2nd, Lord Henry Seymour's Oakstick, Boyce; Baron de Rothschild's Vendredi, Flatman and M. de Savan's Quine, Moss also ran.

Painted with G. B. Campion. Aquatint engraved by C. Hunt. Published by J. Moore, as above, and by Goupil & Co. Boulevard Montmartre, No.15, Paris. 1 October 1841. Approx. 425 × 680 mm.

[125]

74 *Colonel Peel's Slane.
Aquatint after John
Frederick Herring Snr.*

15 Chantilly Derby.

(1)   Preparing to Start.
(2)   They are Off.

*Shows HRH Duke of Orlean's Tragedy, ridden by Edwards;
Lord Henry Seymour's Poetess; M. A. Lupin's Flammetta;
M. Aumont's Beeswing; M. Lupin's Faustus; and M. Depare's
Peter and Prince Paul.*

Aquatints engraved by C. Hunt. Published by J. Moore, as
above, and by Rittner & Goupil, as above. 1 November 1841.
Approx. 425 × 680 mm.

16 A series of winners of the Derby Stakes at Epsom.

(1)   1843. Cotherstone – owned by J. B. Bowes Esq.,
ridden by W. Scott. [*25, page 51*]
(2)   1845. The Merry Monarch – W. Gratwicke Esq.
F. Bell.
(3)   1846. Pyrrhus the First – John Gully Esq. S. Day.
(4)   1847. Cossack. See COOPER **6**.
1848–1881. See HALL 4.

These prints show the racehorses in looseboxes.

Aquatints engraved by: (1), (2) C. Hunt; (3) J. R. Mackrell.
Published by: (1), (2) A. H. & C. E. Baily, Cornhill, London;
(3) Baily Brothers, Royal Exchange Buildings, Cornhill,
London, and Gambart, Junin & Co., Paris. Not Dated.
Approx. 380 × 510 mm.

17 A series of winners of the Doncaster Great St Leger.

(1)   1843. Nutwith – owned by Mr Wrather, ridden by
Job Marson.
(2)   1844. Foig-a-Ballagh – E. H. Irwin Esq., F. Bell.
(3)   1847. Van Tromp – Lord Eglinton, Job Marson.
1848–1881. See HALL **5**.

These prints show the racehorses in looseboxes.

Aquatints engraved by C. Hunt. Published by: (1) A. H. &
C. E. Baily, 83 Cornhill and 18 Change Alley, London; (2)
A. H. & C. E. Baily, Cornhill, London; (3) Baily Brothers,
3 Royal Exchange Buildings, Cornhill, London. Not Dated.
Approx. 380 × 510 mm.

18 Portraits of racehorses, mainly in looseboxes, winners of
Classic races and Gold Cups, with details of pedigrees and
performances.

(1)   Slane – owned by Colonel Peel. Waterloo Shield,
Goodwood, 1837. [*74*]
(2)   Beeswing – the late William Orde Esq. Ridden by
Cartwright. Ascot Gold Cup, 1842.
(3)   Poison – George Samuel Ford Esq. Oaks, 1843.
(4)   Nutwith – S. Wrather Esq. J. Marson. St Leger,
1843.
(5)   Princess – Colonel the Hon. G. Anson. F. Butler.
Oaks, 1844.
(6)   Alice Hawthorn – Mr Salvin. S. Templeman.
Goodwood Cup, 1844.
(7)   Sweetmeat – Mr A. W. Hill. Whitehouse. Ascot
Gold Vase, 1845.

(8)   Gladiator – Colonel the Hon. G. Anson.
(9)   Pyrrhus the First – John Gully Esq. S. Day. Derby, 1846.
(10) Alarm – C. C. Greville Esq. Nat Flatman. The Emperor's Plate, 1846.
(11) The Hero – Mr John Day. The Emperor's Plate and Goodwood Cup, 1847, and Emperor's Plate 1848.

Aquatints engraved by: (1), (7), (9), (10) J. Harris; (2)–(6), (11) C. Hunt; (8) J. R. Mackrell. The majority shown as coloured by C. Simpson. Published by: (1)–(4) A. H. & C. E. Baily, 83 Cornhill, London; (5)–(11) Baily Brothers, 3 Royal Exchange Buildings, Cornhill, London; and (1), (3), (4), (7), (9) by Gambart, Junin & Co., Paris. Not dated, except (2): 19 November 1842. Approx. 380 × 510 mm.

19 'Fores's National Sports'.

1   The Start for the Memorable Derby of 1844. (*With names of horses and jockeys*). [26, page 53]
2   Steeple Chase Cracks. (*Showing Jem Mason on Lottery leading the 'cracks' of the period*).
3–6 (Fox Hunting).
7   Racing – Plate 1. Saddling. (*Showing, left to right:*

The Flying Dutchman; Voltigeur; West Australian; and others, with their trainers and jockeys).
8   Racing – Plate 2. A False Start. (*Showing the same horses as in Plate 1*).
9   Racing – Plate 3. The Run In. (*Showing the same horses as in Plate 2, with Job Marson on Teddington leading*). [*Plate 12*]
10   Racing – Plate 4. Returning to Weigh. (*Showing Teddington; West Australian; The Flying Dutchman; and others. Herring portrays himself on the far left with his son, Charles Herring, behind him*).

Plate 2, left to right: Salute – violet, white sleeves, violet and white cap, ridden by Captain Powell; Discount – black, orange cap, T. Olliver; Switcher – light blue, drab stripes, black cap, Lord Strathmore; Cigar – white, blue stripes, black cap, Captain Broadley; Peter Simple – scarlet, light blue cap, P. P. Rolt Esq.; Brunette – crimson, black cap, Mr A. McDonough; Pioneer – purple, orange cap, Captain Peel; Culverthorpe – scarlet, white cap, Rowlands Esq.; Tramp – black, white sleeves & cap, J. Bradley; Marengo – purple, black cap, P. Barker; Lottery – blue, black cap, James Mason (foreground). Reissues of this plate, using different colours for some of the jockeys, include P. P. Rolt on Peter Simple (Grand National, 1849 and 1853).

75 *The Race for the Emperor's Cup, Value 500 Sovs. at Ascot, June 12th 1845, showing l to r : Alice Hawthorn; Foig-a-Ballagh; and The Emperor. Aquatint after John Frederick Herring Snr.*

76 *Thorough Breds. Aquatint after John Frederick Herring Snr.*

Plates 7–10 are 'composites' in which the leading horses of the years 1845–1853 are portrayed.

Aquatints engraved by: 1 C. Hunt; 2 J. Harris; 7 J. Harris & C. Quentery; 8–10 J. Harris & W. Summers. Published by Messrs Fores, 41 Piccadilly, corner of Sackville Street, London. 1: 28 May 1845; 2: 25 October 1847; 7: 13 May 1856; 8–10: 1 September 1856. Approx. 540 × 1080 mm.

Plate 1 was reprinted without '1844' in the title.

All plates reprinted by Messrs Fores at later dates.

A smaller version of 7–10 was published by Messrs Fores on 1 September 1866. Approx. 340 × 630 mm.

20 'Fores's Racing Scenes'.

(1) The Race for the Emperor's Cup, Value 500 Sovereigns at Ascot, June 12th 1845. *(Showing l. to r: Alice Hawthorn; Faugh-a-Ballagh; and The Emperor.)* [75]

The race was won by Lord Albemarle's The Emperor, ridden by Whitehouse; 2nd, Mr Irwin's Faugh-a-Ballagh, H. Bell; 3rd Mr Salvin's Alice Hawthorn, J. Robinson.

(2) The Flying Dutchman and Voltigeur Running the Great Match at York on the 13th May, 1851, for 1000 Sovereigns a Side [*Plate 9*]

Lord Eglinton's Flying Dutchman ridden by C. Marlow beat Lord Zetland's Voltigeur, Nat Flatman. Their trainers, John Fobert and Robert Hill respectively, are shown on the rails as is Herring himself, near the judge's box.

Aquatints engraved by J. Harris. Published by Messrs Fores, as above. 1: 17 September 1845; 2: 31 July 1851. Approx. 460 × 700 mm.

Reprinted by Messrs Fores at later dates.

21 'The British Stud'. Portraits of pairs of stallions and mares in landscapes, with names of their breeders and details of their pedigrees. See LAPORTE 2.

Pl 1 *Sir Hercules* (and) Bee's Wing.
Pl 2 *Touchstone* (and) Emma. [*Plate 7*]
Pl 3 Languish (and) *Pantaloon.*
Pl 4 *Camel* (and) Banter.
Pl 5 Rebecca (and) *Muley Moloch.*
Pl 6 *Lanercost* (and) Crucifix.
Pl 7 Barbelle (and) *Bay Middleton.*

The names of the stallions are in italics. *The point of this series is that the animals shown were the sire and dam of: 1 Old Port; 2 Cotherstone; 3 Ghuznee; 4 Touchstone; 5 Alice Hawthorn; 6 Crozier; and 7 The Flying Dutchman.*

Pl 1 painted by G. H. Laporte. Aquatints engraved by J. Harris. Published by Messrs Fores, as above, and by Goupil and Vibert, 15 Boulevard Montmartre, Paris. 1 March 1844 to 10 February 1846. Approx. 455 × 700 mm.

Reprinted by Messrs Fores at later dates.

22 'Fores's Stable Scenes'.

Plate 1 (The Mail Change).
Plate 2 (The Hunting stud).
Plate 3 Thorough Breds. *(Showing four horses with their jockeys and trainers, including far right West Australian with his trainer John Scott, F. Butler up).* [76]
Plate 4 (The Team).

Aquatints engraved by J. Harris. Published by Messrs Fores, as **19** above. Plate 3: 17 March 1846. Approx. 445 × 685 mm.

[128]

77 The Earl of Eglinton's The Flying Dutchman, with his trainer J. Fobert and jockey Charles Marlow. Derby 1849. Aquatint after John Frederick Herring Snr.

Smaller versions of these plates were published by Messrs Fores on 1 July 1875. Approx. 205 × 305 mm.

23 Brunette. Portrait of a racehorse owned by Mr Meiklam.

Aquatint engraved by J. Harris. Published by Messrs Fores, 41 Piccadilly, London. 28 April 1847. Approx. 450 × 700 mm.

24 Inheritress. Portrait of a racehorse owned by James Meiklam Esq.

Aquatint engraved by J. Harris. Published by E. Gambart & Co., 25 Berners Street, London. 1 August 1848. Approx. 465 × 610 mm.

25 'Fores's Celebrated Winners'.

(1)   The Flying Dutchman. Portrait of a racehorse owned by the Earl of Eglinton, winner of the Derby (and St Leger) 1849, shown with his jockey, Charles Marlow, and trainer, John Fobert. [77]

(2)   Teddington. Portrait of a racehorse owned by Sir Joseph Hawley, winner of the Derby 1851, shown with his jockey, J. Marson, and trainer, Alec Taylor.

Aquatints engraved by J. Harris. Published by Messrs Fores 41 Piccadilly, corner of Sackville Street, London. (1): 2 August 1849; (2): August 1851. Approx. 450 × 580 mm.

26 Racing scenes.

(1)   'Before'. (*Jockey saddles a horse held by a trainer*).
(2)   'The Beginning'. (*Starter with flag down; two horses running*).

(3)   'The End'. (*Two horses running*).
(4)   'After'. (*Trainer leads winner away*).

Chromolithographs by V. Brooks. Published by Lloyd Bros & Co., Ludgate Hill, and 96 Gracechurch Street, London. 1 December 1853. Approx. 180 × 270 mm.

27 Return from the Derby.

This scene is of Clapham Common, London.

Aquatint engraved by J. Harris. Published by Henry Graves & Co., 6 Pall Mall, London. 1 May 1862. Approx. 525 × 1010 mm.

Steeplechasing

28 Steeple Chase Cracks. See **19.2** above.

Benjamin Herring

Racing

1 A series of portraits of racehorses with names of their owners and details of their pedigrees and performances.

(1)   Hermit – owned by H. Chaplin Esq. Ridden by J. Daly. Derby, 1867. Published 1867.
(2)   Achievement – Colonel Pearson. T. Chaloner. St Leger (and 1,000 Gns and Doncaster Cup), 1867. 1868.
(3)   Blue Gown – Sir Joseph Hawley, Bart. J. Wells. Derby, 1868. 1868.
(4)   Formosa – Mr W. Graham. T. Chaloner. Oaks and St Leger (and 2,000 and 1,000 Gns), 1868. 1868.

Aquatints engraved by C. G. Lewis. Published by J. McQueen, 37 Great Marlborough Street, Regent Street, London. Approx. 415 × 525 mm.

2 'McQueen's Sportings'.
  Racing scene. For pair, see **3** below.

The Silks and Satins of the Turf. With dedication by the Publisher, Thos McLean.

Aquatint engraved by J. Summers. Published by J. McQueen, as above, and John Harrop Jnr. Manchester and Stiefbold & Co., Berlin. 21 October 1867. Approx. 500 × 1090 mm.

Steeplechasing

3 'McQueen's Sportings'.
  Steeplechasing scene. For pair, see **2** above.

The Silks and Satins of the Field. With dedication by the Publisher, Thos McLean.

Aquatint engraved by J. Summers. Published by J. McQueen, as above, 20 October 1868. Approx. 500 × 1090 mm.

*Presumably this plate and **2** above were first published in conjunction with Thos McLean. I have not seen them with only McLean's publication line.*

4 'McQueen's Steeple Chasings'.

  Steeplechasing scenes.

  (1) Restive at the Post.
  (2) Over the Fence in Good Style.
  (3) Green-Sleeves leads the Way.
  (4)

Aquatints engraved by C. Hunt & Sons. Published by G. P. McQueen, 37 Great Marlborough Street, London. 22 April 1873. Approx. 345 × 590 mm.
Reissued by G. P. McQueen, as above on 27 February 1875.

HESTER, Edward Gilbert (alias E. GILBERT), 1843–c1910

Hester was an engraver in mezzo- and aquatint. He also painted, exhibiting pictures at the Royal Academy between 1882 and 1902 from addresses at Chiswick and Hammersmith, London. After 1891 he appears to have spent part of his time near St Albans. Edward's son, Robert Wallace Hester, followed his father as an engraver.

Perhaps failing to find an artist to paint the winner of the 1881 Derby, the print publisher G. P. McQueen turned to Hester, whom he had employed previously

as an engraver, to try his hand at horse portraiture. This was not an unusual practice and any experienced engraver with a little talent would quite easily draw a horse and call it his own – in this case Iroquois. The following year an 'E. Gilbert' appears as the artist in McQueen's publication line; probably a thinly disguised pseudonym for the versatile Hester. Both plates are heavily engraved, lacking vitality; typical of the efforts of artists of the period who felt they had to ape photography.

1 Iroquois. Portrait of a racehorse owned by Mr. Pierre Lorrillard. Winner of the Derby 1881, ridden by F. Archer.

Aquatint engraved by the artist. Published by G. P. McQueen, 70 Berners Street, London. 24 June 1881. Approx. 435 × 525 mm.

2 Shotover. Portrait of a racehorse owned by the Duke of Westminster. Winner of the Derby 1882, ridden by T. Cannon.

Aquatint engraved by the artist (E. Gilbert). Published by G. P. McQueen, 37 Great Marlborough Street, Regent Street, London. 7 July 1882. Approx. 380 × 500 mm.

HILLYARD, J. W., fl 1833–1861

Hillyard exhibited a few paintings at the Royal Society of British Artists and one, in 1833, at the Royal Academy, *Horses with a coming storm*. It is also recorded that he is the author of a print, *The Last Heat*, which was published by R. Ackermann in September 1839, but I have not seen it.

1 Portraits of racehorses, winners of Classic races and Gold Cups, with details of pedigrees and performances. Some titled 'Moore's Celebrated Winners'. See BRETLAND **1**; COOPER **5**; DAVIS H. T. **1**; DE PRADES **1**; HALL **3**; HERRING, J. F. **11**; SHAYER **1**; SMITH, C. N. **1**.

  (1) Chanticleer – owned by James Merry Esq. Goodwood Stakes and Doncaster Cup, 1848.
  (2) The Flying Dutchman – owned by the Earl of Eglinton. Ridden by C. Marlow. Derby, 1849 (and St Leger, 1849). Published 4 July 1849.

(2) shown in a loosebox.

Aquatints engraved by C. Hunt. Published by J. Moore, 1 & 2 corner of West Street, upper St Martin's Lane, London. Approx. 380 × 505 mm.

HILTON, T. (of York), op 1815

Nothing is known of T. Hilton; however, this may be

James Hilton who was practising as a portrait painter near St John's, Micklegate, York in 1787.

1 Haphazard. Portrait of a racehorse, bred by Mr Legh, owned by the Earl of Darlington, with details of pedigree and performance.

Mixed method engraving by J. Whessell. Published by J. Harris, Sweetings Alley & 8 Old Broad Street, London. 5 March 1815. Approx. 355 × 480 mm.

HOLIDAY, Charles Gilbert Joseph, 1879–1937

Gilbert Holiday was the son of the distinguished civil servant Sir Frederick Holiday, whose brother was the artist Henry Holiday. Gilbert's mother also painted. After an education at Westminster School, Gilbert Holiday attended the Royal Academy Schools before becoming a press illustrator. His quickness at sketching the essentials of any passing scene, not least as a war artist for the *Graphic* at the beginning of the First World War, was immediately recognised as out of the ordinary. After the war, in which he subsequently served in the Royal Field Artillery, he turned from military subjects to sport, in particular racing, hunting and polo. His impressionistic technique using a mixture of pastel and watercolour gives his horses and riders more movement even than that shown in the work of Lionel Edwards (*qv*). He fell while out hunting with the Woolwich Drag in 1932 and thereafter was confined to a wheelchair. This fortunately had very little effect on his continuing output of brilliant sketches in which the horse predominates. Many of the prints shown below appeared first in *The Tatler* or *Illustrated Sporting and Dramatic News* in the late 1920s; in print form they are very rare. Although often in pain, Holiday remained a cheerful and buoyant character until his early death at the age of 58.

Racing

1 Racing scenes.

Triple vignette with printed remarques.

Colour reproduction. Approx. 375 × 510 mm.

2 Sandown Park.

Colour reproduction. Approx. 235 × 370 mm.

3 Epsom – The Derby.

Colour reproduction. Approx. 160 × 255 mm.

4 The 1931 Derby – A Furlong from the Post.

The race was won by Mr J. A. Dewar's Cameronian, ridden by F. Fox; 2nd, Sir J. Rutherford's Orpen, R. A. Jones; 3rd, Lord Rosebery's Sandwich, H. Wragg.

Colour reproduction. Approx. 160 × 255 mm.

5 HH The Aga Khan's Diophon, by Grand Parade – Donnetta (G. Hulme up). 2,000 Gns, 1924.

Colour reproduction. Approx. 240 × 370 mm.

Steeplechasing

6 Aintree.

Colour reproduction. Approx. 235 × 400 mm.

7 Punchestown – The Stone Wall.

    (1) (The Downshire Wall) [*31a, see page 62*]
    (2) (The Old Double)

Colour reproductions published by Eyre and Spottiswoode. Approx. 270 × 405 mm.

8 The Grand National.

    (1) The Start.
    (2) The Water Jump.
    (3) The Chair.
    (4) The Canal Turn.

Colour reproductions published by The Sporting Gallery, 7 Grafton Street, Bond Street, London. Approx. 230 × 405 mm.

9 The Grand National.

Colour reproduction published by The Sporting Gallery, as above. Approx. 240 × 425 mm.

10 The Grand National.

Colour reproduction published by The Sporting Gallery, as above. Approx. 260 × 430 mm.

HONE, Nathaniel, RA, 1718–1784

Whether the print below is by this Nathaniel Hone is difficult to say. Hone was born in Dublin in 1718. His father was a merchant, and his son taught himself to paint before coming to England to seek work. He was a successful painter in oils, a miniaturist and enameller of portraits, and was among the foundation members of the Royal Academy. He died at his home in Rathbone Place, London on 14 August 1784.

1 Jason. Portrait of a racehorse owned by the Duke of Cumberland and later Sir Harry Harpur. With details of pedigree and performance.

78 *Finish of the Race. Aquatint after Samuel Howitt.*

Mezzotint engraved by Edward Fisher. Published by Robert Sayer, Fleet Street, London. 1758. Pl. approx. 355 × 350mm.

Republished by Laurie & Whittle, 53 Fleet Street, London. 12 May 1794.

HOWARD, Frank, 1805–1866

Frank Howard was principally an historical painter who practised in London, although he died in Liverpool. The print of 'The Derby Won, 1833' is much on the lines of both James Pollard's (*qv*) and J. F. Herring's (*qv*) views of pre- and post-race activity in front of the stands.

1 The Derby Won, 1833. ('Dangerous'). Portraits of the first five horses below the Stand at Epsom after the Derby, 1833.

The race was won by Mr I. Sadler's Dangerous, ridden by J. Chapple; 2nd, Mr J. Scott's Connoisseur, S. Templeman; 3rd, Mr Rawlinson's Revenge, T. Cowley.

Aquatint engraved by E. Duncan. Published by Charles Tilt, Fleet Street, London and W. Darling, Epsom. 28 May 1834.

HOWITT, Samuel, 1756–1822

Samuel Howitt, who was married to Thomas Rowlandson's (*qv*) sister, had a little of that artist's ability and much of his character. Apparently largely self-taught, although he must have been helped by his companions George Morland, Rowlandson and John Raphael Smith, Howitt's watercolours of hunting, shooting and racing have a delightful (amateur) spontaneity. An enthusiastic sportsman himself, he had sufficient family money to paint at first only for his and his friends' pleasure. However, this fortune was quickly dissipated and Howitt moved to London where he became a drawing master at Mr Goodenough's Academy in Ealing. Unreliable in his attendance, it is likely that Goodenough sacked Howitt after only a short time in his employment.

Howitt managed to cobble together a living, partly by etching at which he was extremely skilled. As an artist he was prolific. More than 150 of his designs were published in *The Sporting Magazine*. He illustrated Beckford's *Thoughts on Hunting*, and other books, including *Orme's Collection of British Field Sports*; *Oriental Field Sports* after the drawings by Captain Thomas Williamson; and *The British Sportsman*.

The light touch of his pen, the delicacy of his brushwork and his experience of field sports ensured all that he drew was animated and accurate.

1 Racing scenes.

    (1) Starting Posts.
    (2) Breaking the Course.
    (3)
    (4) (The Finish). [*78*]

Aquatints engraved by W. M. Fellows. 1792. Approx. 280 × 380 mm.
    Reissued by P. Brown, 5 Pall Mall, London. 1805.

2 *Orme's Collection of British Field Sports* (20 Plates).

    2. Horse Racing.

Aquatint engraved by J. Godby & H. Merke. Published by E. Orme, Bond Street, corner of Brook Street, London. 1 January 1807. Approx. 305 × 440 mm.

3 *The British Sportsman* (72 Plates).

    27. Racing P.1.
    28. Racing P.2.
    29. Racing P.3.
    30. Racing P.4.

Line engravings by the artist. Published by E. Orme, as above. 1812. Approx. 315 × 365 mm.

HUBBARD, Bennett, 1806–1870

Bennett Hubbard, the son of M. B. A. Hubbard, was a pupil of William Etty and John Varley. He painted in both oils and watercolour in his native town, Louth in Lincolnshire. His work comprised portraits, animals and scenery, and he was said to wear a flowered dressing gown while painting! His brother, Richard Hubbard, was an engraver, lithographer and cattle painter. Bennett Hubbard exhibited portraits of dogs and ponies at the Royal Academy between 1839 and 1846.

1 Cure-All. Portrait of a racehorse belonging to Mr William J. Loft. Winner of the Grand National, 1845 ridden by his owner.

William Loft bought Cure-All for £50 when he was badly lame after a fall. Loft's groom, Kitty Crisp, restored the horse to fitness and Loft discovered how good his purchase was while out hunting. Mr W. Stirling Crawfurd's entry for the National was injured during training and Cure-All was given the nomination, running in Crawfurd's name. Cure-All was walked by Kitty Crisp from Lincolnshire to Liverpool (and back again). As a complete outsider, not quoted in the betting, Cure-All won by two lengths in front of Mr Thornton's Peter Simple on a freezing afternoon.

Aquatint engraved by J. Harris. Published by R. Ackermann, 191 Regent Street, London. *c*1845.

HUNT, Charles (Snr), 1803–1877
HUNT, George Charles, fl 1860–1880

The Hunts (George, Charles Snr and Jnr, and George Charles and his son) were predominantly engravers rather than artists. However, like many before them, once engraving a plate had been thoroughly mastered, it was not difficult to copy, pirate or invent 'original' designs and masquerade as a painter! This may sound unkind, but no family of engravers were more prolific in the nineteenth century than the Hunts, nor more practised in turning out engraved plates to order, almost by the dozen. Every publisher of the period engaged the indefatigable Charles Hunt (Snr) to engrave hundreds of topographical, military and sporting plates. Generally, they are of good quality. However, Charles Hunt's engravings after his own work – presumably in watercolour or directly onto the plate from sketches since no original oils have ever been seen – lack spontaneity, and his portraits of racehorses are instantly recognisable by their unnaturally large and fishy eyes. (Charles Hunt should not be confused with the Victorian genre painter of the same name whose work was exhibited at the Royal Academy between 1860 and 1890.)

The Hunts lived and worked in London, first in the artists' colonies around Covent Garden and later south of the Thames in Surrey. Certainly they dominated the field of aquatint engravers, excepting John Harris (1811–1865), from 1820 to 1860, but as painters their efforts can best be regarded as an additional record of racing and steeplechasing in a period well served by other, better artists.

Charles Hunt

Racing

1 Grand Stand, Goodwood (Coming in for the Gold Cup, 1838).

With names of the winner, Harkaway, and of the next seven finishers. The race was won by Mr Ferguson's Harkaway, ridden by Wakefield; 2nd, Lord Exeter's Adrian; 3rd, Mr Worrall's Dormouse.

Aquatint engraved by the artist. Published by J. Moore, corner of West Street, Upper St Martin's Lane, London. 1 January 1839. Approx. 505 × 740 mm.

Reprinted in 1853, and reprinted by L. Brall, 6 Great Prescott Street, London in 1870 representing contemporary races. See TURNER 4.

2 'Ackermann's Series of National Races'.

No 1   The Derby, 1847.

With portraits of the winner, Mr Pedley's Cossack ridden by S. Templeman; 2nd, Mr Bouverie's War Eagle, W. Boyce; 3rd, Lord Eglinton's Van Tromp, J. Marson.

Aquatint engraved by the artist. Published by R. Ackermann, 191 Regent Street, London. 1847. Approx. 505 × 760 mm. Reprinted as Blink Bonny, winner of the Derby & the Oaks in 1857.

3 'Hunt's Series of National Races'.

No 2   The Derby, 1848.

With portraits of the winner, Lord Clifden's Surplice ridden by S. Templeman; 2nd, Mr J. Bowes's Springy Jack, F. Butler; 3rd, Mr B. Green's Shylock, S. Mann.

Aquatint engraved by the artist. Published by J. W. Laird, 2 Barge Yard, Bucklesbury. No date. Approx. 505 × 760 mm.

4 'Hunt's Series of Derby Winners'

(1)   The Flying Dutchman owned by the Earl of Eglinton. Winner of the Derby Stakes at Epsom, 1849, ridden by C. Marlow.

Aquatint 'Drawn and engraved by Charles Hunt, Engraver of Derby & St Leger Winners for the last 20 years'. Published by Charles Hunt, 96 Cheapside, London. (1849). Approx. 595 × 725 mm.

(2)   Daniel O'Rourke owned by J. Bowes Esq. Winner of the Derby Stakes at Epsom, 1852. Ridden by F. Butler.

Aquatint 'Drawn and engraved by Charles Hunt, Engraver of Derby & St Leger Winners for the last 25 years'. Published by Charles Hunt & Co., 78 Long Acre, London. July 1852. Approx. 515 × 760 mm.

5 Doncaster Grand Stand, West Australian winning the Great St Leger, 1853.

Aquatint engraved by the artist. Approx. 550 × 820 mm.

6 A series of portraits of racehorses with names of their owners and details of their pedigrees and performances.

(1)   Blink Bonny – owned by William I'Anson Esq. Ridden by John Charlton. Derby & Oaks, 1857. Published 15 July 1857.
(2)   Skirmisher – Lord Zetland. Ascot Gold Cup, 1857. 7 September 1857.

(3)   Beadsman – Sir Joseph Hawley, Bart. J. Wells. Derby, 1858. 9 July 1858.
(4)   Fisherman – Mr Tom Parr. J. Wells. Ascot Gold Cup, 1858 (and 1859). 15 September 1858.
(5)   The Promised Land – William Day Esq. Alfred Day. 2,000 Gns and Goodwood Cup, 1859. [*Plate 13*] 10 September 1859.
(6)   Thormanby – James Merry Esq., MP. H. Custance. Derby, 1860. 16 July 1860.
(7)   St Albans – Lord Ailesbury. L. Snowden. St Leger, 1860. (1860).

Aquatints engraved by the artists, C. Hunt & Sons. Published by E. Gambart & Co., 25 Berners Street, Oxford Street, London and (1)–(4): 8 Rue de Bruxelles, Paris; and (5)–(7): 8 Rue D'Assas, Paris. Approx. 505 × 675 mm.

7 A series of portaits of racehorses with names of their owners and details of their pedigrees and performances.

(1)   Caractacus – owned by Mr Charles Snewing. Ridden by J. Parsons. Derby, 1862. Published 12 August 1862.
(2)   Tim Whiffler – owned by Lord William Powlett. Ridden by Ralph Bullock. Doncaster Cup, 1862. 12 May 1863.
(3)   Macaroni – C. Naylor Esq. T. Chaloner. 2,000 Gns, Derby and Doncaster Cup, 1863. (1863).
(4)   Hermit – H. Chaplin Esq. J. Daley. Derby, 1867. 27 July 1867.
(5)   Kingcraft – Lord Falmouth. T. French. Derby, 1870. (1870).

Aquatints engraved by C. Hunt & Son. Published by Moore, McQueen & Co., 25 Berners Street, Oxford Street, London, and (1), (2): Chez Francoise Delarne, 18 Rue J. J. Rousseau, Paris. Approx. 500 × 670 mm.

8 Exciting Race for the Middle Park Plate, Newmarket, 1869.

The race was won by Mr Lyndon's Frivolity, ridden by T. Chaloner; 2nd, Mr Merry's Sunshine, J. Daley; 3rd, Lord Falmouth's Kingcraft, T. French.

Aquatint engraved by C. Hunt & Son. Published by J. McQueen, 37 Great Marlborough Street, Regent Street, London and 22 Rue de Dunkerque, Paris. 1 March 1870.

9 Hawthornden. Portrait of a racehorse owned by T. V. Morgan Esq. Winner of the St Leger, 1870, ridden by J. Grimshaw.

Aquatint engraved by C. Hunt & Son. Published by J. McQueen, as above. 13 January 1871. Approx. 375 × 505 mm.

Steeplechasing

10 Lottery. Portrait of a racehorse owned by Mr John Elmore. Winner of the Liverpool Grand National Steeple Chase, 1839, ridden by Mr Jem Mason.

Aquatint engraved by the artist. Published by J. Moore, as above. 22 April 1839. Approx. 435 × 550 mm.

11 Liverpool Grand Steeplechase, 1839.

   1   Stone Wall: First Round.
   2   Brook 2nd: Second Round.
   3   Brook 3rd: Second Round.
   4   Coming In.

In 1 Captain Marshall's Railroad, ridden by Mr Powell is shown leading Mr J. Elmore's Lottery, Jem Mason. The race was won by Mr J. Elmore's Lottery; 2nd, Sir George Mostyn's Seventy Four, ridden by Tom Olliver; 3rd, Mr Theobald's Paulina, Mr Martin.

Aquatints engraved by the artist. Published by J. W. Laird, 1 Leadenhall Street, London. 1 June 1839. Approx. 460 × 690 mm.
   Reprinted by Barnett, Moss & Co., Leman Street, Goodman's Field, London.

12 Cheltenham Annual Grand Steeple Chase.

   (1)   The Start.
   (2)   The Frogmill Brook.
   (3)   The Brook Forded.
   (4)   Coming In.

The race was won by Mr Elmore's Lottery, ridden by Mr J. Mason; 2nd, Mr Evans's Seventy-Four, Captain Vivian; 3rd, Mr Robertson's Cigar, Mr A. McDonough.

Aquatints engraved by the artist. Published by J. W. Laird, as above. 1841. Approx. 505 × 665 mm.
   Reprinted at later dates.

13 Northamptonshire Grand National Steeple Chase, 1840.

   Plate No 1   The Start.
   Plate No 2   The Brook.
   Plate No 3   The Fence.
   Plate No 4   Coming In.

The race was won by Mr Elmore's Lottery, ridden by Mr J. Mason; 2nd, Mr Robertson's Cigar, Mr W. McDonough; 3rd, Mr Holmes's Croxby, Captain Skipworth.

'Drawn on the spot and engraved by Chas. Hunt'. Published by J. W. Laird, as above. 1841. Approx. 400 × 610 mm.
   Reprinted by Barnett, Moss & Co., as above.

14 'Ackermann's Series of National Steeple-Chases'.

   (1)   The Liverpool, 1840.

       (a) Charging the Stone Wall.
       (b) Leap the 9th Rail – Bank and Artificial Ditch, 18 feet. Published 15 June 1840.

The names of the riders, their colours and horses are given and (a) shows Valentine leading; Lottery and The Nun both falling. (b) shows Columbine leading, Hasty following, The Sea and Seventy Four clearing in good style, Arthur refusing, Lottery, Nun, Jerry and Valentine bringing up the rear. The race

was won by Mr Villebois' Jerry, ridden by Mr Bretherton; 2nd, Mr Barry's Arthur, Mr A. McDonough; 3rd, Mr A. Power's Valentine ridden by the owner.

   (2)   The Leamington, 1840.
       (a) The Start.
       (b) Coming In. 20 October 1840.

(a) gives the names of the riders, horses and colours. (b) shows 1st, Mr Mason on Lottery; 2nd, Mr Powell on Seventy Four; 3rd, Marquis of Waterford on Columbine; and 4th, Mr Bretherton on Jerry.

   (3)   The Herefordshire and Monmouthshire Grand Hunt Steeple Chase.

       (a) The Start.
       (b) Coming In. 28 April 1845.

   (4)   The Royal Birthday Stakes, Worcester, March 14th, 1856.

       (a) Grand Stand. Made Brook.
       (b) Coming In. 16 May 1856.

   (5)   The Dublin.

       (a) Charging the Stone Wall.
       (b) Leap the 9th Rail – Bank and Artificial Ditch, 18 feet. 15 June 1856.

(5) is a reprint of (1) above.

Aquatints designed and engraved by the artist. Published by Ackermann & Co., 96 Strand, London and (3); W. H. Vale, High Town, Hereford. (1), (5): approx. 375 × 515 mm; (2): approx. 380 × 535 mm; (3): approx. 460 × 610 mm; (4): approx. 430 × 520 mm. (3) reprinted with same publication line; (4) reprinted with same publication line and without publication line; (5) reprinted with and without 'late' in the publication line.

15 The Grand Military Steeple Chase near Northampton, March 24th, 1841.

   (1)   The Start.
   (2)   The Fence.
   (3)   The Brook.
   (4)   Coming In.

The race was won by Captain Sir J. G. Baird's (10th Hussars) Carl, ridden by the Owner; 2nd, Mr Maddock's (9th Lancers) Creole, Owner; 3rd, Mr W. de Winton's (2nd Life Guards) Primrose, Owner.

Aquatints engraved by the artist. Published by Ackermann & Co., as above. 15 November 1841. Approx. 405 × 610 mm.
   Republished by J. W. Laird, as above.
   Republished by Barnett, Moss & Co., as above.

16 The Grand Military Steeple Chase near Newmarket, March 24th 1856. (20 horses started).

   Plate I   The Start.
   Plate II   Double Brook – Little Billing.
   Plate III Double Stone Wall – Little Billing.
   Plate IV Coming In.

Each with names of horses, jockeys and colours shown.

Aquatints engraved by the artist. Published by Ackermann & Co., as above. 15 November 1856. Approx. 360 × 510 mm.

George Charles Hunt & Son

1 Steeplechasing scenes.

(1) The Paddock. Published 23 August 1877.
(2) The First Fence. 15 January 1877.
(3) The Stone Wall.
(4) The Brook. 28 February 1877.
(5) The Last Fence.
(6) An Exciting Finish.

Aquatints engraved by the artists. Published by G. P. McQueen, 49 Great Marlborough Street, London. Approx. 230 × 360 mm.

HUNT, Edwin Henry & Son, fl 1880–1890

Very little is known of Edwin Henry Hunt except that he was not a member of the large family of Charles and George Hunt, artists and predominantly engravers. However, like Charles Hunt (*qv*), Edwin engraved portraits of racehorses (and greyhounds) after his own designs. His drawing of horses and their jockeys is often weak but as an engraver he had considerable skill at a time when others were producing too heavily etched and unattractive plates.

1 Portraits of racehorses with jockeys up, winners of Classic and other races, with details of pedigrees and performances. See POWELL 1; WOMBILL 1.

(1) Robert the Devil – owned by Mr C. Brewer. Winner of the Rous Memorial Stakes at Goodwood, 1879 (and St Leger, 1880, ridden by T. Cannon). Published 1880.
(2) Bend Or – Duke of Westminster. Ridden by F. Archer. Derby, 1880. [*27, page 56*] 19 July 1880.
(3) The Great Contest between Bend Or and Robert the Devil at Epsom. (*Epsom Gold Cup – Bend Or won*). 28 January 1882.
(4) Dutch Oven – Lord Falmouth. F. Archer. St Leger, 1882. 29 September 1882.
(5) St Blaise – Sir Frederick Johnstone. C. Wood. Derby, 7 June 1883.

Aquatints engraved by the artists. Published by George Rees: (1), (2), (4), (5) 41, 42, 43 Great Russell Street, Covent Garden, and 115 Strand, London; (3) Savoy House, 115 Strand, London. (1), (2), (4), (5) approx. 480 × 645 mm; (3) approx. 335 × 490 mm.

JONES, Adrian, MVO, 1845–1938

Born at Ludlow, Shropshire in 1845, Adrian Jones spent his youth in country pursuits and hunting with the Ludlow Foxhounds. He was keen to draw and paint, but his father sent him to the Royal Veterinary College in London where he qualified in 1866. He was gazetted into the Royal Horse Artillery and served in this and other regiments in India, Africa (the Boer War), Egypt and the Sudan as well as at home. During his time in the Army he had made a reputation for himself as a sculptor; his commission from Sir Coutts Lindsay to model a four-horsed chariot (quadriga) drawn by an Assyrian was exhibited at the Royal Academy in the year he left the Army, 1891.

His work as a sculptor prospered except that Academicians resented his success without formal training. However, the Royal Family admired his work and encouraged him. He was also commissioned to paint portraits of Persimmon (Derby, 1896); his own brother Diamond Jubilee (Derby, 1890), and Ambush II (Grand National, 1900) owned by the Prince of Wales, among other less formal portraits. The work for which he is best known is the immense Quadriga of Peace on the Decimus Burton Arch at Hyde Park Corner.

He tried to enlist in the Remount Corps in 1914 but was considered too old. Receiving commissions for monumental sculptures during and particularly after the First World War, he continued to practice his art until his death at the age of ninety-three.

1 The Household Brigade Cup. A large scale group portrait.

Painted with H. J. Brooks, see BROOKS 3. Photogravure. Published by The Leadenhall Press Ltd. February 1901. Approx. 410 × 900 mm.

KILLINGBECK, Benjamin, fl 1769–1783

Benjamin Killingbeck exhibited paintings in London between 1769 and 1783. They comprise landscapes, human and horse portraits, the last owing their style to both James Seymour (*qv*) and, later, George Stubbs (*qv*). Although his pictures were sent in from London addresses, it is known that he had a number of patrons in the north of England.

Killingbeck was also an accomplished engraver. In 1794 the publishers Laurie & Whittle reprinted a collection of earlier plates from various sources, but I have not seen the print below in anything but this version.

1 High-Flyer. Portrait of a racehorse owned by Mr Tattersall.

Mezzotint engraved by B. Killingbeck. Published by Laurie & Whittle, 53 Fleet Street, London. 12 May 1794. Approx. 255 × 350 mm.

LAMBERT, E. F., fl 1823–1875

An E. F. Lambert exhibited paintings at the Royal Academy from a London address between 1823 and 1846. They were mainly human and equestrian portraits. It seems a little surprising that the two prints listed below are from a so much later date. It is just possible that the painter of these engravings could be the son of the Royal Academy exhibitor, rather than one and the same person painting over a period of more than fifty years.

1 Formosa. Portrait of a racehorse owned by William Graham Esq. Winner of the 1,000 Gns, Oaks and St Leger, 1868. In the 1,000 Gns (when owned by Mr G. Jones) and in the Oaks, ridden by G. Fordham; in the St Leger by T. Chaloner.

Aquatint engraved by G. Brown. Published by George Rees, 57 Drury Lane, London WC. c1868. Approx. 395 × 515 mm. Reprinted by Dixon & Ross, 70 Hampstead Road, London.

2 Galopin. Portrait of a racehorse owned by Prince Batthyany. Winner of the Derby, 1875, ridden by J. Morris.

Aquatint engraved by C. Hunt. c1875. Approx. 315 × 430 mm. Reprinted without the names of the artist or engraver, and without a publication line.

LAMI, Eugène, 1800–1890

This talented French artist, who had studied under Horace Vernet, first visited England in 1826, resulting in the publication of two delightful sets of lithographs depicting all kinds of sports and coaching. He became court painter to Louis-Philippe, returning to England in 1849 with the Royal Family in exile after the Revolution. He painted in both oils and watercolour.

1 Chantilly Races.

Aquatint engraved by N. Fielding. Published by Ackermann & Co., 96 Strand and R. Ackermann, 191 Regent Street, London. 13 May 1841. Approx. 400 × 630 mm.

LAPORTE, George Henry, 1802–1873

George Henry Laporte came from an artistic family but it is difficult to discover why he turned to sport for the subjects of many of his paintings. He lived in London, exhibiting there from the age of seventeen. The proprietor of *The Sporting Magazine* used his work and later in life he was appointed animal painter to the King of Hanover and to the Duke of Cumberland. His horses are usually well drawn if a little uninspiring. They have a prettiness in common with the small heads and arched necks so loved by a fellow-Londoner, F. C. Turner (*qv*); both painted scenes of the first Grand National Steeple Chase, 1839.

Racing

1 Sir Hercules. Portrait of a stallion owned by H. O. Wheatley Esq., with details of pedigree and dedication to Prince Esterhazy.

Aquatint engraved by J. Harris. Published by Messrs Fores, 41 Piccadilly, London. Not Dated. Approx. 230 × 300 mm.

2 'The British Stud'. Portraits of pairs of stallions and mares in landscapes, with names of their breeders and details of their pedigrees. See HERRING, J. F. **21**.

Pl. 1. *Sir Hercules* (and) Bee's Wing.

The name of the stallion is in italic. The horses were sire and dam of Old Port.

Aquatint engraved by J. Harris. Published by Messrs Fores, as above, and by Goupil and Vibert, 15 Boulevard Montmarte, Paris. 1 March 1844. Approx. 455 × 700 mm.

3 Racing scenes.

   (1)   The Start.
   (2)   Winning.

Aquatints engraved by H. A. Papprill. 1 March 1860. Approx. 310 × 565 mm.
   Reprinted at a later date.

Steeplechasing

4 Liverpool Grand National Steeple Chase, 1839.

   I   The Brook, by the Canal.
   II   The Stone Wall, opposite the Grand Stand.
   III   The Ditch.
   IV   The Finish, at the Winning Post.

The race was won by Mr J. Elmore's Lottery, ridden by Jem Mason; 2nd, Sir George Mostyn's Seventy-Four, T. Olliver; 3rd, Mr Theobald's Paulina, Mr Martin.

Aquatints engraved by R. G. & A. W. Reeve. Published by Messrs Fores, as above. Not Dated. Approx. 365 × 630 mm.
   Reprinted with '1839' removed from title and dated 2 March 1853.

LORAINE, Nevison Arthur, RBA fl 1889–1908

Loraine appears to have lived much of his life at Grove Park, Chiswick, London before moving to Esher in Surrey. He sent in paintings to the Royal Academy and the Royal Society of British Artists between 1889 and 1903 from both addresses. The subjects of these pictures were what might be described as 'outdoor rustic'. The pair of bold chromolithographs shown below are out of the ordinary and modern for their time; although Cecil Aldin (*qv*) and Alfred Munnings (*qv*) also used flat areas of colour in a similar manner in their humourous 'nursery' pictures and posters respectively.

1 Portraits of racehorses.
   (1) Ambush II. Winner of the Grand National, 1900. Ridden by A. Anthony. [*28, page 58*]
   (2) Diamond Jubilee. Winner of the Triple Crown, 1900. Ridden by Herbert Jones. [*29, page 58*]

Each print includes a portrait of the Prince of Wales, the owner of both horses.

Chromolithographs. Published by Thomas McLean, 7 Haymarket, London. July and September 1900. Approx. 430 × 600 mm.

LUCAS-LUCAS, Henry Frederick, 1848–1943

H. F. Lucas-Lucas is often referred to as 'of Rugby', an adopted domicile after leaving his wife and children at Spalding in Lincolnshire in about 1878. He obtained a number of commissions painting all types of horses in every sporting activity. However, few show much fun perhaps reflecting the rather lonely and grey life which he appears to have followed in trying to make a living from his brushes. Some of his paintings now attract high prices. It is hard to understand why except that the dearth of good horse painters at the end of the last century makes anybody with competence appear to shine!

1 'Fores's Celebrated Winners'. See HAVELL 1; WHEELER, A. 1; WHEELER, J. A. 1.

   (1) Bendigo. Portrait of a racehorse owned by Major H. T. Barclay. Winner of the Cambridgeshire, 1883. With details of pedigree and performance.

Photogravure. Published by Messrs Fores, 41 Piccadilly, London. Approx. 425 × 570 mm.

MARSHALL, Benjamin, 1768–1835

As a young man, Ben Marshall was a schoolmaster at Seagrave in Leicestershire. His artistic ability was soon noticed and in 1791 he studied portraiture for a short time in London under Lemuel Francis Abbott. The origin of his being attracted to paint horses is not known but it is thought that at some stage he may have received some tuition from John Boultbee (*qv*).

Marshall worked in London from 1795 to 1812 where John Ferneley (*qv*) and Abraham Cooper (*qv*) were his pupils, the former becoming a lifelong friend. He exhibited occasionally at the Royal Academy, and from 1796 to 1832 provided sixty designs for engravings in *The Sporting Magazine*. His paintings at the turn of the century are his best work: vigorous, colourful and, in many cases, romantic in his treatment of light and atmosphere. His portraits of horses and their jockeys, trainers and owners have immense vitality, their straightforward realism giving the characters of animals and humans portrayed.

Marshall moved to Newmarket in 1812 to reduce the time he was continually spending in travelling from London to undertake commissions at the home of the turf. The artist was badly hurt in a coaching accident in 1819 but made a remarkable and courageous recovery, enabling him to continue painting as before, but perhaps with a smaller output. At this time he was also writing about racing in *The Sporting Magazine* using the pseudonym 'Observator'.

Ben Marshall returned to London in 1825 at which time he was encouraging and teaching his son Lambert (1809–1870) to paint. His own ability declined and pictures from this period begin to lose the sparkle of his earlier work. Whether this resulted in part from his accident is debatable, but sadly presaged a time of sorrow. His wife died in 1827 and the daughter who subsequently looked after him was burnt to death before him when her nightdress caught fire. This was the year before his death in 1835.

The evolution of the racing portrait advanced enormously in the hands of Ben Marshall, linking those who followed with Stubbs. The strings of winners by Ferneley, Cooper, Charles Hancock (*qv*), J. F. Herring (*qv*) and Harry Hall (*qv*) owe much to Marshall. If he had lived in a later generation, the print publishers would undoubtedly have engaged him to contribute to their series of winners. As it is, the list of engravings below are individually beautiful but their production is rather like the Earl of Darlington's horse – Hap-hazard!

1 Portraits of horses.

    (1) Adonis – owned by Mr M. A. Taylor.
    (2) Bungay.

Mezzotints engraved by C. Townley. Published by Taplin. 1796. Approx. 380 × 455 mm.

2 Lop. Portrait of a stallion owned by the Duke of Beaufort, with details of pedigree and performance. [*17, page 38*]

Stipple engraving by J. Whessell. Published by J. Harris, 3 Sweetings Alley, East end of Royal Exchange and 8 Old Broad Street, London. 1 January 1802. Approx. 365 × 485 mm.

3 Oscar. Portrait of a racehorse bred by Ex. Turnor Esq., with details of pedigree and performance.

Stipple engraving by J. Whessell. Published by J. Harris, as above. 13 May (*c*1802). Approx. 365 × 490 mm.

4 Portraits of racehorses.

    (1) Hap-hazard. A racehorse owned by the Earl of Darlington, with his trainer Sam. Wheatley and Jockey Wm. Pierse, with details of pedigree and performance.
    (2) Muly Moloch. A racehorse owned by the Earl of Darlington, with portraits of Messrs Trotter, Hardy and Thompson, well known turfites of the day, with details of pedigree and performance.

Stipple and line engravings by W. & G. Cooke. Published by B. Marshall, 23 Beaumont Street and W. & G. Cooke, 2 Clarence Place, Pentonville, London. 15 April 1805. Approx. 455 × 605 mm.

5 *The History and Delineation of the Horse* by John Lawrence.

    13   Race Horse. To Sir Charles Bunbury, Bart, this Portrait of his Celebrated Mare Eleanor.

Line engraving by John Scott. Published by James Cundee & John Scott, London. 1 January 1809. Approx. 140 × 200 mm.

  For other engravings of racehorses from this book, see GILPIN **6**; SARTORIUS, J. N. **17**; and STUBBS **16**.

6 Diamond. Portrait of a racehorse owned by Mr Joseph Cookson.

Mezzotint engraved by W. Barnard. Published by Thos Palser, Surrey Side, Westminster Bridge, London. 1 January 1811. Approx. 440 × 555 mm.

7 Pericles. Portrait of a racehorse owned by Hon. George Watson.

Aquatint engraved by R. Reeve. Published by S. Knight, 3 Sweetings Alley, Cornhill, London. 1 March 1815. Approx. 400 × 430 mm.

8 Pericles. Portrait of a racehorse bred by Chas Tibbits Esq. William Arnull up.

Mezzotint by W. Ward. Published by C. Tibbits, Barton Seagrove, Northamptonshire. 13 March 1816.

9 Racing scenes.

    (1) Filho da Puta and Sir Joshua. Portraits of the two racehorses, with details of pedigrees and performances.
    (2) Match for One Thousand Guineas!!! Scene of Hon. R. Neville's Sir Joshua beating Mr Houldsworth's Filho da Puta over the Rowley Mile at Newmarket. Sir Joshua ridden by W. Arnull; Filho da Puta, T. Goodisson.

Mezzotint engraved by W. Ward. Published by S. Knight, as above. 1 June 1818. Approx. 500 × 595 mm.

10 Oscar. Portrait of a racehorse bred by Ex. Turnor Esq., with details of pedigree and performance. See STUBBS **17** for pair.

Line engraving by (?) J. Whessell. Published by Thos Kelly, 17 Paternoster Row, London. 1820. Approx. 145 × 180 mm.

11 Dick Andrews. Portrait of a racehorse owned by Viscount Sackville, with Richard Goodisson up.

Mezzotint engraved by C. Turner. Published by M. Colnaghi, 23 Cockspur Street, Charing Cross, London. 26 March 1826. Approx. 420 × 540 mm.

12 A Comparative View of English Racers and Saddle-Horses. See CHALON **12**; SEYMOUR **13**; STUBBS **18**.

    Pl 11   Muly Moloch – owned by the Earl of Darlington.
    Pl 13   Pericles – bred by Charles Tibbits Esq.

Lithographs drawn by H. B. Chalon. Printed by C. Hulmandell. Published by Thos Hookham, 15 Old Bond Street, London. 1836. Approx. 200 × 250 mm.

MARTIN, A. Anson, fl 1840–1872

Anson Martin is probably best known for his large painting of the members of the Bedale Hunt at a 'meet' in 1840; the picture was engraved by W. H. Simmons in 1842. This painting and those of the jockeys of the north and south of England suggest that Martin was a portrait painter first and an equestrian artist second.

  Much of his work originates from Yorkshire, but his name is recorded in a Birmingham *Directory* in 1864. As with a number of sporting artists, his value as a 'recorder' is greater than as a painter, although the composition of his pictures is always well thought out, if a little static.

1 Portraits of Jockeys.

    (1) Jockeys of the South of England.
    (2) Jockeys of the North of England. [79]

Thirty-one 'miniatures' of jockeys in their colours, in scrolled frames each on one sheet. The name of the jockey on each 'frame'.

Lithographs drawn by G. B. Black. Published by the artist at 17 Gate Street, Lincoln's Inn Fields, London. *c*1850. Approx. 356 × 505 mm.

2 Clementina, The Well Known Steeple Chase Mare, 10 Years Old. With dedication to Mr John Mewburn, Rounton Grange, Near Northallerton, Yorkshire.

Lithograph drawn by G. B. Black. Probably published by the artist. *c*1860. Approx. 375 × 540 mm.

MASON, William, fl 1724–1797

It seems probable that William Mason the poet was also William Mason the artist here. Mason was an Honorary Exhibitor at the Royal Academy between 1782 and 1786 where his subjects included *A Review*; *Portrait of a Highwayman*; and *Scene in a Country Town*. The prints listed below are full of life and fun, which makes one wish that more of his work was known and engraved.

1 Racing scenes.

    (1) A Country Race Course with Horses Preparing to Start.
    (2) A Country Race Course with Horses Running.

Mixed engravings by J. Jenkins & F. Jukes. Published by R. Pollard, Braynes Row, Spa Fields, London. 20 May 1786. Approx. 450 × 650 mm.

A similar pair was published by J. Phillips.

The same scenes, in smaller format, with titles 'Preparing to Start' and 'Horses Running', were published by Bowles & Carver, No. 69 in St Paul's Churchyard, London. 14 February 1796. Approx. 245 × 350 mm.

79 Jockeys of the North of England. Lithograph after A. Anson Martin.

MITCHELL, J. A., fl 1826–1835

It is probable that this Mitchell is the artist who painted one or two hunting portraits in the 1820s. An historical subject painted by a J. A. Mitchell was exhibited at the Royal Academy in 1832, and a portrait at the Royal Society of British Artists in 1835. The Royal Academy exhibit was sent in from a London address; otherwise, little is known about the artist.

1 Capt. Becher on Vivian. Portrait of a steeplechaser owned by Captain Lamb, with details of pedigree and performance.

Aquatint engraved by G. & C. Hunt. Published by J. Moore, 1 West Street, St Martin's Lane, London. *c*1837. Approx. 425 × 555 mm.

MORIER, David, *c*1705–1770

Morier was a Swiss who came to England in 1743. He painted a number of equestrian military subjects and the Duke of Cumberland became his principal patron. Cumberland paid Morier £100 annually and commissioned the painting from which the print below is taken. Morier exhibited at the Society of Artists from 1760 to 1768, but after Cumberland's death he lost his pension and died in the Fleet Prison (where debtors were incarcerated) in 1770.

1 The Portraiture of the Bay-Arabian, the Property of the Right Honble the Earl of Godolphin etc.

This horse is the Godolphin Arabian. It is probable that the original picture or this print was used by George Stubbs for his later painting of the horse. See STUBBS 14.

Mezzotint engraved by I.F. (John Faber?). 1752. Approx. 240 × 350 mm.

MUNNINGS, Sir Alfred James, KCVO, PRA, 1878–1959

Paintings by Munnings are familiar to all. Their colour and bravura reflect their author's character. As a young man, Munnings was apprenticed to a Norwich firm of lithographers where he learnt, in particular, the use of bold colour in poster-work. He also attended night school at the Norwich School of Art, the Atelier Julian in Paris, and spent some time among the Newlyn group of artists. At the beginning of the First World War he served with the Remount Depot at Reading under Cecil Aldin (*qv*). Later, in 1918, he became the official war artist to the Canadian Cavalry Brigade. His successful portrayal of Major General Seeley led to many commissions for equestrian portraits after the war. These were mainly from the hunting fraternity.

He next turned to the turf where he was attracted by the excitement and again the bright colours, and opportunities to paint scenes under summer skies. An association with the print publishers Messrs Frost and Reed of Bristol started in 1924, from where a steady flow of reproductions continued until shortly before his death.

Little need be written about the Sir Alfred's tenure as President of the Royal Academy, except that his outspoken dislike of the work of many modern artists and their inexplicable pictures unfortunately led to a reaction to sporting painting by the 'art world' which still exists today. A larger than life man, Munning's ability to paint horses and the countryside approached, in his own style, those of Stubbs and Constable rolled into one. He died at this home, Castle House, Dedham (now the Art Museum of his work) in his beloved Suffolk in 1959.

Racing

1 Humorist. Portrait of a racehorse being led out at Epsom, owned by Mr J. B. Joel. Winner of the Derby, 1921, ridden by Steve Donoghue.

The painting was exhibited at the Royal Academy in 1923.

Colour reproduction. Published by Frost & Reed Ltd. 1924. Approx. 440 × 555 mm.

2 Solario. Portrait of a racehorse owned by Sir J. Rutherford, going out at Ascot with Joe Childs up. Winner of the St Leger, 1925 and Ascot Gold Cup, 1926.

Colour reproduction. Published privately. *c*1927. Approx. 380 × 410 mm.

3 Foxlaw. Portrait of a racehorse owned by Sir Abe Bailey, going out at Ascot. Winner of the Ascot Gold Cup, 1927, ridden by Brownie Carslake.

Colour reproduction. Edition of 25 privately published by Sir Abe Bailey. Approx. 455 × 480 mm.

4 Pennycomequick. Portrait of a racehorse owned by Lord Astor, in a loosebox. Winner of the Oaks, 1929, ridden by H. Jelliss.

Colour reproduction. Published privately. *c*1930. Approx. 355 × 485 mm.

5 The Paddock at Epsom, Spring Meeting.

Colour reproduction. Published by Frost & Reed Ltd. 1932. Approx. 400 × 510 mm.

80 *October Meeting. Newmarket. Colour reproduction after Sir Alfred Munnings* KCVO, PRA.

6 Going Out at Epsom. Two racehorses with jockeys up going out past the number board.

Colour reproduction. Published by Frost & Reed Ltd. 1932. Approx. 475 × 480 mm.

7 Unsaddling at Epsom, Summer Meeting. [*Plate 16*]

Colour reproduction. Published by Frost & Reed Ltd. 1932. Approx. 395 × 505 mm.

8 Crème Brûlée. Portrait of a racehorse held by his groom in the paddock at Salisbury, jockey and trainer in attendance.

Colour reproduction. Published privately. *c*1933. Approx. 355 × 460 mm.

9 Brown Jack, with his lad Alfie Garratt. Portrait of a racehorse in a landscape. Winner of the Queen Alexandra Stakes, Ascot from 1929–1934; and Goodwood and Doncaster Cups, 1930.

Colour reproduction. Published by Frost & Reed Ltd. 1935. Approx. 460 × 560 mm.

10 Lovely Rosa. Portrait of a racehorse owned by Sir Abe Bailey, on the course at Epsom. Winner of the Oaks, 1936, ridden by Tommy Weston.

Colour reproduction. Published privately by Sir Abe Bailey. Approx. 405 × 460 mm.

11 After the Race. Two racehorses being unsaddled in a racecourse paddock.

Colour reproduction. Published by Frost & Reed Ltd. 1951. Approx. 490 × 630 mm.

12 Before the Start, Newmarket. Seven racehorses with jockeys up.

Colour reproduction. Published by Frost & Reed Ltd. 1953. Approx. 405 × 630 mm.

13 Warren Hill, Newmarket. Racehorses being exercised.

Colour reproduction. Published by Frost & Reed Ltd. 1953. Approx. 405 × 630 mm.

14 October Meeting. Five racehorses with jockeys up preparing to start at Newmarket. [*80*]

Colour reproduction. Published by Frost & Reed Ltd. 1957. Approx. 440 × 750 mm.

Steeplechasing

15 The Saddling Paddock, Cheltenham, March Meeting. [*Plate 16*]

Colour reproduction. Published by Frost & Reed Ltd. 1952. Approx. 400 × 630 mm.

NEVILLE, A. W., fl 1860–1870

These prints, similar to some after John Sturgess, also published by McQueen, are attractive, typical of their time, and suffer slightly from the heavy engraving also of their period. I have been unable to discover anything about their author.

1 'McQueen's Steeple Chasings'.
    (1)   The First Flight – All Plain Sailing. [*Plate 14*]
    (2)   The Last Ditch – Difficulty, Danger & Doubts. [*81*]

Aquatints engraved by W. Summers. Published by J. McQueen, 37 Great Marlborough Street, Regent Street, London. (1) 21 October 1867; (2) 20 October 1868. Approx. 440 × 770 mm.
    Reissued by J. McQueen on 24 June 1871.

NEWMARCH (NEWMARSH?), G. B., fl 1828–1849

From the few oils seen by this artist, he was competent if uninspiring. Henry Pyall was primarily an engraver who, like others of his craft, set up a number of publishing partnerships which rarely survived for very long. This print seems to be from one such essay.

1 Sharper. Portrait of a racehorse bred by Lord Egremont in 1819.

Sharper was sent to Russia in 1825 where he and Mina were matched against two Cossack horses to run the equivalent of nearly fifty miles on the public road near St Petersburg. Mina, falling lame, was pulled up early in the race, which Sharper won with ease. One of the Cossack horses fell at twenty-five miles and then died.

Aquatint engraved by H. Pyall. Published by Pyall & Stroud, 16 Great Russell Street, London. 1 May 1828.

NOYES, Robert, 1780–1843

Robert Noyes was a descendant of an old Wiltshire and Sussex family who gave up a career in banking to paint. He was also a lithographer who earned his living as a drawing master with his school and studio in Church Street, Wolverhampton. As well as being a prolific landscape painter working in Wales, Shropshire and Staffordshire, he taught a wide range of skills and provided a 'basic design' course aimed at apprentices employed as decorators in the local manufacturing

81 *The Last Ditch – Difficulty, Danger & Doubts. Aquatint after A. W. Neville.*

industries, (notably japanned lacquer ware and enamelling).

He was drawing master for Wolverhampton School between 1822 and 1831, and was succeeded there by his son Henry Noyes who also taught at Shrewsbury.

1 Wolverhampton Race Course. With dedication to Thomas William Gifford Esq. of Chillington and Henry Horden Esq. of Wolverhampton, then Stewards. [82]

Lithograph drawn by T. M. Baynes, 41 Burton Street, London. Printed by C. Hullmandell. 12 August 1835. Approx. 390 × 630 mm.

O'BRYAN LOMAX, J., fl 1853–1888

A J. O'Bryan Lomax exhibited four seascapes at the Royal Academy between 1853 and 1888, and other coastal scenes at the Royal Society of British Artists during the same period. Whether this is one and the same artist as the author of the lithograph below – of a very different subject – is a matter of conjecture.

1 Hurdling scene.

Bognor, September 17th, 1853. (The Finish).

Lithograph drawn by the artist. Printed by C. Moody, 257 Holborn, London. c1853. Approx. 280 × 360 mm.

PALMER, James Lynwood, 1868–1941

The son of a Lincolnshire parson, Lynwood Palmer's career as an equestrian artist began when his talent was recognised while breaking horses in the USA as a young man. As well as painting pictures of racehorses for American owners, he was also commissioned by the Duke of Portland, King Edward VII, Lord Derby and the Aga Khan. His knowledge of anatomy ensured his portraits of horses were outstanding, but the poor landscape backgrounds and figures in a number of these paintings reduce the overall impact which is sometimes distinctly muddy.

He was an accomplished driver of a four-in-hand, a dandy in his dress and one of the few in his profession to be financially successful. In Lynwood Palmer's case, this was achieved through sheer hard work in a life lived to the full.

Racing

1 Volodyovski. Portrait of a racehorse owned by Mr W. C. Whitney. Winner of the Derby, 1901, ridden by Lester Reiff.

Chromolithograph. Published by Thomas McLean, 7 Haymarket, London. November 1901. Approx. 665 × 480 mm.

Steeplechasing

2 Kellsboro' Jack. Portrait of a steeplechaser in a landscape

owned by Mrs F. Ambrose Clark. Mr F. Ambrose Clark and the jockey, D. Williams, standing by the horse. Winner of the Grand National Steeple Chase, 1933.

Colour reproduction. Published by Frost & Reed, Bristol. 1933. Pl. approx. 445 × 610 mm.

PAYNE, Charlie Johnson ('Snaffles'), 1884–1967

Charlie Johnson Payne was the fourth son of a bootmaker, shopkeeper and licensee, first in Warwickshire, where Snaffles was born, and later at Oxford. The family was interested in music, painting and literature. The last two subjects provided a firm base on which the young artist could build his lifelong occupation of drawing horses and people. Payne tried to enlist at the outbreak of the Boer War, but he was too young. In 1901 he joined the Royal Garrison Artillery at Aldershot until forced to leave with a disability in 1906. Throughout his life his wish to be in the thick of any conflict was always to be frustrated by ill-health. In 1908 Fores Gallery in Piccadilly became his agent and he submitted a stream of illustrations, often humourous, to the *Graphic*, *Punch*, *Illustrated Sporting and Dramatic News*, and *The Field*. Both in depicting scenes of war and of his well loved hunting and steeplechasing, his interest and compassion for people and their predicaments shine out of his watercolours and gouaches.

After the First World War in which he went to Northern France in 1914 and later served in the RNVR camouflaging ships, he travelled extensively in Ireland and India. He wrote and illustrated a great many books of his experiences and thoughts both before and after the Second World War. In 1939 he helped camouflage aerodromes and other potential targets, and joined the Home Guard in Wiltshire.

It is believed that much of his work was lost in fires in London during the Second World War, and certainly some was destroyed when a VE Day celebration firework fell on a warehouse in Exeter! Snaffles, the name he used to sign his work from an early point in his career, continued painting to the end of his life despite failing eyesight. He died at his home, Orchard Cottage, Tisbury, Wiltshire on 30 December 1967.

1 The Worst View in Europe.

Oh Murther! The dhrink died out of me and the wrong side of Bechers.

Arthur Nightingall on the winner of the 1901 Grand National

(Mr B. Bletsoe's Grudon) approaches Becher's with a loose horse in front of him and another falling beyond the fence.

Colour reproduction published by Messrs Fores. c1922. Approx. 405 × 660 mm with remarque.

A very similar print was also published in c1922. Each is often paired with one of the four versions of 'The Finest View in Europe', showing foxhounds running hard in Leicestershire from a viewpoint in the saddle.

2 The Grand National. The Canal Turn – A Memory of the Old Serjeant and Geoffrey Bennet.

1926. The Canal Turn, second time round, left to right: Mrs M. Partridge's Sprig, ridden by T. E. Leader (4th); Mr A. C. Schwartz's Jack Horner, W. Watkinson (1st); Mr W. Parsonage's Master Billie, E. Foster (6th); Admiral Sir Hedworth Meux's White Surrey, Farragher (falling); No 12, Major F. R. Samson's Darracq, F. Gurney (5th); No 17, Lord Stalbridge's Thrown In, Mr H. Grosvenor (8th); Mrs W. H. Dixon's Old Tay Bridge, J. R. Anthony (2nd); and Mr S. Sanford's Brights Boy, E. Doyle (3rd).

In 1925 Old Serjeant ran for the seventh and final time in the National, then being fifteen. The horse was killed in an accident at Bogside in 1926. Captain G. N. 'Tuppy' Bennet, a vet and leading amateur jockey, rode Serjeant Murphy to victory in 1923. Bennet died as the result of a fall in the same year.

Colour reproduction published by Messrs Fores. 1927. Approx. 450 × 833 mm with remarque.

3 Sandown. Asking 'Em the Question.

The last fence at Sandown in a Military Steeplechase. A composite showing Captain Nobbie Brownhill (cross-belts); Captain Dick McCreery (chequers); and Major Lumsden (royal blue).

Colour reproduction published by Messrs Fores. 1928. Approx. 420 × 670 mm with remarque.

4 A National Candidate.

The chestnut, Mr S. Sanford's Sergeant Murphy, winner of the Grand National in 1923, being led in the parade ring with Captain Bennet (?) up.

Colour reproduction published by Messrs Fores. 1932. Approx. 470 × 430 mm with remarque.

One of a series of five miscellaneous subjects published under the title ''Osses and Obstacles'.

POLLARD, James, 1792–1867

James Pollard was the youngest son of Robert Pollard (1755–1838). The latter had come south to London from Newcastle as a young man and at the time of James's birth was an established engraver and print publisher at Spa Fields, Islington, London. At the age of fifteen James was copying the work of Ben Marshall and already enamoured with painting horses. He continued in this line until 1816 using both watercolour and oils, but with little financial success. To make a better living he then turned to engraving, sometimes after his own watercolours but more often after the work of other artists and for publishers other than his father. The firm of R. Pollard and Sons, now of Holloway Place, was struggling again in the early 1820s until the success with which James began to paint stage and mail coaches and other contemporary carriages quickly improved the position. A stream of coaching paintings followed, many of which he engraved himself. From 1821 he exhibited a small number of pictures at the Royal Academy and the British Institution which brought him more patrons.

Between 1830 and 1840 James also painted a number of racing pictures and some of the earliest scenes of steeplechasing on purpose-made courses, many recording the prowess of the few professional and more amateur riders of the day. In 1838 and 1839 he collaborated with J. F. Herring (qv) in painting the spectators and background to Herring's racehorses in *The Doncaster Cup*; *The Grand Stand, Ascot*; *The Doncaster Great St Leger*; and *An Extraordinary Trotting Match against Time*, of which the last three were engraved by Charles Hunt (qv). These plates are particularly fine examples of the turf of the period providing a contemporary record of courses, stands and the evolving mechanics of organised racing.

In 1838 James's father died and two years later he suffered the double blow of the death of his wife and a daughter. He barely recovered and from that time painted very little and on a small scale as though he had neither the enthusiasm nor the energy to tackle the large, crowded scenes of the past. In *Derby Day, Tits and Trampers on the Road to Epsom*, James Pollard can be seen mopping his balding brow; a self-portrait trick which he either learnt from or imparted to Herring who also included a picture of himself in some of his sporting paintings. James fell on hard times and in 1859 called for help from the Artists' Benevolent Institution of which his father had been a founder member. Finally he went to live with his son James Robert and died at his home in Sidney Street, Chelsea on 15 October 1867.

In their own way, portraits of racehorses by James Pollard have a similar naivity to those of James Seymour. Despite their rather oddly combined stiff and dancing movement they have character and life; but it is Pollard's large racing scene which really takes off and into which one can gaze and discover a microcosm of the turf.

Racing

1 Sir Joshua & Filho da Puta. Portraits of racehorses owned by the Hon. R. Neville and Mr Houldsworth respectively.

Aquatint engraved by C. Rosenberg. Published by E. Orme, Bond Street, corner of Brook Street, London. 1 July 1816. Approx. 285 × 380 mm.

2 Match for One Thousand Guineas!!! Sir Joshua beating Filho da Puta.

Aquatint engraved by R. Havell Snr. Published by R. Pollard, Holloway, London. 1 July 1816. Approx. 355 × 480 mm.

3 The Student. Portrait of a racehorse owned by Mr J. R. Udny. Claret Stakes, 1819.

Aquatint engraved by R. Havell Snr. Published by R. Pollard as above. Approx. 355 × 430 mm.

4 Specimens of Horsemanship. (Ten subjects on one plate).

Aquatints engraved by M. Dubourg. Published by E. Orme, as above. 1 November 1816. Approx. 90 × 620 mm.

5 Doctor Syntax. (The Winner of Twenty Gold Cups!!!). Portrait of a racehorse owned by Ralph Riddell Esq. Details of pedigree and performance.

Aquatint engraved by the artist. Published by R. Pollard & Sons, Holloway Road, London. 5 January 1817. Approx. 320 × 450 mm.
Reissued by R. Pollard in 1822.

6 Racing scenes.

   (1) Epsom Races. Published 25 April 1818.
   (2) Ascot Heath Races. [*20, page 41*] 28 September 1818.
   (3) Newmarket Races. 1 February 1819.

Aquatints engraved by the artist. Published by R. Pollard & Sons, as above. Approx. 305 × 450 mm.
Reprinted by J. Moore, 1 West Street, Upper St Martin's Lane, London.

7 A series of portraits of Classic winners, with names of owners and jockeys, mainly with jockeys up. Details of pedigrees and performances.

   (1) Tiresias – owned by the Duke of Portland. Ridden by W. Clift. Derby 1819. Published 6 July 1819.
   (2) Gustavus – Mr J. Hunter. S. Day. Derby, 1821. 19 July 1821.
   (3) Moses – Duke of York. T. Goodisson. Derby, 1822. 22 June 1822.
   (4) Emilius – J. Udney Esq. F. Buckle. Derby, 1823. 8 July, 1823.

83 *Mr Richard Watt's Memnon, with W. Scott up. St Leger 1825. Aquatint after James Pollard.*

(5) Barefoot – Richard Watt Esq. T. Goodisson. St Leger, 1823. 20 October 1823.

(6) Figaro – Mr Farquarson. Doncaster Cup, 1823.

(7) Cedric – Sir John Shelley, Bart. J. Robinson. Derby, 1824. 1 July 1824.

(8) Jerry – R. O. Gascoigne Esq. B. Smith. St Leger, 1824. 11 October 1824.

(9) Middleton – Lord Jersey. J. Robinson. Derby, 1825. 14 June 1825.

(10) Wings – General Grosvenor. S. Chifney Jnr. Oaks, 1825. June 1825.

(11) Memnon – Richard Watt Esq. W. Scott. St Leger, 1825. [*83*] 2 October 1825.

(12) Matilda – Hon. E. Petre. J. Robinson. St Leger, 1827. 25 October 1827.

Aquatints engraved by the artist. Published by R. Pollard & Sons, as above. Approx. 320 × 445 mm.

(3), (4), (5), (8) & (12) reprinted at a later date.

8 Racing scenes.

(1) (Training).

(2) (Preparing to start).

(3) (Running).

(4) (After Running).

Etchings. Published by R. Pollard & Sons, as above. 20 September 1821. Approx. 100 × 350 mm.

Reissued by R. Pollard on 5 March 1822.

Republished by J. Kendrick, 54 Leicester Square, London.

9 Racing scenes.

(1) Training.

(2) Starting.

(3) Running.

(4) After Running.

Aquatints engraved by G. Hunt. Published by J. Watson, 7 Vere Street, Bond Street, London. 5 February 1822. Approx. 220 × 355 mm.

10 Racing scenes.

1 The Subscription Rooms at Newmarket.

2 A View on the Road to Newmarket.

3 Training Ground at Newmarket. [*84*]

4 Race for the Claret Stakes. (*Showing Moses, Morisco, Swap, Posthuma and Ajax; sixth and last in the race was 'brother to Antonio'*).

Aquatints engraved by the artist. Published by R. Pollard & Sons, as above. 1, 2, 3: 7 March 1825; 4: 29 May 1823. Approx. 180 × 445 mm.

1 Republished as lithograph by McQueen and later by Richard Powell, 6 Grove Road, Brixton, London SW.

11 Racing scenes.

Plate 1 Training.

Plate 2 Preparing to Start.

Plate 3 Starting.

Plate 4 Racing.

Aquatints engraved by the artist. Published by Dean & Munday. 1823. Approx. 190 × 255 mm.

12   The Derby Pets.

    1   Sale of the Colt.
    2   The Trial.
    3   The Arrival.
    4   The Winner.

Aquatints engraved by the artist. Published by R. Ackermann, 101 Strand, London. 25 April 1825. Approx. 305 × 445 mm.

13   Doncaster. Race for the Great St Leger Stakes.

In 1824 the St Leger was won by R. Gasgoigne Esq's Jerry, ridden by B. Smith.

Aquatint engraved by the artist. Published by R. Pollard & Sons, as above. 20 July 1825. Approx. 320 × 645 mm.

14   Racing scenes.

    (1)   Epsom, Race for the Great Derby Stakes.

The 1826 Derby was won by Lord Egremont's Lapdog, ridden by G. Dockeray; 2nd, Mr West's Shakespeare; 3rd, Duke of Grafton's Dervise.

    (2)   Ascot Heath, Race for His Majesty's Gold Plate.

This race was in fact a standard King's Plate of 100 Gns. The race was won by Mr Wyndham's Chateau Margeaux, ridden by W. Arnull; 2nd, Mr Heathcote's Nigel; 3rd, Mr Mockford's Velasquez.

Aquatints engraved by the artist. Published by R. Pollard & Sons, as above. 1 August 1826. Approx. 315 × 635 mm. Republished by J. Moore, as above.

15   Race for One Thousand Pounds!!! Lord Darlington's Memnon beating Lord Exeter's Enamel, 14th May 1827.

Aquatint engraved by the artist. Published by R. Pollard & Sons, as above. 2 June 1827.

16   Epsom Races. The Derby Stakes.

The race in 1827 was won by Lord Jersey's Mameluke, ridden by J. Robinson; 2nd, Lord Jersey's Glenartney, H. Edwards; 3rd, Mr Yates's Edmund, W. Scott.

Aquatint engraved by the artist. Published by J. Watson, as above. 12 June 1827. Approx. 220 × 625 mm.

17   Race for the Derby Stakes at Epsom, 1828. Cadland beating The Colonel.

At first there was a dead heat; in the decider, the Duke of Rutland's Cadland, ridden by J. Robinson, beat Mr Petre's The Colonel, W. Scott. No 3rd place was given officially but M. W. Chifney's Zinganee was third past the post.

Aquatint engraved by R. G. Reeve. Published by Thos McLean, 26 Haymarket, London. (1828). Approx. 330 × 430 mm.

18   The Colonel. Portrait of a racehorse owned by the Hon. E. Petre. Great St Leger, 1828.

Aquatint engraved by the artist. Published by Thos McLean, as above. 6 October 1828. Approx. 330 × 440 mm.

19   Race for the Derby Stakes at Epsom, 1829.

The race was won by Mr Gratwicke's Frederick, ridden by J. Forth; 2nd, Mr Forth's The Exquisite, F. Buckle; No 3rd place was given. Forth trained both first and second, rode the former and owned the latter.

Aquatint engraved by J. Gleadah. Published by Thos McLean, as above. 20 June 1829. Approx. 365 × 460 mm.

84 *Training Ground at Newmarket. Aquatint after James Pollard.*

85 *The Celebrated Horse Glaucus at Ascot Races Beating Rockingham and Samarcand. Ascot Gold Cup 1834. Aquatint after James Pollard.*

Republished by Barnett, Moss & Co., Leman Street, Goodman's Fields, London. 31 December 1852.
*May be a Pair with **20** below.*

20 Race for the Gold Cup at Ascot.

In 1829 the race was won by Lord Chesterfield's Zinganee, ridden by S. Chifney Jnr.; 2nd, Mr Gully's Mameluke; no horse was officially placed 3rd.

Aquatint engraved by J. Edge. Published by Thos McLean, as above. 24 July 1829. Approx. 355 × 460 mm.
Republished by Barnett, Moss & Co., as above. 31 December 1852.
*May be a Pair with **19** above.*

21 Mr G. Osbaldeston Riding his Horse Against Time at Newmarket.

Aquatint engraved by the artist. Published by T. Helme, 81 Paul Street, Finsbury, London. 5 November 1831. Approx. 330 × 445 mm.
Reprinted by Barnett, Moss & Co., as above on 31 December 1852 with a slightly different title, including '200 Miles Against Time'. Also reprinted without engraver's name or publication line.

22 Doncaster Races.

(1) Horses Starting for the Great St Leger.
(2) Passing the Judge's Stand.

Aquatints engraved by R. W. Smart & C. Hunt. Published by S. & J. Fuller, 34 Rathbone Place, London. (1): 1 June 1832; (2): 25 October 1833. Approx. 345 × 625 mm.
Reprinted in 1834.

23 Epsom Races. The Race for the Derby Stakes. 1833.

The Race was won by Mr I. Sadler's Dangerous, ridden by J. Chapple; 2nd, Mr J. Scott's Connoisseur, S. Templeman. 3rd, Mr Rawlinson's Revenge, T. Cowley.

Aquatint engraved by H. Pyall. Published by Thos McLean, as above. 1 November 1833. Approx. 335 × 635 mm.

24 Racing scenes.

(1) Goodwood Races (Goodwood Cup, 1833). Rubini, the Property of Mr Kent, winning the Cup.

Rubini was ridden by F. Boyce; 2nd, Mr C. C. Greville's Whale; 3rd, Lord Exeter's Beiram.

(2) Ascot Races (Ascot Gold Cup, 1834). Glaucus beating Rockingham and Samarcand. [85]

Glaucus was owned by Lord Chesterfield, ridden by W. Scott; 2nd, Mr Theobald's Rockingham, J. Chapple; 3rd, Sir Gilbert Heathcote's Samarcand, F. Buckle.

(3) Epsom Races (Derby, 1834). Plenipotentiary beating Shilelagh and Glencoe.

Plenipotentiary was owned by Mr S. Batson, ridden by P. Con-

olly; 2nd, Duke of Cleveland's Shilelagh, S. Chifney Jnr; 3rd, Lord Jersey's Glencoe, J. Robinson.

Aquatints engraved by (1): C. Pyall; (2), (3): H. Pyall. Published by Thos McLean, as above. (1): 1 February 1834; (2): 4 October 1834; (3): 1 November 1834. Approx. 355 × 620 mm.

25 A View of the Grand Stand, Doncaster, with portraits of the Winning Horses of the St Leger, 1815–1834.

Aquatint engraved by H. Pyall. Published by Thos McLean, as above. January 1835. Approx. 360 × 620 mm.

26 Epsom Races.

(1) Now They're Off. (Start for the Derby).
(2) Here They Come. (Passing Tattenham Corner).

Aquatints engraved by R. W. Smart & C. Hunt. Published by S. & J. Fuller, as above. 2 June 1834. Approx. 355 × 625 mm. Reprinted at a later date.

27 A Prospective View of Epsom Races.

I Saddling in the Warren.
II The Betting Post. Published 1835.
III Preparing to Start.
IV The Grand Stand.
V The Race Over.
VI Settling Day at Tattersall's.

IV. The Grand Stand shows the finish of the Derby, 1835 won by J. Bowes Esq's Mundig, ridden by W. Scott; 2nd, Lord Orford's Ascot, Nat Flatman. No horse was placed 3rd, but Lord Jersey's Ibrahim ridden by J. Robinson and Lord Warwick's Pelops, G. Calloway, were well up.

Aquatints engraved by C. Hunt. Published by Ackermann & Co., 96 Strand, London. 1 February 1836. Approx. 295 × 465 mm.
Reprinted with all plates dated 1836. Reprinted by Messrs Fores, 41 Piccadilly, London, undated.

28 British Horse Racing.

Plate I Goodwood Grand Stand – Preparing to Start.

In 1836 the Goodwood Gold Cup was won by Lord Chesterfield's Hornsea, ridden by W. Scott; 2nd, Lord Lichfield's Elis; 3rd, Lord Chesterfield's Bampfylde.

Plate II Doncaster Grand Stand – Race for the Gold Cup.

In 1836 the Doncaster Cup was won by the Marquis of Westminster's Touchstone; 2nd, Lord Chesterfield's Carew; 3rd, Mr J. Day's Venison.

Plate III Ascot Grand Stand – The Coming In.

In 1836 the Ascot Gold Cup was won by the Marquis of Westminster's Touchstone, ridden by J. Day; 2nd, Mr Theobald's Rockingham, Macdonald; 3rd, Mr Robertson's Lucifer, W. Scott.

Plate IV Epsom Grand Stand – The Winner of the Derby Stakes.

In 1836 the Derby was won by Lord Jersey's Bay Middleton, ridden by J. Robinson; 2nd, Lord Wilton's Gladiator, W. Scott. No horse was officially placed 3rd, but Mr J. Day's Venison finished in that position.

Aquatints engraved by R. G. Reeve. Published by Thos McLean, as above. 1 November 1836. Approx. 265 × 370 mm.
Reprinted by Barnett Moss & Co. in 1852.

29 Doncaster Races. Race for the Great St Leger Stakes, 1836.

Plate 1 Vexation – The False Start.
Plate 2 Approbation – Off in Good Style.
Plate 3 Anticipation – Who is the Winner?
Plate 4 Joy & Desperation – All over but Settling.

In 1836 the St Leger was won by Lord Lichfield's Elis, ridden by J. B. Day; 2nd, Mr W. Scott's Scroggins, W. Scott; 3rd, Mr Orde's Bee's Wing, R. Johnson.

Aquatints engraved by J. Harris. Published by Ackermann & Co., as above. 24 May 1837. Approx. 380 × 630 mm.
Reprinted at a later date.

30 Scenes on the Road, or Trip to Epsom and Back.

Plate I Hyde Park Corner.
Plate II The Lord Nelson Inn, Cheam.
Plate III The Cock, at Sutton.
Plate IV Kennington Gate.

Aquatints engraved by J. Harris. Published by Ackermann & Co., as above. 30 May 1838. Approx. 325 × 500 mm.

31 The Derby Day. Tits and Trampers on the Road to Epsom. [86]

This print shows James Pollard as a 'Tramper', mopping his brow.

Aquatint engraved by J. Harris. Published by R. Ackermann, 191 Regent Street, London. 25 May 1842. Pl. approx. 250 × 355 mm.
Reprinted by G. W. Landau, 157 Waterloo Road, London.

32 Racing scenes.

(1) Mr Bowes's Horse 'Cotherstone' Winning the Derby, 1843.
(2) The Desperate Race for the St Leger, 1843. (*Won by Mr Wrather's Nutwith with Job Marson up*).
(3) The Race for the Plate, the Gift of HM the Emperor of Russia, 1845. (*At Ascot, won by The Emperor, also the winner in 1844 when the trophy was the Gold Cup*).
(4) The First Time of Saddling in Front of the Grand Stand at Epsom, 1846.
(5) Dismounting in the Enclosure at Ascot, 1846.

86 *The Derby Day.*
Tits and Trampers on
the Road to Epsom.
(James Pollard mops
his brow.) Aquatint
after James Pollard.

(6)   The Merry Monarch. Portrait of a racehorse owned by Mr Gratwicke. Winner of the Derby, 1845.

(7)   Alarm. Portrait of a racehorse owned by Mr C. C. Greville, Winner of the Emperor's Plate, Ascot, 1846.

Lithographs. Published by Dean & Co., Threadneedle Street, London. (1)–(5) approx. 330 × 330 mm; (6), (7) approx. 245 × 340 mm. See ROGERS 2 for similar prints.

Steeplechasing

33   St Albans Grand Steeple Chase, March 8th 1832.

Plate 1   Preparing to Start. The Turf Hotel.
Plate 2   First Leap.
Plate 3   Turning an Angle.
Plate 4   Struggle at the Bank.
Plate 5   Within View.
Plate 6   The Winning Post.

With further description below each scene, and keys. The race was won by Mr Elmore's Moonraker, ridden by Mr Seffert; 2nd, Captain Evan's Grimaldi, Mr Mostyn; 3rd, Mr Thomas's Corinthean Kate, Captain Becher.

Aquatints engraved by: 1, 5, 6 G. & C. Hunt; 2, 4 H. Pyall; 3 C. Bentley. Published by J. Moore, West Street, St Martin's Lane, London. Approx. 300 × 430 mm.

34   Northampton Grand Steeple Chase, March 23rd 1833. (With verses).

Plate 1   This was a Noble Sight . . . . (the Start).
Plate 2   Crossing the Brook . . . .
Plate 3   Crossing this Lane . . . .

Plate 4   This was a Tremendous leap . . . .
Plate 5   At this Fence . . . .
Plate 6   On the top of the Hill called Cottesbrooke Cow Pasture . . . . (The Finish) [87]

With further description below each scene and key to Plate 1, (Plate 7). 1st, Daring Ranger, Mr Solway up; 2nd, Moses, Jem Shirley; 3rd, Enterprise, W. Ivens.

Aquatints engraved by H. Pyall. Published Thos McLean, as above. 2 September 1833. Approx. 205 × 290 mm.

A contemporary advertisement describes this set comprises seven plates.

35   St Albans Tally Ho! Stakes, 1834. (A Hurdle Race)

1   The First Leap.
2   The Second Leap.

The race was won by Mr Tom Colman's Figurante; 2nd, Mr Deakin's Latitat; 3rd, Mr Tilbury's Pompey.

Aquatints engraved by G. & C. Hunt. Published by J. Moore, Corner of West Street, Upper St Martin's Lane, London. 22 May 1834. Approx. 305 × 430 mm.

36   The Aylesbury Grand Steeple Chase, The Light Weight Stake, 11 February 1836.

Plate I   Starting Field.
Plate II   The Brook.
Plate III   Down a Bank – The Pony Leading.
Plate IV   Winning – Captain Lamb's Vivian Winning.

With names of horses and riders. The race was won by Captain Becher on Vivian; 2nd, Grimaldi; 3rd, The Pony.

[151]

Aquatints engraved by J. Harris. Published by Ackermann & Co., as above. 30 March 1836. Approx. 345 × 500 mm. Reprinted at a later date.

37 Chances of the Steeple Chase.

1   Captain Becher and Vivian.
2   Mr Seffert and Moonraker.
3   Mr Powell and Saladin.
4   Mr Cooper and The Pony, at Aylesbury, 1836.
5   Mr Seffert and Grimaldi, at Aylesbury.
6   Mr Rice and Red Deer.
7   Mr Mason and Lottery.
8   Mr Martin and Paulina.

Aquatints engraved by: 1, 3, 4 C. Rosenberg; 2, 5 C. Hunt; 6 G. Hunt; 7, 8 no engraver's name. Published by G. S. Tregear, 96 Cheapside, London. 1–6: 1837; 7, 8: 29 April 1839. Approx. 350 × 485 mm.
Reprinted by Tregear and Lewis; by Lewis and Johnson; and by Lewis; also without publication line.

38 St Albans Grand Steeple Chase, 1837.

1   The Start.
2   Coming into the Second Field.
3   Last Field – Desperate Struggle.
4   Death of the Celebrated Horse Grimaldi after Passing the Winning Post.

The race was won by Mr Anderson's Splendour, ridden by Mr Solloway; 2nd, Captain Fairlie's Spicey, Captain Becher; 3rd, disputed between Cinderella and Speculation.

Aquatints engraved by: 1 R. G. Reeve; 2–4 C. Hunt. Published by J. W. Laird, 1 Leadenhall Street, London. 1 June 1837. Approx. 350 × 475 mm.
Reprinted at a later date; also by T. Helme, as above in 1838; and without the names of the artist or engraver.

39 St Albans Grand Steeple Chase, 1838. (20 December 1838).

1
2
3
4

The race was won by Mr Elmore's Yellow Dwarf, ridden by Mr J Mason; 2nd, Mr Webb's Pauline, Mr Smith; 3rd, Mr Thomas's Napoleon, Carlin.

Aquatints. Published by T. Helme, as above. (1838). Approx. 205 × 290 mm.

40 Incidents of the Steeplechase.

(1)   Liverpool, 5th April 1840.
(2)   Cheltenham, 1840.

Aquatints. Published by T. Helme, as above. (1840). Approx. 310 × 440 mm.

87 *Northampton Grand Steeple Chase, March 23rd 1833. (The Finish.) Aquatint after James Pollard.*

The Winning Post. Gladiateur's Derby, 1865. Aquatint after Henry Alken Jnr.

PLATE 14   *The First Flight – All Plain Sailing. Aquatint after A. W. Neville.*

PLATE 15

The Grand National, (1920). Valentine's. Colour reproduction after Cecil Aldin.

(above)
*The Saddling Paddock.
Cheltenham, March
Meeting.
Colour reproduction
after Sir Alfred
Munnings, KCVO, PPRA.*

PLATE 16

*Unsaddling at
Epsom, Summer
Meeting.
Colour reproduction
after Sir Alfred
Munnings, KCVO, PPRA.*

POWELL, R., fl 1880–1896

Powell is known for his paintings of greyhounds, also engraved by Edwin Hunt and published by George Rees. As well as the double portrait detailed here, Powell is said to have published a print of his own painting of the racehorse Persimmon in 1896.

1 Portraits of racehorses. See HUNT, E. H. 1; WOMBILL 1.

St Gatien and Harvester. Dead Heat for the Derby, 1884.

St Gatien – owned by Mr J Hammon, ridden by C Wood. Harvester – Sir John Willoughby. S. Loates.

Aquatint engraved by Edwin Hunt & Son. Published by George Rees, Savoy House, 115 & 116 Strand, London. 1 August 1884. Approx. 335 × 490 mm.

ROBERTS, James, fl 1708–1760

James Roberts and his brother Henry (?) were principally engravers and publishers. The 'originality' of James's work is questionable, its quality poor. The line engravings are of very little value to those wishing to study the early development of the racehorse in England, but they provide some useful information in the detail of the pedigrees and performances which accompany the prints. The majority of the prints also include attractive vignettes.

1 The Sportsman's Pocket Companion. 'A Striking Likeness or Portraiture of the most Eminent Race Horses & Stallions, that ever were in this Kingdom . . . . .' With their owners, pedigrees and performances. The majority of these details are the same as those given with the thirty-four line engravings after Seymour. Where this is not so, the names of the owners are included here. See SEYMOUR 1.

Portraits of:
1   Basto.
2   Bay Bolton.
3   Old Scar.
4   Brocklesby Betty.
5   Fox.
6   Molly.
7   Flying Childers.
8   Lamprie.
9   Old Partner.
10 Bald Charlotte or Lady Legs.
11 Buckhunter of the Carlisle Gelding.
12 Crab.
13 Bonny Black.
14 Starling. (Duke of Bolton's).
15 Fearnought.
16 Old Cartouch.
17 Conqueror.
18 Young Cartouch.
19 Second.
20 Spanking Rorger. (*Correct spelling is Roger*).
21 Lath.
22 Sedbury.
23 Volunteer.
24 Squirrel.
25 Torrismond – owned by Mr Crofts.
26 Starling. (Duke of Ancaster's).
27 Moorcock.
28 Regulus – Mr Martindale.
29 Sportley.
30 Babraham.
31 Bajazet.
32 Little Driver.
33 Silver Leg.
34 Othello or Black & All Black.
35 Whynot – Lord Onslow.
36 Sampson – Mr Robinson.
37 Victorious.
38 Sportsman – Lord Strange.
39 Cato – Marquis of Rockingham.
40 Bay Arabian. (*This is the Godolphin Arabian*).

Line engravings by H. Roberts. Published by H. Roberts, near Hand Alley, opposite Great Turn Stile, Holborn, London. (*c*1760). Approx. 210 × 135 mm.

2 Portraits of racehorses with names of their owners.

(1) Sportsman – owned by Lord Strange.
(2) True Blew – Sir Charles Sedley. Winner of Hunters' Prizes.
(3) Bolton Starling – Duke of Bolton.
(4) Creeping Molly – Duke of Bolton.
(5) Sampson – Mr Robinson.
(6) Garland.

Line engravings by H. Roberts. Printed for R. Sayer, opposite Fetter Lane, Fleet Street, London. Approx. 155 × 255 mm.

3 '12 Prints of High-Bred Running Horses, Drawn from Life, with an Account of the number of Matches won by them'. Portraits of racehorses, with names of their owners and details of performances.

1   Shakespear – owned by Mr Meredith. [*88*]
2   Sampson – Mr Robinson.
3   Skim – Earl of Portmore.
4   Grenadier – Mr Witty.
5   Silver Leg – Capt. Jennison Shaftoe.
6   Antelope – Sir Marmaduke Wyvill.
7
8   Othello – Mr Prior.
9
10
11 Little Driver – Aaron Lamego Esq.
12

Plate numbers not known for : True Blew – Sir Charles Sedley ;

88 *Mr Meredith's Shakespear. Line engraving after James Roberts.*

Bandy – Lord Grosvenor; Victorious – Earl of Onslow; and Whynot – Earl of Onslow.

Line engravings by H. Roberts. Printed for R. Sayer, as above. Approx. 155 × 260 mm.

ROGERS, J. Snr, fl 1825–1845

J. Rogers is recorded as having painted in oils, but I believe his particular skill was in drawing and lithography. His lightness of touch in depicting galloping horses is delightful. It is a pity we know so little about this artist.

1 Portraits of racehorses with names of their owners and details of performances.

(1) Longwaist – lately owned by Fulwar Craven Esq.
(2) Rubens – HRH the Prince of Wales.
(3) Cadland – Duke of Rutland. Derby, 1828.

Lithographs drawn by J. Rogers. Printed by C. Hulmandell. Published by T. McLean, Haymarket, London. (3): 1828. Approx. 320 × 420 mm.
   According to Siltzer (see Bibliography), (3) was published by Dean & Munday.

2 Portraits of racehorses with names of their owners and details of performances.

(1) Blue Bonnet, by Touchstone by Camel. The Property of Lord Eglinton. Winner of the Great St Leger Stakes at Doncaster, 13 September 1842.
(2) Cotherstone – owned by J. Bowes Esq. Winner of the Derby Stakes at Epsom, 1843.
(3) Poison – Mr G. Ford. Winner of the Oaks Stakes at Epsom, 1843.
(4) Running Rein – Mr Eli Goodman. Winner of the Derby Stakes at Epsom, 1844.
(5) Orlando – Colonel Peel. Derby Winner, 1844 after Running Rein's disqualification.
(6) Emperor. The Property of Lord Albermarle. Winner of the Gold Cup at Ascot, June 6th 1844.

(4) Running Rein, who ran in the name of Mr A. Wood, was a four-year-old named Maccabaeus (unknown to Wood, switched by the gambler Eli Goodman Levy) and was disqualified later; Orlando, 2nd, owned by Colonel Peel, was declared the winner.

Lithographs. Published by Dean & Co., Threadneedle Street, London. (1843 & 1844). Approx. 245 × 340 mm. See POLLARD **32** for similar prints.

3 Foig-a-Ballagh, owned by Mr Irwin. Winner of the Great St Leger, 1844, ridden by H. Bell. By Sir Hercules, out of Guiccioli.

Lithograph. Printed by Mourilyan & Casey, Mitre Court, Fleet Street, London. Published by Lewis & Co., 79 Leadenhall Street, London. No date. Approx. 300 × 400 mm.

ROOK, John, 1807–1872

By 1847, John Rook was describing himself as a 'Painter, Landscape and Marine', working in Whitehaven.

[154]

He was also an illlustrator of natural history subjects including a large series of fish and shell studies completed in 1870. He has become the drawing master at the Grammar School in nearby St Bees in 1854.

1 The Whitehaven Races, September 7th, 1852.

The print represents one of the races on the opening day of the 1852 meeting on the Harras Moor Racecourse. The first race was the Whitehaven Castle Stakes run over 1½ miles, won by Mr J. J. Henderson's Needle in a field of three runners. The second race was the West Cumberland Stakes and the third, the Whitehaven Plate. The fourth race on the card, the Farmers' Plate, did not take place due to a lack of entries. The last meeting at Whitehaven took place on 26 May 1890.

Lithograph drawn by M. & N. Hanhart. Published by M. & N. Hanhart, 64 Charlotte Street, Rathbone Place, London. (c1852). Approx. 260 × 375 mm.

ROWLANDSON, Thomas, 1756–1827

Thomas Rowlandson was born in 1756 and at an early age was admitted to the Royal Academy Schools. He visited France, continued his studies in England and by 1775 was exhibiting 'serious' pictures at the Royal Academy. However, when thrown upon his own resources, and having wasted half a fortune left to him by an aunt, he fell back on the quickness of his pen and brush to produce innumerable drawings and sketches. Rudolph Ackermann Snr employed him and, it could be said, looked after him in all financial matters, being well aware of Rowlandson's recklessness and love of gambling. 'Master Rolly', as he was known to his friends, was as happy drawing buildings and trees as people or animals, but racing scenes which were subsequently engraved are few. He etched many of the plates himself, but I doubt if it was within his nervous temperament to manage the tedious and painstaking work of aquatinting. A number of his plates were engraved in this manner by Samuel Alken Snr. At the end of two years of illness, Rowlandson died in London on 22 April 1827.

1 Racing scenes.
   (1)   The Start.
   (2)   The Finish.

Etchings by the artist. Published by H. Brookes, Coventry Street, Haymarket, London. 1 June 1785. Approx. 190 × 300 mm.

89 *Race Ground. (Probably at Brighton.) Aquatint after Thomas Rowlandson.*

[155]

90 *The Jockey Club or Newmarket Meeting. The central figure is Denis O'Kelly. Aquatint after Thomas Rowlandson.*

Republished by E. Jackson, No. 14 Mary-le-bone Street, Golden Square, London. 23 August 1786.

2 The High Mettled Racer (*each with verses*).

  1 The Racehorse.
  2 The Hunter.
  3 The Hack.
  4 The Cart-horse.

Aquatints engraved by J. Hassell. Published by S. W. Fores, 3 Piccadilly, London. 20 July 1789. Approx. 260 × 355 mm.

3 Race Ground. [*89*]

This scene of the finish of a race before a small stand, with the sea beyond, is probably of Brighton.

Aquatint tinted by Alken. Published by Messrs Robinsons, Paternoster Row, London. 1 June 1790.

4 Racing scenes.

  (1) (Starting).
  (2) (Nearing the Finish).

Etchings by T. Rowlandson. Published by S. W. Fores, 9 Piccadilly, London. 1 November 1791. Approx. 190 × 300 mm.

5 Racing scenes.

  (1) Racing.
  (2) Weighing.
  (3) Mounting.
  (4) Between Heats.
  (5) Running out of the Course.
  (6) Betting.

Etchings by T. Rowlandson. Published S. W. Fores, 50 Piccadilly, corner of Sackville Street, London. 1 January 1799. Approx. 180 × 260 mm.

6 The Jockey Club or Newmarket Meeting. [*90*]

A scene of Members of the Jockey Club in their rooms at Newmarket. The central figure is Dennis O'Kelly.

Etching. Published by Thos Tegg, 111 Cheapside, London. (*c*1810). Approx. 235 × 340 mm.

7 Racing scenes.

    (1)   Preparing to Start.

    (2)   Racing.

Etchings by T. Rowlandson. Published by Thos Tegg, 111 Cheapside, London. 20 October 1811. Approx. 230 × 340 mm.

SARTORIUS, Francis, 1734–1804
SARTORIUS, John Nost, 1759–1828

Francis Sartorius, the son of John Sartorius, was born in Nuremburg; his grandfather was an engraver practicing between 1694 and 1737. John Sartorius brought his family to London in the mid-eighteenth century. Francis exhibited paintings of racehorses, hunters and hacks in London between 1773 and 1791, including twelve pictures at the Royal Academy. His work bridges the gap between the 'primitive' work of James Seymour (*qv*) and the realism of George Stubbs (*qv*).

John Nost Sartorius, the only son of Francis, developed the realism a little further although some of his pictures were based on those painted by his father and other earlier artists. John Nost lived for much of his life at Carshalton in Surrey from where he exhibited no less than seventy-four paintings at the Academy; thirty-two elsewhere. Among his patrons were the Prince of Wales, Lord Derby and Christopher Wilson.

Scenes of races in progress by both Francis and John Nost Sartorius have a particular charm, accurately portraying the state of the turf in their times.

John Francis Sartorius, one of John Nost's sons, was also a sporting painter but not often of equestrian subjects.

Francis Sartorius

1 Bay Malton beating Gimcrack in a Match for 1,000 Guineas at Newmarket, 1st October 1765, with pedigrees and performances of the horses. [*6, page 24*]

91 *Bay Malton beating King Herod, Turf and Askam in a Sweepstakes for 500 Guineas each over the Beacon Course at Newmarket, 21st April 1767. Mezzotint after Francis Sartorius.*

92 *Marc Anthony beating Chalkstone over the Beacon Course at Newmarket, 7th May 1774. Mezzotint after Francis Sartorius.*

93 *Epsom, Derby Sweepstakes. Aquatint after John Nost Sartorius.*

Mezzotint engraved by R. Houston. Published by R. Heber, Chancery Lane and R. Sayer, Fleet Street, London. 10 March 1766. Approx. 290 × 455 mm.

2 Portraits of racehorses, with details of pedigrees and performances.

(1) Gimcrack – owned by Earl Grosvenor, held by a groom near a rubbing house.
(2) Careless – the Duke of Kingston. (*Misspelt Carless in the print*).
(3) King Herod – HRH Duke of Cumberland, but now Sir John Moore Bart.

Mezzotints. Published by R. Sayer, 53 Fleet Street, 1 September 1768. Approx. 250 × 350 mm.

3 Portraits of racehorses.

(1) Snap – owned by Mr Jennison Shaftoe.
(2) Nacissus, by Wilson's Arabian – Earl of Northumberland.

Line engraving by Robert Hancock. Published by Robert Sayer at No. 53 Fleet Street, London. 1 October 1768. Approx. 255 × 350 mm. Titles also in French.

4 Bay Malton beating King Herod, Turf and Askam. A Sweepstake of 500 Gns each. Wt. 8st. 7lb. over the Beacon Course at Newmarket, April 21st 1767. [*91*]

Mezzotint engraved by R. How. Published by R. Sayer, as above. 3 May 1769. Approx. 290 × 450 mm. Title also in French.

5 Portraits of racehorses, with details of performances.

(1) Cardinal Puff. The Property of Lord Grosvenor.
(2) This Excellent Horse Tortoise. The Property of Mr Peregrine Wentworth.
(3) This Excellent Horse Marquis, Got by the Godolphin Colt.
(4) The Famous Horse Pumpkin, Got by Matchem out of a Squirt Mare.

Mezzotints. Published by R. Sayer, as above. 10 January 1770. Approx. 215 × 340 mm.

6 Series of portraits of racehorses with names of their owners, and their pedigrees and performances.

1   Pilgrim – owned by the Marquis of Rockingham.
2   Goldfinder – Mr Jennison Shaftoe.
3   Gimcrack – Earl Grosvenor.
4   Bay Malton – Marquis of Rockingham.
5   Cardinal Puff – Lord Grosvenor.
6   Old Traveller – Wm Osbaldeston Esq.
7   King Herod – Sir John Moore Bart.
8   Snap – Mr Jennison Shaftoe.
9   Tortoise – the Hon Richard Vernon.
10   Antinous – Duke of Grafton. (*Misspelt Antonius in the print*).
11   Bellario – Sir Charles Bunbury.

12   Careless – Duke of Kingston. (*Misspelt Carless in the print*).

Line engravings by J. June. Published by R. Sayer, as above. 1 July 1770. Approx. 155 × 260 mm. Reprinted at a later date.

7 Racing scenes.

(1) A Race on the Round Course at Newmarket for the King's Plate.
(2) A Race on the Beacon Course.

Mezzotints engraved by R. Houston. Published by R. Sayer, as, above. 20 August 1770. Approx. 240 × 350 mm.

8 Marc Anthony Beating Chalkstone over the Beacon Course at Newmarket. 7 May 1774. [*92*]

Mezzotint. Published by R. Sayer and J. Bennett, London. 10 October 1774. Approx. 255 × 350 mm.

9 Mr Wm Clarke's Dark Chestnut Horse, Hylas, bred by the Duke of Grafton, with details of pedigree and performance.

Hylas won the King's 100 Gns at Burford in 1775.

Mezzotint engraved by H. Kingsbury. Published by R. Sayer, as above. 1788. Approx. 215 × 355 mm.

10 Portraits of racehorses.

(1) Tantrum – owned by Mr Blake.
(2) Firetail – Thomas Foley Esq.

Mezzotints. Published by Robt Sayer, 53 Fleet Street, London. 1788. Approx. 255 × 350 mm.

These two prints may be reissues since (2) above has been seen as published by Sayer and Bennett in 1774 – see 8 above.

11 Brilliant. Portrait of a racehorse owned by William Crofts Esq.

There is doubt about who is the author of this print. It is catalogued under Shaw – see SHAW **1**.

12 After taking over Robert Sayer's establishment at 53 Fleet Street, Laurie & Whittle published, on 12 May 1794, a series of portraits of racehorses in book form. These were re-issues of some of **6** above, Nacissus (**3** (2)) and by other artists.

13 A series of racehorses successful at stud, in or outside their looseboxes, with details of pedigrees and performances. See HERRING, J. F. **10**.

(1) Eclipse – bred by HRH William, Duke of Cumberland.

Aquatint engraved by C. Hunt. Published by S. & J. Fuller, 34 Rathbone Place, London. 1840. Approx. 240 × 300 mm. Republished as one of *Sheldon's Celebrated Racing Sires*, by James Sheldon, 31 Ely Place, London.

John Nost Sartorius

1 Portraits of racehorses.

    (1) Old Traveller, bred by William Osbaldeston Esq.
    (2) Careless – Duke of Bolton.

Mezzotints engraved by R. Houston. Published by R. Sayer. 1 September 1786. Approx. 255 × 355 mm.

2 Sir Thomas. Portrait of a racehorse owned by HRH the Prince of Wales. (Derby 1788).

Aquatint engraved by J. W. Edy. Published by J. Harris, Sweetings Alley, Cornhill, London. 1788. Approx. 305 × 420 mm.

3 Rockingham. Portrait of a racehorse owned by Mr Wentworth, ridden by L. Barrymore. With details of pedigree and performance.

Aquatint engraved by J. W. Edy. Published by J. Harris, as above and 8 Broad Street, London. 25 April 1789. Approx. 305 × 420 mm.

4 Racing scenes.

    (1) Grey Diomed beating Traveller.
    (2) Traveller beating Meteor.

Aquatints engraved by J. W. Edy. Published by J. Harris, as above. 23 October 1790. Approx. 405 × 510 mm.

5 Portraits of racehorses.

    (1) Escape – owned by the Prince of Wales. Published 24 February 1792.
    (2) Grey Diomed – owned by the Duke of Bedford. 9 April 1792.

Aquatints engraved by R. Dodd. Published by R. Pollard, Spa Fields, London. Approx. 395 × 520 mm.

6 Racing scenes.

    (1) Ascot, Oatlands Stakes, 28 June 1791. [*9, page 29*]

The race was won by the Prince of Wales's ('Mr Lake's') Baronet, ridden by S. Chifney; 2nd, Mr Barton's Express; 3rd, Lord Barrymore's Chanticleer.

    (2) Epsom, Derby Sweepstakes. [*93*]

The 1791 Derby was won by the Duke of Bedford's Eager, ridden by Stephenson; 2nd, Lord Foley's Vermin; 3rd, Lord Egremont's Proteus; and 4th, the Prince of Wales's St David.

Aquatints engraved by J. W. Edy. Published by J. Harris, Sweetings Alley and 8 Broad Street, London. 28 June 1792. Approx. 360 × 525 mm.

7 Portraits of racehorses, with details of their pedigrees and performances.

    (1) Skylark.
    (2) Skyscraper, by Highflyer. Derby, 1789.

    (3) Buzzard, by Woodpecker.
    (4) Lurcher, by Dungannon.

Mezzotints. Published by Laurie & Whittle, 53 Fleet Street, London. (1) and (4): 24 August 1795; (2) and (3): 12 October 1795. Approx. 235 × 355 mm.

8 Skyscraper. Portrait of a racehorse with his trainer. Winner of the Derby in 1789.

Mezzotint engraved by R. Houston. Approx. 255 × 355 mm.

9 Cormorant. Portrait of a racehorse. Winner of 19 races for Lord Foley and Charles James Fox.

Mezzotint engraved by E. Bell. Published by J. Aitkin, Castle Street, Leicester Square, London. 1 March 1795. Approx. 455 × 560 mm.

10 Racing scenes.

    (1) Sir Henry Vane Tempest's Hambletonian Preparing to Start against Mr Cookson's Diamond over the Beacon Course at Newmarket.
    (2) The Famous Match between Sir Henry Tempest Vane's Hambletonian beating Diamond the Property of Joseph Cookson Esq. at Newmarket for 3,000 Gns.

Aquatints engraved by J. W. Edy. Published by J. Harris, 3 Sweetings Alley, Cornhill and 8 Old Broad Street, London. 21 August 1799. Approx. 350 × 525 mm.

Written on (2): 'Large Portraits are now engraving of the above horses and may be had from the publisher.'

11 Portraits of racehorses, with details of pedigrees and performances.

    (1) Hambletonian, owned by Sir Henry Vane-Tempest, with trainer and jockey.
    (2) Diamond, owned by Mr Joseph Cookson, with trainer and jockey.

Stipple engravings by J. Whessell. Published by J. Harris, as above. 1 November 1799. Approx. 370 × 490 mm.

12 Portraits of racehorses, with details of pedigrees and performances.

    (1) Hambletonian – owned by Sir Henry Vane-Tempest, with jockey up. (St Leger 1795).
    (2) Diamond – Mr Cookson.

Mezzotints. Published by Laurie & Whittle, as above. 12 December 1799. Approx. 230 × 355 mm.

13 Racing scenes.

    (1) Sir Harry Tempest Vane's Horse Hambletonian, preparing to start against Mr Cookson's Diamond, over the Beacon Course at Newmarket on 25 March 1799. [*11, page 31*]
    (2) The Famous Match between Sir Harry Tempest Vane's Horse Hambletonian rode by Mr Buckle

beating Diamond, the property of Joseph Cookson Esq., etc., for 3,000 Gns.

Stipple engravings by J. Whessell. Published by John Harris, 3 Sweetings Alley, Cornhill and 8 Old Broad Street, London. 1 March 1800. Approx. 350 × 520 mm.
  Reissued.

14 Portraits of racehorses, with details of their pedigrees.

  (1) Champion – owned by Christopher Wilson Esq., by Pot-8-Os, with his trainer. (Derby and St Leger, 1800). [*14, page 35*]
  (2) Warter, by King Fergus. Oatlands Stakes, 1799.

Mezzotints. Published by Laurie & Whittle, as above. 1 January 1802. Approx. 240 × 355 mm.

15 Moll Tomson and Hare Foot. Portraits of racehorses, with a View of the Well Gap, Newmarket.

Line engraving by Scott. Published by J. Whittle, Warwick Square, London. May 1804. Approx. 100 × 140 mm.

16 Mrs Thornton on Vingarillo beaten by Mr Flint's Brown Mare Thornville on Knavesmire Course, at York Meeting, August 25th 1804.

Published by Colnaghi.

17 *The History and Delineation of the Horse* by John Lawrence.

11 Eclipse . . . Shakespear. To the Gentlemen of the Turf.
12 King Herod . . . Flying Childers. To his Grace the Duke of Devonshire.

Line engravings by John Scott. Published by James Cundee & John Scott, London. 1 January 1810. Approx. 140 × 200 mm.
  For other engravings of racehorses from this book, see GILPIN **6**; MARSHALL **5**; and STUBBS **16**.

18 Smolensko. Portrait of a racehorse owned by Sir Charles Bunbury, with details of pedigree and performance. 2,000 Gns and Derby, 1813.

A portrait of Smolensko painted by the artist was exhibited at the Royal Academy in 1814.

Mezzotint engraved by W. Ward. Published by S. Knight, Sweetings Alley, Cornhill, London. 20 September 1813. Approx. 400 × 500 mm.

SEALY, Allen Culpepper, 1850–1927

Sealy exhibited over fifty paintings during his lifetime of which nineteen were shown at the Royal Academy, many of them landscapes. He was a fine painter of racehorses and their accompanying trainers and jockeys,

94 Weathergage, with his trainer Tom Parr. Aquatint after William A. Sextie.

as well as being the author of some spirited hunting scenes which have suffered through cheap reproduction. Some of his paintings were reproduced in the Badminton Library series.

1 Flying Fox. Portrait of a racehorse owned by the Duke of Westminster. Winner of the Triple Crown, 1899, ridden by M. Cannon. With details of pedigree and performance.

Photogravure. Published by F. C. McQueen & Son, 37 Great Marlborough Street, London. 8 May 1900. Pl. approx. 350 × 460 mm.
   Reprinted by Messrs Fores, 41 Piccadilly, London.

SEXTIE, William A., fl 1848–1857

William Sextie exhibited one picture at the Royal Academy (1848) of a hack belonging to the Earl of Granville; but otherwise he concentrated on painting racehorses. Their detailed, dull realism is the advance guard of the work of his late Victorian successors!

1 Weathergage. Portrait of a racehorse with his trainer Tom Parr, and jockey up. Winner of the Goodwood, Wolverhampton and Cesarewitch Stakes, 1852. [94]

Aquatint engraved by J. Harris. Published by the artist and Ackermann & Co., 96 Strand, London. 1 March 1853. Approx. 480 × 665 mm.

2 Saucebox. Portrait of a racehorse owned by T. Parr Esq. Winner of the St Leger, 1855, ridden by J. Wells. With details of pedigree. [95]

Aquatint engraved by J. Harris & C. Quentery. Published by R. Ackermann, 191 Regent Street, London. 15 May 1857. Approx. 465 × 665 mm.

SEYMOUR, James, c1702–1752

James Seymour, born in about 1702, was the son of a well-to-do banker, goldsmith and jeweller of Mitre Court, Fleet Street, London. Perhaps as part of his 'trade', James Seymour Snr is found inviting subscriptions for plates (races) to be run at Guildford and elsewhere in 1705, suggesting an enthusiasm for the turf which soon rubbed off on his son. Among his other accomplishements Seymour Snr sketched, collected

95 Mr Tom Parr's Saucebox, with J. Wells up. St Leger, 1855. Aquatint after William Sextie.

96 *The Duke of Devonshire's Basto. Line engraving after James Seymour.*

prints and was a fellow member with the artists John Wootton and Peter Tillemans (*qqv*) of the Virtuosi Club of St Luke. From the example of his father springs the character of the son. Seymour Jnr was a lively youth, artistic, interested in the turf, and at home in a circle of sportsmen whose criteria for a happy life included spending as much of their time as they could at Newmarket where coursing, cock-fighting and racing were enjoyed. James Seymour Snr having indulged his son's and probably his own love of gambling and racing too extravagantly was made bankrupt in 1737, dying two years later. Unable to change his ways, James Jnr's luck ran out and he died destitute at his Southwark lodgings on 30 June 1752, surrounded by unfinished paintings.

The vivacity of James Jnr's pencil and ink sketches is lost in his oils. His manner of painting is similar to that of Wootton, but with an even more catholic line surrounding solid, merry-go-round racehorses. However, better than Wootton, his horses would be able to run, having the proper joints and proportions to enable them to do so. This style, combined with immaculately groomed and uniformed figures, both equine and human, results in a naive charm which is almost unmistakable except when aped by Thomas Spencer

(*qv*). The line engravers of his day, lacking the chiaroscuro of mezzotint or stipple grounds, failed to interpret Seymour's paintings with much realism; however, this poor record is better than none.

1 'A View of the Great Horse Match between Conqueror and Looby that was Run at Newmarket on the 6th of October 1735. Conqueror the Property of Thomas Panton Esq.; Looby, the Duke of Bolton.' [*5, page 23*]

Line engraving by R. Rooe. Printed for Carington Bowles in St Paul's Churchyard and John Bowles at the Black Horse, Cornhill. Approx. 375 × 625 mm.

2 Thirty-four racehorses with names of their owners and details of their pedigrees and performances framing the portraits. Those published by Butler, with coat of arms.

 1 Starling – owned by the Duke of Bolton.
 2 Crab – Earl of Portmore.
 3 Bay Bolton – late Duke of Bolton.
 4 Lath – Duke of Devonshire.
 5 Basto – Duke of Devonshire. [*96*]
 6 Carlisle Gelding – Earl of Carlisle.
 7 Second – John Neales Esq.
 8 Young Cartouch – Earl of Portmore.
 9 Spanking Roger – Viscount Weymouth.
10 Bonny Black – the late Duke of Portland.
11 Bal'd Charlotte – Earl of Portmore.

12   Creeping Molly – the late Duke of Rutland.
13   Lamprie – the late Sir Wm Morgan.
14   Childers – Duke of Devonshire.
15   Fearnought – Duke of Bolton.
16   Conqueror – Viscount Weymouth.
17   Old Scar – the late Duke of Devonshire.
18   Old Cartouche – the late Sir Wm Morgan.
19   Fox – Earl of Portmore.
20   Squirril – Richard Williams Esq.
21   Sedbury – Mr Martindale.
22   Molly – Thomas Panton Esq.
23   Brokelsby Betty – Charles Pelham Esq.
24   Volunteer – Sir Marmaduke Wyville Bart.
25   Little Driver – Aaron Lemego Esq.
26   Silver Leg – Nathaniel Curzon Esq.
27   Victorious – Lord Onslow.
28   Sportley – Lord Massereene.
29   Moorcock – Earl of Portmore.
30   Old Partner – Charles Pelham Esq.
31   Babraham – Mr Benjamin Rogers.
32   Bajazet – Earl of March.
33   Starling – Duke of Ancaster.
34   Othello – Sir Ralph Gore Bart.

Line engravings, after paintings by Seymour; 26: J. Wootton (see WOOTTON 3); and 27, 28, 33, 34: T. Spencer (see SPENCER 1).

The majority engraved by R. Parr; 27: Canot ; 28, 33, 34: H. Roberts. Published by John Cheny and Thomas Butler, Pall Mall, London between 1741 and 1754. Approx. 175 × 180 mm.

3 Portraits of racehorses.

(1)   Childers – owned by the Duke of Devonshire.
(2)   Black Legs – Duke of Devonshire.
(3)   Young Windham.
(4)   Terror – Duke of Bolton.

Line engravings by R. Parr. Published by John Bowles at the Black Horse, Cornhill, London. 4 July 1743. Approx. 150 × 190 mm.

4 'The Watering Place at Newmarket with a View of the Course and the String of Horses belonging to his Grace the Duke of Devonshire.' [97]

Line engraving by J. Thompson. Printed for Rbt Sayer at the Golden Buck, Opposite Fetter Lane, Fleet Street, London. c1750. Approx. 300 × 450 mm.
   There are other versions of this print.

5 Set of twelve untitled scenes.

(1)   Two racehorses in stalls with a groom.
(2)   Two racehorses in stalls with a groom approaching.
3   Flying Childers with two grooms by a rubbing house, other racehorses in the background.
4   A horse being walked by a wood with two grooms, other horses in the background. (This horse may be Roxana).

5–9   (A Horse dealer, and four hunting scenes).
10   'Miss Slamerkin, with her colt Othello . . .'.
11   (Hunter and hounds).
12   The finish of a Match.

Mezzotints engraved by T. Burford. 10–12 published 1752. Approx. 250 × 350 mm.

5a Some of these plates were adapted and republished; among them, 12: Careless Beating Atlas.

The race was run on 21 August 1760 when Atlas was defeated for the first time in his career.

Mezzotints. Published by Robert Sayer, Fleet Street, London. 1 May 1767. Approx. 255 × 345 mm.

5b Twelve undated line engravings published by Bowles & Carver include 5 racing scenes of which 3 are after the same original work as above.

5.   ((2) above). The Stables, & two famous Running Horses belonging to his Grace the Duke of Bolton.
6.   ((1)). The Stables, & two famous Running Horses belonging to his Grace the Duke of Grafton.
7.   The Stables, & two famous Running Horses belonging to Sir Jas. Lowther Bart.
9.   Old Partner beat the following Horses at great Odds, Vizt. Sir Robt. Fagg's Horse Barter, Lord Drogheda's Tipler, and the Duke of Bolton's Horse Sloven, he beat twice.
11.   (12). Aaron & Driver, two famous running horses.

The adaption of 11 (12) to Aaron & Driver shows the 3rd Heat in a Match run between Mr Roger's Aaron and Mr Lamego's Driver (the winner) at Maidenhead in August 1754 (two years after Seymour's death).

6 Portraits of racehorses.

(1)   Sedbury. A racehorse owned by Mr Martindale, with details of pedigree and performance.
(2)   Torrismond. A racehorse owned by Mr Martindale, with details of pedigree and performance.

Line engravings. Published by T. Bradford, 132 Fleet Street, London. (1): approx. 360 × 450 mm; (2): approx. 355 × 460 mm.

7 True Blue. Portrait of a racehorse owned by Sir Charles Sedley, with details of performance.

Line engraving by J. Wood. Published 1 October 1753. Approx. 365 × 460 mm.

8 Regulus. Portrait of a racehorse owned by Mr Martindale, with details of pedigree and performance.

Line engraving. Published by Thos Jefferys, The Strand, London. 10 August 1754. Approx. 360 × 460 mm.

9 Series of twelve portraits of racehorses, with names of their

97 'The Watering Place at Newmarket with a View of the Course and the String of Horses belonging to his grace the Duke of Devonshire.' Line engraving after James Seymour.

owners and details of their pedigrees and performances. With engraved ornamental borders and coats of arms.

(1)   Childers – owned by the Duke of Devonshire. Published March 1755.
(2)   Old Partner – Charles Pelham Esq. 10 March 1755.
(3)   Sedbury – Mr Martindale. [*3, page 21*] 10 March 1755.
(4)   Dormouse – Lord Chedworth. 10 March 1755.
(5)   Crab – Earl of Portmore. 10 March 1755.
(6)   Lamprey – the late Sir Wm Morgan. 10 March 1755.
(7)   White-Nose – Earl of Portmore. March 1756.
(8)   Cullen Arabian – Lord Cullen. March 1756.
(9)   Babraham – Earl of Godolphin and Mr Benjamin Rogers. 10 March 1756.
(10)   Bay Bolton – the late Duke of Bolton. 10 March 1756.
(11)   Bald Charlotte – Duke of Somerset. [*4, page 21*] 10 March 1756.
(12)   Chestnut Arabian – Mr Charles Wilson. 26 April 1756.

Mezzotints engraved by R. Houston after paintings by Seymour and (4), (5), (7)–(9), (12): T. Spencer (see SPENCER **2**). Sold by the Proprietors Thos Spencer and Robt Clee, Panton Street, Leicesterfields, London. Image excluding borders, approx. 215 × 290 mm.
    Reprinted at a later date.

10 Star. A Running Horse belonging to His Grace the Duke of Bridgewater. (Foaled in 1725).

Mezzotint engraved by R. Houston. Printed for John Bowles at the Black Horse in Cornhill, London. Approx. 250 × 360 mm.

11 Stable scenes.

(1)   The Stables, and two running horses of his Grace the Duke of Bolton.
(2)   The Stables, and two famous running horses belonging to Sir James Lowther.

Line engravings by W. Cannon. Printed for R. Sayer, Opposite Fetter Lane, Fleet Street, London. Approx. 155 × 260 mm. These engravings are based on **5** (1) and **5** (2) above.

12 'Twelve Prints, representing Managing and Training Horses . . .' etc. See SMITH, T. **2**.

13 A Comparative View of English Racers and Saddle-Horses. See CHALON **12**; MARSHALL **12**; STUBBS **18**.

Pl I   Old Partner – owned by Charles Pelham Esq.
Pl II   Sedbury – Mr Martindale.
Pl III   Racer – Lord Grosvenor.

Lithographs drawn by M. Gauci. Printed by C. Hulmandell. Published by Thos Hookham, 15 Old Bond Street, London. 1836. Approx. 200 × 250 mm.

14 Newmarket Heath. (A map of Newmarket racecourse with other details, including a vignette by Seymour of the finish of a race). With dedication to HRH the Prince of Wales.

[165]

Line engraving and aquatint. Published and sold by John Bodger, Land Surveyor, at Stilton, Huntingdonshire. 29 October 1787. Also sold by Messrs Boydells, 90 Cheapside; Mr Weatherby, 7 Oxendon Street, Haymarket, London; and at the Coffee Room, Newmarket. Approx. 450 × 675 mm.

SHAW, William, FSA, op1756, d1773

Very little is known about William Shaw, who exhibited paintings of horses and other animals at the Society of Artists (of which he was made a Fellow in 1771) from London addresses between 1760 and 1772. Obviously successful in his day with a number of patrons, he advanced the painting of equestrian portraits beyond the stylised work of Seymour (*qv*) and Spencer (*qv*). His subject are nearly always dealt with in a manner sympathetic to both the creatures and their surroundings. This is well demonstrated in his picture of Blank engraved by Houston. In the set (**4** below), I suspect there is more of 'others' than Shaw for Carrington Bowles was adept at putting together series of prints copied from a number of sources!

1 Brilliant. Portrait of a racehorse owned by William Crofts Esq. Winner of 7 races between 1754 and 1756.

Mezzotint. Printed and Sold by Carington Bowles, No. 69 in St Paul's Churchyard, London. Approx. 230 × 355 mm. See SARTORIUS, F. **11**.

2 Blank. Portrait of a racehorse owned by the Duke of Ancaster, with dedication.

Mezzotint engraved by R. Houston. Published May 1757. Approx. 295 × 395 mm.

3 Atlas. Portrait of a racehorse owned by the Duke of Devonshire, with dedication.

Line engraving by J. Miller. Published 27 January 1761. Approx. 290 × 380 mm.

4 Twelve Prints of the most Famous high bred Running Horses by Shaw and others.

1	Chestnut Arabian – owned by Mr Charles Wilson.
2	Brilliant – William Crofts Esq.
3	Sedbury – Mr Martindale.
4	Babraham – Earl of Portmore.
5	Atlas – Duke of Devonshire.
6	Blank – Duke of Ancaster. [*98*]
7	Dormouse – Lord Chedworth.
8	Cullen Arabian – Lord Cullen.
9	Bald Charlotte – Duke of Somerset.
10	White Nose – Earl of Portmore.
11	Childers – Duke of Devonshire.
12	Poor Old Fox.

98 *The Duke of Ancaster's Blank. Line engraving after William Shaw.*

Line engravings. Printed for Carington Bowles, No. 69 in St Paul's Churchyard, London. 2 January 1773. Approx. 155 × 270 mm.

SHAYER, William Joseph, 1811–1892

William Joseph Shayer was the son of the landscape artist, William Shayer (1787–1879). He was born in Chichester where his father was working as an heraldic artist for a coach builder. The family moved to Southampton in about 1820, where his mother died three years later when William Jnr was twelve. Perhaps at first helping his father, Shayer exhibited a *Portrait of a Mare* at Henry Buchan's Hampshire Gallery in Southampton in 1828. Thereafter his paintings were hung at the Royal Academy and British Institution on a number of occasions as well as at Buchan's. In search of more work, William Jnr moved to London but commissions for animals and horse paintings seem to have been few and far between since, of necessity, the artist became a coach driver. It is as a painter of accurate and lively coaching scenes that William Joseph is best known. However, with the passing of the coaching era, Shayer again fell on hard times. He continued painting to the end of his life despite failing eyesight. He died at 77 Amyand Park Road, Twickenham on the 5 November 1892 almost penniless.

His portraits of racehorses are well observed, if a little lifeless.

1 Portraits of racehorses, mostly with jockeys up, winners of Classic races and Gold Cups, with details of pedigrees and performances. Some titled 'Moore's Celebrated Winners'. See BRETLAND **1**; COOPER **5**; DAVIS, H. T. **1**; DE PRADES **1**; HALL **3**; HERRING, J. F. **11**; HILLYARD **1**; and SMITH, C. N. **1**.

(1) Alice Hawthorn – (Mr Salvin, leased from Mr Plummer). Ridden by S. Templeman. Goodwood Cup 1844. Ridden by Bumby. Doncaster Cup, 1844. Hesseltine. Published 6 November 1844.
(2) Charming Polly. 1844.
(3) Orlando and The Princess. Orlando – Colonel Peel. Ridden by Nat Flatman. Derby, 1844. The Princess – Colonel Anson. F. Butler. Oaks, 1844. 1844.
(4) The Emperor – Lord Albemarle. Whitehouse. Ascot Gold Cup, 1844 and Emperor's Plate, Ascot, 1845. 1845.

Aquatints engraved by: (1), (2) J. R. Mackrell; (3), (4) C. Hunt. Published by J. Moore, 1 & 2, corner of West Street, Upper St Martin's Lane, London. Approx. 400 × 515 mm. (1) republished by George Rees, 41, 42, 43, Russell Street, Covent Garden, London.

SMITH, C. N., fl 1848–1855

C. N. Smith was an engraver employed by John Moore of Upper St Martin's Lane, London. Perhaps when there was insufficient time for Moore to engage an artist to paint a winner quickly, Smith stepped in to help his publisher by obligingly drawing the plate as well as engraving it – a practice which was quite common at the time.

1 Portraits of racehorses, mostly with jockeys up, winners of Classic races and Gold Cups, with details of pedigrees and performances. Some titled: 'Moore's Celebrated Winners'. See BRETLAND **1**; COOPER **5**; DAVIS, H. T. **1**; DE PRADES **1**; HALL **3**; HERRING, J. F. **11**; HILLYARD **1**; and SHAYER **1**.

(1) Glen Saddel – owned by the Earl of Eglinton. Ridden by J. Cree. Great Metropolitan Stakes, Epsom, 1848. Published 22 May 1848.
(2) Surplice – Lord Clifden. S. Templeman. Derby, 1848 (and St Leger, 1848 ridden by Nat Flatman). 1 July 1848.

Aquatints engraved by the artist. Published by J. Moore, 1 & 2 corner of West Street, St Martin's Lane, London. Approx. 380 × 515 mm.

SMITH, Thomas, *c*1720, d1767

1 Racehorses.

No 1   The Cullen Arabian etc.
No 2   Brood Mares with Their Foles [*sic*]
No 3   Catching the Colts.
No 4   Subduing, Shoeing, the Cavison and Pillar.
No 5   Bridling, Saddling, Breaking & Training.
No 6   Finish'd Horses, Matchem & Trajan Runing at New-market.

The Match between Matchem and Trajan took place in April 1756.

Line engravings by No. 1: W. Elliott & T. Smith; Nos. 2–6: W. Elliott. No. 1 and No. 6: Published by T. Smith. January 1758. No. 2–No. 5: Published by Parker, Cornhill & Boydell, Cheapside, London. 1769. Approx. 360 × 520 mm.

2 'Twelve Prints, representing Managing and Training Horses, with Coursing, Shooting, Setting Etc.'

1   The Cullen Arabian.
2   Brood Mares with Their Foals.
3   Catching the Colts.
4   Subduing, Shoeing, the Cavison and Pillar.
5   Riding, Sadling, Breaking and Training.
6   Finish'd Horses.
7–12 (Coursing, shooting and a portrait).

Line engravings. Printed and Sold by Carington Bowles,

No 69 in St Paul's Churchyard, London. Approx. 155 × 270 mm.

The authorship of these rather poor, smaller versions of 1 1–6 above, with six additional subjects, are given to Seymour in the Mellon Collection catalogue. However, since the Match between Matchem and Trajan took place four years after Seymour's death this seems unlikely. Presumably this expanded set of prints is after the work of Smith and possibly 'others'.

SNOW, John Wray, fl 1832–1840

Better known for his pictures of hunting, Snow's strength is the common feature of good human portraiture. His racehorses stand awkwardly which detracts from the care he took in painting their coats and heads with some accuracy and feeling.

1 Harkaway. Portrait of a racehorse bred by Mr Ferguson, ridden by George Calloway, with details of pedigree.

Aquatint engraved by C. Hunt. Published by S. & J. Fuller, 34 Rathbone Place London, and to be had of Mr Le Pettet, Dublin; Miss Kernor, Cork; and Mr Hodgson, Belfast. August 1839. Approx. 360 × 455 mm.

SPALDING, C. B., fl 1832–1875

C. B. Spalding exhibited five paintings at the Royal Academy between 1840 and 1849. The first address he gives is that of the print publishers, S. & J. Fuller at 34 Rathbone Place, London for whom he painted Satirist in their series of St Leger winners after J. F. Herring (qv) and, later, Harry Hall (qv). In 1848 his address is in Brighton. He had a number of patrons and in his day was a popular but not very prolific artist.

1 Winners of the Great St Leger at Doncaster. See HERRING, J. F. **3**.

 (28) 1841. Satirist – owned by the Marquis of Westminster, W. Scott up.

The racehorse Coronation is also shown on this print. Coronation (winner of the Derby, 1841) was beaten by a head in the St Leger by Satirist.

Aquatint engraved by C. Hunt. Published by S. & J. Fuller, 34 Rathbone Place, London. 1 November 1841. Approx. 310 × 425 mm.

SPENCER, Thomas, 1700–1763

In style, if not in fact, Thomas Spencer may be considered as a follower of Seymour (qv). He may also have been employed by Thomas Butler of Pall Mall, the print publisher. Butler put his name to a few portraits of horses while advertising that he and his assistants could undertake commissions to paint 'horses, dogs, living and dead game' executed in a 'more elegant and newer taste than has been yet'.

Spencer's manner of painting is in some ways more engaging than that of Seymour since his horses appear more fluid than those by his contemporary, although their attendants can be quite stiffly portrayed. What is gained in grace is lost in realism since it is unlikely that the racehorses he portrayed would have lasted long even in a kind trainer's hands! His apparent habit of painting a lively scene of racing or hunting (including the subject of the foreground) as a background to his static portraits, is particularly attractive.

1 Thirty-four racehorses with names of their owners and details of their pedigrees and performances framing the portraits. Some with coats of arms. See SEYMOUR **2**.

 27 Victorious – owned by Lord Onslow.
 28 Sportley – Lord Massereene.
 33 Starling – Duke of Ancaster.
 34 Othello – Sir Ralph Gore Bart.

Line engravings by H. Roberts. Published by T. Butler, Pall Mall, London. Approx. 175 × 180 mm.

2 Series of twelve portraits of racehorses with names of their owners and details of their pedigrees and performances. Engraved ornamental borders and coats of arms. See SEYMOUR **9**.

 (4) Dormouse – owned by Lord Chedworth. Published 10 March 1755.
 (5) Crab – Earl of Portmore. 10 March 1755.
 (7) White-Nose – Earl of Portmore. March 1756.
 (8) Cullen Arabian – Lord Cullen. March 1756.
 (9) Babraham – Earl of Godolphin and Mr Benjamin Rogers. 10 March 1756.
 (12) Chestnut Arabian – Mr Charles Wilson. 26 April 1756.

Mezzotints engraved by R. Houston. Sold by the Proprietors Thos Spencer and Robt Clee, Panton Street, Leicesterfields, London. Image excluding borders, approx. 215 × 290 mm.

3 Miss Doe, a Mare of Sir Edward O'Brien, Bart., she beat the Duke of Bolton's famous horse Starling.

Mezzotint engraved by R. Houston. Printed for John Bowles in London. c1750. Approx. 410 × 480 mm.

STOCK, C. R., fl 1880–1902

Primarily an engraver during the last years of the aquatint, C. R. Stock could also design a reasonable likeness of a racehorse. This was in a period when competition among equestrian portrait painters was by no means severe!

1 Portraits of racehorses with jockeys up. Winners of Classic and other races, with details of pedigrees and performances.

> (1) Isinglass – owned by Mr H. M. McCalmont. Ridden by T. Loates. Triple Crown, 1893.
> (2) Mrs Butterwick – Duke of Portland. J. Watts. Oaks, 1893.

Aquatints engraved by the artist. Published by P. Sufrini, 20 High Holborn, London. Printed by J. Ross & Son. Not dated. Approx. 330 × 405 mm.

STUBBS, George, ARA, 1724–1806

It seems superfluous in a book of this nature to write much about George Stubbs, the pre-eminent sporting artist of all time. Born in Liverpool, he was mainly self-taught and at the start of his career worked in the north of England. Studying anatomy with remarkable dedication and zeal, he published his results in 1766. His *Anatomy of the Horse* provided the 'groundwork' for all his paintings of racehorses. He settled in London in 1760. So far as racing prints are concerned, Stubbs's contribution might have been greater if his projected series of portraits of famous horses for his *Turf Review* had been more successful and not come to a halt after sixteen paintings and fifteen prints, the latter engraved by his son George Townley Stubbs. Together with other plates published in his lifetime, his determination for overall perfection set a standard which others could neither achieve nor afford; the last factor being part of the reason for the failure of the *Turf Review*.

His paintings provided examples for his successors to follow but for realism and a sense of grandeur no artist could quite emulate his work, and few later prints have a similar serene yet vibrant quality.

1 Gimcrack. Portrait of a racehorse with Mr John Pratt up, riding groom to Viscount Bolingbroke.

Mezzotint engraved by W. Pether. Published by Thos Bradford. 17 May 1766. Approx. 350 × 455 mm.

2 An Arabian – owned by Lord Grosvenor.

Published by W. W. Ryland, 27 Cornhill, London. 20 February 1771.

3 Marske. Portrait of a stallion owned by the Earl of Abingdon.

Mezzotint engraved by G. Stubbs Jnr. Published by J. Welson, Lichfield Street, Soho, London. 24 February 1771.

4 The Terrible Horse Trentham, a racehorse owned by Charles Ogilvy Esq., with details of performance. [99]

Mezzotint engraved by G. T. Stubbs. Published by Robt Sayer, 53 Fleet Street, London. 1 January 1772. Approx. 230 × 345 mm.

5 Eclipse. Portrait of a racehorse owned by Denis O'Kelly Esq., with details of pedigree and performance.

Mezzotint engraved by T. Burke. Published by J. Welson, as above. 7 February 1772. Also by R. Sayer, as above. 1 October 1773. Approx. 430 × 565 mm.
Republished by R. H. Laurie, 53 Fleet Street, London.

6 Brown Horse Mask. Portrait of a stallion, with details of pedigree.

Mezzotint engraved by G. Stubbs Jnr. Published by R. Sayer, as above. 24 October 1773. Approx. 400 × 550 mm.

7 Jupiter. Portrait of a stallion owned by Colonel Thornton. Mezzotint engraved by G. T. Stubbs. Published G. T. Stubbs at Mr Torrand's, 18 Wells Street, Oxford Street, London. 20 September 1776.
Reissued 1 January 1777.

8 Brood Mares. The Property of the Hon Colonel Parker.

Mezzotint engraved by Benjamin Green. Printed for R. Sayer and J. Bennett, 53 Fleet Street, London. 14 November 1776. Approx. 415 × 555 mm.

9 Arabian horses.

> (1) An Arabian – owned by Mr Gregory.
> (2) An Arabian – John Warde Esq.

Mezzotints. Published by R. Sayer and J. Bennett, 53 Fleet Street, London. 2 June 1777. Approx. 255 × 355 mm.
> (1) Reissued by Laurie and Whittle. 12 May 1794.

10 Portraits of racehorses.

> (1) Bandy – owned by Lord Grosvenor.
> (2) Pangloss – Lord Grosvenor.

Mezzotints. Printed for R. Sayer & J. Bennett, 53 Fleet Street, London. 2 June 1777. Approx. 245 × 345 mm.
> Reprinted by Sayer in June 1790.
> Republished by Laurie & Whittle, 53 Fleet Street, London. 12 May 1794.

11 Portraits of stallions, with details of their performance as racehorses.

> (1) Mambrino – owned by the Earl of Grosvenor.
> (2) Protector – Earl Grosvenor.

99 *Charles Ogilvy Esq's The Terrible Horse Trentham. Mezzotint after George Stubbs.*

Mezzotints engraved by C. H. Hodges. Published by John & Josiah Boydell, 90 Cheapside, London. 1 September 1788. Approx. 370 × 470 mm. See GILPIN **4** for a similar print.

12 Portraits of racehorses or stallions with details of pedigrees and performances.

(1) Pyrrhus – owned by Mr Foley, (and others).
(2) Shark – Robert Pigott Esq.
(3) Johnny – Lord Clermont.
(4) Mask, aged 20 – Earl of Abingdon.
(5) Sweet William – Lord Grosvenor.

Aquatints with stipple engraved by G. T. Stubbs. Published by J. Harris, Sweetings Alley, London. 1 January 1789. Approx. 245 × 350 mm.

13 Mambrino. Portrait of a stallion owned by Earl Grosvenor with details of performance as a racehorse.

Aquatint engraved by G. T. Stubbs. Published by J. Harris, as above. 23 March 1791. Oval, approx. 225 × 280 mm.

14 *The Turf Review* (A Review of the Turf from 1750 to the present time). Portraits of racehorses or stallions.

(1) Godolphin Arabian – (owned by the Earl of Godolphin). [*Plate 1*] Published 20 February 1794.
(2) Baronet – (HRH the Prince of Wales). [*Plate 3*] 20 February 1794.
(3) Protector – (Earl Grosvenor). 20 February 1794.
(4) Pumpkin – (Lord Foley). [*Plate 3*] 20 February 1794.
(5) Dungannon – (Colonel O'Kelly). 20 May 1794.
(6) Mambrino – (Earl Grosvenor). 20 May 1794.
(7) Sharke – (Robt Pigott Esq). 20 May 1794.
(8) Anvil – (HRH the Prince of Wales). December 1794.
(9) Sweetbryer – (Earl Grosvenor). December 1794.
(10) Volunteer – (Colonel O'Kelly). [*13, page 32*] December 1794.
(11) Sweetwilliam – (Earl Grosvenor). 30 July 1796.
(12) Eclipse – (Colonel O'Kelly). 1 September 1796.
(13) Gimcrack – (Earl Grosvenor). 1 September 1796.
(14) Marske – (Earl of Abingdon) [*12, page 32*] 1 September 1796.

(*1*) *Godolphin Arabian was neither a racehorse nor thoroughbred, but rightfully takes his place here as an important sire.*

Stipple engravings by G. T. Stubbs. Printed in black and

some in colours. Published by Messrs Stubbs, Turf Gallery, Conduit Street, London. (2)–(14): approx. 395 × 505 mm. Also (1)–(14): approx. 190 × 250 mm.

All were republished by Edward Orme, New Bond Street, London. 4 June 1817.

15 Eclipse. Portrait of a racehorse owned by Captain O'Kelly, with details of performance.

This appalling print is derived from 5 above.

Published by Laurie & Whittle, 53 Fleet Street, London. 1804. Approx. 235 × 350 mm.

16 *The History and Delineation of the Horse* by John Lawrence.

> 4 Godolphin Arabian. To the Right Honble Lord Francis Godolphin.

Line engraving by John Scott. Published by James Cundee & John Scott, London. 1 December 1809. Approx. 140 × 200 mm.

For other engravings of racehorses from this book, see GILPIN **6**; MARSHALL **5**; and SARTORIUS, J. N. **17**.

17 Sharke. Portrait of a racehorse owned by Robt Pigott Esq. See MARSHALL **10** for pair.

Line engraving. Published by Thos Kelly, 17 Paternoster Road, London. Approx. 135 × 175 mm.

18 A Comparative View of English Racers and Saddle-Horses. See CHALON **12**; MARSHALL**12**; SEYMOUR **13**.

Pl IV	Mambrino.
Pl 5	Sweetbryer
Pl 6	Sweetwilliam.
Pl 7	Volunteer.
Pl 8	Protector.
Pl IX	Sharke.
Pl 10	Johnny.
G	Gimcrack.
Pl XVI	Portrait (of a hunter).

Lithographs drawn by M. Gauci. Pls IV, 5–8: H. B. Chalon. Printed by C. Hulmandell. Publised by Thos Hookham, 15 Old Bond Street, London. 1836. Approx. 200 × 250 mm.

19 Eclipse. Portrait of a racehorse with pedigree and performance.

Aquatint by C. Hunt. Published by J. Moore, corner of West Street, Upper St Martin's Lane, London. 12 November 1839. Approx. 320 × 425 mm.

20 A series of Famous Sires. See WOOTTON **5**.

> (1) Godolphin Barb.
> (2) Eclipse.
> (3) Diomed.

Photogravures. Published by Messrs Fores. Approx. 280 × 355 mm.

STURGESS, John, fl 1869–1903

Surprisingly little is known about John Sturgess. As an illustrator for many periodicals and books including the *Sporting and Dramatic News, Illustrated London News* and volumes of the Badminton Library, it might be hoped that, at worst, an obituary would have been written outlining what must have been a successful career. He seems to have been based in London for most of his life. His pictures of racehorses in motion have considerably more vitality than those painted by John Beer (qv) but, like him, Sturgess does not appear to have studied Muybridge's treatise on the action of galloping horses.

Racing

1 Blair Athol. Portrait of a racehorse owned by William I'Anson Esq. Winner of the Derby, 1863, ridden by J. Snowden, with details of pedigree.

Lithograph. (c1864). Approx. 360 × 485 mm.

2 Silvio. Portrait of a racehorse owned by Lord Falmouth. Winner of the Derby, 1877, ridden by F. Archer, with details of pedigree.

Lithograph drawn by the artist. Published by Arthur Ackermann, 191 Regent Street, London. 9 June 1877. Approx. 300 × 410 mm.

3 Racing scenes.

> (1) Rounding the Bend.
> (2) The Struggle for Victory.

These are composite scenes showing the racehorses Cremorne; Lord Clifden; Blair Athol; Gladiateur; Doncaster; Favonius; and Pretender, with names of jockeys.

Aquatints engraved by E. G. Hester. Published by L. Brall & Sons, 6 Great Prescott Street, Goodman's Fields, London. (1): 30 August 1873; (2): 20 October 1873. Approx. 610 × 860 mm.

Steeplechasing

4 Steeplechasing scenes.

> (1) Impending Danger.
> (2) A Match.

Aquatints engraved by C. Hunt. Published by J. McQueen, 37 Great Marlborough Street, London. (1): 18 December 1871; (2): 21 January 1872. Approx. 410 × 355 mm.

5 Steeplechasing scenes.

> (1) The Liverpool Grand National Steeplechase.
> (2) The Doncaster Grand Steeple Chase.

Aquatints engraved by E. G. Hester. Published by L. Brall

& Sons, as above. September 1872. Approx. 610 × 860 mm.

6 Punchestown, Conyngham Cup, 1872. With a dedication to the Marquis of Drogheda.

(1) The Start.
(2) The Stone Wall.
(3) The Double.
(4) The Finish. [*100*]

Each plate shows the names of the horses and riders.

The race was won by Heraut d'Armes, ridden by Captain Smith; 2nd, Curragh Ranger, Mr G. Moore; 3rd, Bashfull, Mr Whyte; 4th, Waterford, Captain MacFarlane.

Aquatints engraved by E. G. Hester. Published by Thomas Cranfield, 115 Grafton Street, Dublin and Arthur Ackermann, 191 Regent Street, London. 1 June 1874. Approx. 400 × 760 mm.
Reprinted at a later date.

SWANDALE, George, fl 1824–1844

George Swandale was a successful portrait painter who exhibited at the Royal Academy from a London address between 1824 and 1844. He was also the author of a portrait of Queen Victoria which was engraved in

mezzotint by Giller and published by R. Ackermann in 1838. The racehorse portrait below is a little stiff but has a certain charm, particularly in placing the animal and the jockey in a stall, which is unusual. A few years later Harry Hall painted Voltigeur with Job Marson and included the trainer in a similar stable scene.

1 Foig-a-Ballagh. Portrait of a racehorse owned by E. H. Irwen Esq., in his stall with his jockey. Winner of the St Leger 1844, ridden by H. Bell, with details of pedigree.

Aquatint engraved by C. Hunt. Published by J. Moore, 1 & 2 corner of West Street, St Martin's Lane, London. 6 November 1844. Approx. 310 × 510 mm.

TATTERSALL, George W., 1817–1849

George Tattersall was the younger son of the owner of Tattersall's Horse Repository, Richard Tattersall. Better known for his architectural work, George Tattersall illustrated, with Henry Alken Snr (*qv*), *Reminiscences of Nimrod* and R. S. Surtees's *Hillingdon Hall*. He was editor of *The Sporting Magazine* in the 1840s and drew groups of contemporary racehorses which were engraved and published. He used the

100 *Punchestown. Conyngham Cup 1872. The Finish. Aquatint after John Sturgess.*

pseudonym of 'Wildrake' for many of these diverse activities.

1 Goodwood, the Race for the Goodwood Stakes, 1846, with names of horses and riders, and result: 1st, Jonothan Wild; 2nd, The Hero; 3rd, Dulcet.

Aquatint engraved by J. Harris. Published by R. Ackermann, 191 Regent Street, London. 20 August 1846. Approx. 370 × 455 mm.

Siltzer records a pair: Epsom.

TILLEMANS, Peter, 1684–1734

Tillemans came to England from Antwerp in 1708. His first commissions were to paint topographical views of palaces, important buildings and the country seats of nobility and gentlemen. Each required figures to give life to the well-painted landscapes and what was more natural than to show some of these people mounted. Tillemans ability to paint horses was unremarkable, but his large and busily populated pictures of New-market Heath have considerable charm. The influence of his friend John Wootton (qv) is most pronounced in his horse portraiture while his compositions owe something to Francis Barlow (qv).

Tillemans' patrons included all the principal race-horse owners of the period and he spent much of his time travelling the length and breadth of the country completing their commissions. He must have known Newmarket well, already established as the home of the turf. He died at the comparatively young age of fifty, having suffered from asthma since a child.

Tillemans' influence on later sporting artists is considerable; although less innovative than Barlow he was more imaginative than Wootton. The engravings after his Newmarket paintings provide a fascinating record of training and horse management when the turf was developing quickly in the hands of the aristocracy of the period.

1 Set of four.

   (1) View of a Horse-Match over the Long-Course at New-Market from the Starting Post to ye Stand . . .

   (2) View of the Round-Course or Plate-Course with divers Jockeys and Horses in different Actions and Postures . . .

   (3) View of the Noblemens and Gentlemens several Strings or Trains of Running Horses taking their Exercise . . . [*2, see page 15*]

   (4) (Hunting).

Line engraving by: (1) & (4) Claude du Bosc; (2) & (3)

J. Sympson Snr. Printed for John Bowles at 13 in Cornhill and Carington Bowles at 69 in St Paul's Churchyard, London. No Date. Approx. 425 × 1105.

Reissued as published by Carington Bowles. Each engraving is made from two copper plates. All give a dedication, and the inscriptions are repeated in French. A similar set in reduced size (approx. 285 × 420 mm) was sold by J. Sympson at The Dove, Russell Court, Drury Lane, London and J. Lord in Dublin c1730. Siltzer records that the smaller set was reissued by Elizabeth Foster at the White Horse, Ludgate Hill, London in 1752.

There is another plate, probaby for export to France, which shows the right half of (3) with an extension of the view. This print is also after Tillemans, engraved by J. Sympson, with the title in French only. Approx. 430 × 540 mm.

2 Part of a series of portraits of racehorses with the names of their owners. See ANON **1**; WOOTTON **1**.

   (1) Childers – owned by the Duke of Devonshire.
   (2) Windham – Duke of Somerset.
   (3) Robson – Earl of Tankerville.
   (4) Creeping Molly – Duke of Rutland.
   (5) Light Foot – A Fine Breeding Mare owned by Mr Shepard.
   (6) Diamond – Duke of Somerset.

Line engravings by J. Sympson Snr & Jnr. Sold by J. Sympson at The Dove, Russell Court, Drury Lane, London. c1730. Approx. 165 × 205 mm.

3 'A Beautiful Running Horse Belonging to His Grace the Duke of Bolton'.

Line engraving by Tomson. Published 1738. Two plates joined: approx. 570 × 915 mm.

4 Portraits of racehorses.

   (1) Bonny Black – owned by the Duke of Rutland.
   (2) Judgement – Sir William Morgan.

Line engravings by R. Parr. Printed by John Bowles, 13 Cornhill, and sold by Robt Sayer, Opposite Fetter Lane, Fleet Street, London. c1740. Approx. 160 × 190 mm.

5 Set of eight unnamed racehorses; each print showing one, two or three horses.

Line engravings by S. Ravenet. Published for and sold by R. Sayer at the Golden Buck, Opposite Fetter Lane, Fleet Street, London. 1753. Approx. 115 × 165 mm.

6 King George I at Newmarket. (In 1722.)

Photogravure. Published by Messrs Fores, 41 Piccadilly, London. 1 September 1914. Approx. 335 × 835 mm.

101 *Orville, lately owned by HRH the Prince of Wales. St Leger 1802. Line engraving after Clifton Tomson.*

TOMSON, Clifton, (of Nottingham), 1775–1828

Clifton Tomson was born in Nottingham where he established himself as a sporting artist. His father was a skilled craftsman, a frame-maker in the local hosiery business, which gives no positive indication of why his son turned to painting. Working quietly in Nottingham, Tomson was first recognised outside the confines of his native town when *The Sporting Magazine* published engravings after his portraits of the racehorses Moorcock in August 1801 and Sir Soloman two months later. The *Magazine* continued to publish his pictures sporadically during his lifetime. In 1812, Tomson's fine painting of Earl Fitzwilliam's Orville was printed as a line engraving by a William Bishop. The artist's favourite race meetings were those at Nottingham, York and Doncaster, and it was at the last where he painted at least two large panoramas: one of the finish of the St Leger, 1812 and another of the Start of the St Leger, 1816, both of which were later published by Edward Orme of Bond Street, London. He married in 1797 and his wife Grace (Brailsford) bore him nine children; of his four sons, two died in infancy, one when aged twenty-two and the fourth, Clifton, two years before his father who died in September 1828, aged fifty-three.

While Clifton Tomson can be correctly described as a 'provincial' painter, the condescension this term sometimes implies is misplaced since, at his best, he had the same ability as many of his contemporaries such as George Garrard (*qv*) and C. H. Schwanfelder (1773–1837). In particular, his sympathetic observation of racehorses is often outstanding.

1 Orville. Portrait of a racehorse lately owned by HRH George, Prince of Wales, with dedication to Earl FitzWilliam. Details of pedigree and performance. (St Leger, 1802). [*101*]

Line engraving by J. Scott. Printed by Wm Bishop. 20 August 1812. Approx. 435 × 610 mm.

2 Panoramic View of British Horse Racing, The Race for the St Leger Stakes of 1812, on Doncaster Course. [*19, page 40*]

Names of horses, owners and jockeys shown. 1st, Mr Robb's Otterington, ridden by R. Johnson; 2nd, Lord Strathmore's Benedict, T. Goodisson; 3rd, Mr Beckwith's Herrington, J. Jackson.

Aquatint engraved by J. Clark & M. Dubourg. Published by E. Orme, Bond Street, corner of Brook Street, London. 1 May 1815. Two plates, approx. 500 × 1365 mm.

A small version of this panorama was engraved by J. Pollard & M. Dubourg and published by Orme, as above on 1 March 1816. Approx. 90 × 630 mm.

3 Preparing to Start for the St Leger Stakes.

Names of the horses, owners and jockeys shown at the start of the 1816 St Leger which was won by Sir B. R. Graham, Bart's The Duchess, ridden by B. Smith; 2nd, Mr R. Watt's Captain Candid, J. Jackson; 3rd, Duke of Leeds's Rasping, J. Shepherd.

Aquatint engraved by M. Dubourg. Published by E. Orme, as above. 1 March 1818. Approx. 90 × 620 mm. This print is often found as a pair to the smaller version of **2** above.

TOWNE, Charles, 1763–1840

Charles Towne (or Town, as he wrote his name until about 1800) was born in Wigan in 1763, the son of a poor currier. As a young man he sought work in Liverpool and Manchester but with little success until being employed in decorating coaches by a John Latham, from which he progressed to being a Japanner and painter on his own account in Liverpool.

Towne first exhibited a picture at the Liverpool Society in 1787 and a few years later obtained some notoriety by his outstanding copies of George Stubbs's two masterpieces, *Harvesters*, and *Reapers*. By 1795 he was an accomplished painter and his imaginative landscape settings for his animal portraits were extremely competent. He moved to London in 1797 where, falling in with George Morland and his rowdy circle, he was soon in financial difficulties and other scrapes. Nine of his paintings were exhibited at the Royal Academy between 1799 and 1804.

Towne returned to Liverpool in 1810, by which time he was receiving portrait commissions from a number of patrons. However, he was also devoting too much of his energy to painting delightful but unsaleable landscapes. He was a founder member of the Liverpool Academy and two years later became their Vice-President in 1812. He showed portraits at their annual exhibitions until 1822 and landscapes with animals at the Royal Manchester Institution from 1827 to 1833.

His paintings are varied in quality. The best have a similar serenity to the work of Stubbs. It is sad that his set of four pictures of the *Life of a Racehorse* were not engraved since they tell us much about training in his day. *Newton Races* (below) is a lively scene and its concentration on group portraiture is out of the ordinary.

Charles Towne died in 1840, almost as poor as he was in his youth.

1 Newtown Races, 1831, Fylde beating Halston and Recovery, for the Gold Cup given by Thos Legh Esq, MP.

The proper name of this race was 'The Lord of the Manor's Gold Cup'.

Aquatint engraved by C. Hunt. Published by Agnew & Zanetti, Exchange Street, Manchester and S. & J. Fuller, 34 Rathbone Place, London. December 1832. Approx. 500 × 735 mm.

TURNER, Francis Calcraft, c1782–1846

A contemporary of Henry Alken Snr (*qv*), Turner's oils of hunting, shooting, racing and steeplechasing are similar in style and have some of the gaiety, but not humour, as those of his more famous peer. Turner claimed, as did Alken, a considerable personal experience of field sports, particularly hunting.

London based, he exhibited paintings at the Royal Academy, the British Institution and the Royal Society of British Artists from 1810 to the year of his death. He also provided almost eighty designs which were engraved in *The Sporting Magazine* as well as being engaged by the important publishers: Moore; McLean, Ackermann; and, near the end of his life, McCormick.

His pictures of thoroughbreds can often be identified by the animals' small heads and, whenever he had the opportunity to paint a standing horse, the over-emphasised arched neck denoting their Arabian ancestry.

Racing

1 Portraits of racehorses with names of their owners and details of their pedigrees and performances.

 (1) Cyprian – owned by Mr J. Scott. W. Scott up. Oaks, 1836.
 (2) Hornsea – Earl of Chesterfield. W. Scott up. Goodwood Gold Cup, 1836. [*Plate 5*]

Aquatints engraved by: (1) C. & G. Hunt; (2) G. Hunt. Published by J. Moore, corner of West Street, St Martin's Lane, London. (1) July 1836; (2) Not Dated. Approx. 315 × 425 mm.

2 Racing scenes.

 (1) Heaton Park Races, 1835.
 (2) Ascot Heath Races, 2 June 1836.

(1) Heaton Park was Lord Wilton's house near Manchester. The winner was George Osbaldeston on Rust; 2nd, Lord Wilton on Lady Le Gros; 3rd, Mr Serdefield on Giovanni.

(2) William IV stands in the box on the right. The Ascot Gold Cup, 1836 was won by the Marquis of Westminster's Touchstone, ridden by J. Day; 2nd, Mr Theobald's Rockingham, Macdonald; 3rd, Mr Robertson's Lucifer, J. Robinson.

[175]

102 *Coming in for the Derby. (1837.) Aquatint after Francis Calcraft Turner.*

Aquatints engraved by R. G. Reeve. Published by J. McCormick, 147 Strand, London and (1): Joseph Gale, King Street, London; Thos Dewhurst, Market Street, Manchester; Henry Lacey, Liverpool. (1) Not Dated; (2) June 1837. Approx. 360 × 610 mm.

3 Racing scenes.

    (1)   The Start of the Derby.
    (2)   Coming in for the Derby. [*102*]

The Derby, 1837 was won by Lord Berners's Phosphorous, ridden by G. Edwards; 2nd, Lord Suffield's Caravan, A. Pavis; no horse was officially placed 3rd.

Aquatints engraved by C. Hunt. Published by J. Moore, 1 West Street, St Martin's Lane, London. 1 February 1838. Approx. 600 × 800 mm.
    Reprinted by L. Brall & Sons, 9 Great Prescott Street, London on 1 August 1870.

4 Racing scenes.

    (1)   Grand Stand, Goodwood. (Coming in for the Gold Cup, 1838).

With names of the horses and jockeys. The Goodwood Gold Cup, 1838 was won by Mr Ferguson's Harkaway, ridden by Wakefield; 2nd, Lord Exeter's Adrian; 3rd, Mr Worrall's Dormouse.

    (2)   Grand Stand, Ascot.

With names of horses and jockeys. The Ascot Gold Cup, 1839 was won by the Hon. Captain Berkeley's Caravan, ridden by J. Robinson; 2nd, Mr Thornhill's St Francis; 3rd, Colonel Peel's Ion.

Aquatints engraved by C. Hunt. Published by J. Moore, as above, and by (1) E. Cooper, Chichester. (1) 1 January 1839; (2) September 1839. Approx. 510 × 745 mm.
    Reissued representing a contemporary race in 1853 and 1870. See HUNT, C. 1.

5 Race for the Tradesmen's Plate, Chester, 1839. With names of horses and colours of jockeys.

The race was won by Lord Westminster's Cardinal Puff, ridden by Darling; 2nd, Sir T. Stanley's Cowboy. S. Templeman; 3rd, Mr Price's Zillah, M. Jones.

Aquatint engraved by J. Harris. Published by Thos McLean, 26 Haymarket, London and T. Hulme, Manchester. 1 February 1839. Approx. 520 × 735 mm.

6 Race for the Wolverhampton Stakes, 1839.

The race was won by the Duke of Richmond's Confusionee, ridden by Howlett; 2nd, Lord George Bentinck's Ratsbane.

Aquatint engraved by G. A. Turner. Published by Thos

McLean, 26 Haymarket, London. 2 August 1840. Approx. 520 × 760 mm.

7 The Great St Leger Decisive Heat at Doncaster, 1839, between Charles XIIth and Euclid. [*103*]

After the initial dead heat, Major Yarburgh's Charles XII, ridden by W. Scott beat Euclid, P. Connolly in the run off.

Aquatint engraved by G. A. Turner. Published by Ackermann & Co., 96 Strand, London. 7 May 1840. Approx. 513 × 760 mm.

8 Portraits of racehorses with names of their owners and details of their pedigrees and performances.

(1) Conolly on Coronation, Winning in a Canter – owned by A. Rawlinson Esq. Derby, 1841. Published 18 August 1841.
(2) Ghuznee, with Characteristic Portraits of Mr John Scott & Mr William Scott. 1 October 1841.
(3) Scott on Satirist – Lord Westminster. St Leger, 1841. 1841.
(4) Attila – Hon. Col Anson. Rode by W. Scott. Derby, 1842.
(5) Our Nell – Mr G. Dawson. T. Lye up. Oaks, 1842. 1 September 1842.

Aquatints engraved by J. R. Mackrell. Published by Ackermann & Co., 96 Strand, London. Approx. 450 × 600 mm.

(1)–(3) reprinted at a later date.

9 Arab horses.

(1) Godolphin Arabian – Scham. Owned by Earl Godolphin.
(2) Darley Arabian – Roxana. Owned by Earl Godolphin.

The descriptions below these plates are not in the least accurate and muddle the relationships of the horses named.

Aquatints engraved by J. R. Mackrell. Published by J. McCormick, 90 Strand, and by E. Gambart & Co., 25 Berners Street, Oxford Street, London, and E. Gambart, Junin & Co., Paris. (1) 1 September 1842; (2) 15 September 1842. Approx. 420 × 530 mm.

10 Portraits of racehorses with the names of their owners and details of their pedigrees and performances.

(1) Alice Hawthorn (Queen of the Turf) – owned by J. Plummer Esq., ridden by R. Hesseltine. Goodwood Cup, 1844. [*104*]
(2) Refraction – Duke of Richmond. H. Bell. Oaks, 1845.
(3) The Baron – G. Watts Esq. F. Butler. St Leger, 1845.

Aquatints engraved by G. A. Turner. Published by J. McCormick, 90 Strand, London. (c1845). Approx. 430 × 530 mm.

103 *The Great St Leger Decisive Heat at Doncaster, 1839, between Charles XII and Euclid. Aquatint after Francis Calcraft Turner.*

104 *J. Plummer Esq's Alice Hawthorn, with R. Hesseltine up. Aquatint after Francis Calcraft Turner.*

105 *(below) Leamington Grand Steeple Chase, 1837. Third Fence. Aquatint after Francis Calcraft Turner.*

Steeplechasing

11 Vale of Aylesbury Steeple Chase, Second Day, Thursday 11th February 1836. (Lightweights).

Plate 1   Blackgrove Farm.
Plate 2   Fleet Marston Brook.
Plate 3   Mr Simmond's Berry Field Farm.
Plate 4   Mr Josh Terry's Long Furlong field.

With descriptions of each scene and names of horses and riders. The race was won by Captain Becher on Vivian; 2nd, Grimaldi; 3rd, The Pony.

Aquatints engraved by: Plates 1 & 2 C. & G. Hunt; Plates 3 & 4 G. & C. Hunt. Published by J. Moore, 1 West Street, Upper St Martin's Lane, London. Not Dated. Approx. 335 × 550 mm. Reprinted at a later date.

12 Leamington Grand Steeple Chase, 1837.

Plate 1   (Starting, head-on view).
Plate 2   Third Fence. [*105*]
Plate 3   (Over a stream).
Plate 4   (Running in to the Finish).

With dedication to John Creighton Esq., and names of horses and riders. The race was won by Mr Anderson's Jerry, ridden by Mr J. Mason; 2nd, Captain Lamb's Vivian, Capt Becher; 3rd, Mr Coke's Flacrow, Mr W. Haycock.

Aquatints engraved by C. Hunt. Published by Thos McLean, 26 Haymarket, London. June 1837. Approx. 370 × 600 mm. Reprinted at a later date.

13 The Liverpool Great National Steeple-Chase, 1839.

Plate I   (Preparing to Start, by the Grand Stand).
Plate II   (Over the rail and brook).
Plate III   (Over the wall, view from the rear). [*23, page 46*]
Plate IV   (The run in).

William Lynn who promoted the race and Lord Sefton who acted as Starter can be seen on the far left of Plate I. Having fallen on Captain Childe's Conrad, Captain Becher can be seen in Plate II struggling out of the brook thereafter given his name. The race was won by Mr J. Elmore's Lottery, ridden by Jem Mason; 2nd, Sir George Mostyn's Seventy Four, Tom Olliver; 3rd, Mr Theobald's Paulina, Mr Martin.

Aquatints engraved by J. Harris. Published by Thos McLean, as above. 1 May 1839. Approx. 405 × 675 mm.

Reprinted with title 'The Liverpool Grand National, 1852' (names of horses and owners omitted) by Barnett, Moss & Co., Leman Street, Goodman's Fields, London. (*c1852*).

14 Ackermann's Series of National Sports'.

The Windsor Grand Military, 1840.

(1)   The Start.
(2)   Coming In.

The race, on 14 December, was for horses the property of and ridden by Officers of the Royal Household Brigade. The winner was Sir W. W. Wynne's Amazon, ridden by Mr Hood; 2nd, Mr De Winton's Nimrod, ridden by the Owner.

Aquatints engraved by G. A. Turner. Published by Ackermann & Co., 96 Strand, London. 1 May 1841. Approx. 380 × 535 mm.

VEAL, George, fl 1880–1890

Veal painted a number of equestrian group portraits of racehorses with jockeys up which sadly lack much recognisable life. The 'gentlemen' riders are almost always mutton-chop-whiskered men looking into the middle distance in a bored manner. The paintings are usually large which, if anything, accentuates their dullness. The prints provide a record, but only just!

1 'McQueen's Racings'.

(1)   Our Leading Jockeys of the Day.

A parade with jockeys up, with facsimile signatures including George Fordham; Sam Loates; Fred Archer; John Osborne; and James Goater.

(2)   Our Gentlemen Steeple Chase Riders.

A group of steeplechasers having cleared a fence.

(3)   Our North Country Jockeys.

Preparing to start, with facsimile signatures including James Woodburn; Walter Glover; George Woodburn; James Snowden; and James Griffiths.

(4)   Our Gentlemen Riders.

A group of riders, with facsimile signatures.

Aquatints engraved by: (1), (2) E. G. Hester; (3), (4) C. R. Stock. Published by F. C. McQueen & Sons, 181 Tottenham Court Road, London; Stiefbold & Co., Berlin; M. Knoedler & Co., New York. (1) 1 May 1885; (2) 1 December 1885; (3) 24 May 1887; (4) 31 May 1888. Approx. 505 × 920 mm.

VOSS, C. J., fl 1850–1855

1 Bourton. Portrait of a racehorse owned by Mr William Moseley. Winner of the Grand National, 1854, ridden by J. Tasker.

Aquatint engraved by C. Hunt. *c1854*. Approx. 455 × 675 mm.

106 *Sir John Shelley's Phantom. Lithograph by and after James Ward* RA.

WALSH, Thomas N. H., fl 1885–1890

Thomas Walsh was a prolific artist, mainly in watercolour. His pictures of racing and hunting are often very well executed, sometimes with humour. Walsh does not appear to have exhibited any paintings, but he was employed by a number of print publishers in a successful but what may have been a short life.

1 Dodson's Racing Incidents.

(1) 'Saddling the Favourite'.
(2) 'Preparing to Start'.
(3) 'Left at the Post'.
(4) 'A Close Finish'.

Aquatints engraved by C. R. Stock. Published by R. Dodson, 147 Strand, London. 1 November 1887. Approx. 210 × 355 mm.
Reprinted at a later date.

WARD, James, RA, 1769–1859

The apparently complex character of James Ward is simplified if one discards the opinions of some early biographers who both maligned him and denigrated his ability unfairly. Born in October 1769, the second son in what was to be the large family of a London fruit warehouseman until he lost his job through drink, James's early life was not an easy one. When aged eleven he started work in the studio of the successful engraver John Raphael Smith, to whom his older brother was apprenticed. Somehow the situation improved and a move to Kensal Green resulted in meeting George Morland (1763–1804). The friendship between the families was cemented by the marriages of James's sister Anne to the artist, and his brother William to Morland's sister, Maria. James was immediately attracted to Morland's style of painting. He now turned from engraving to oils, obtaining commissions to portray animals in landscapes and attempting large allegorical subjects with mixed success both financially and from the viewpoint of public acclaim. During his lifetime he exhibited more than 300 pictures at the Royal Academy and was elected an RA in 1811.

He left London in 1829 for Cheshunt in Hertfordshire where he hoped to find fresh commissions, but he was not successful. He began writing, and in considerable financial difficulties applied for a pension from the Royal Academy, which he was granted. He died in 1859 and lies buried in Kensal Green cemetery, not far from where he had lived for many years.

In 1823 Ward had engraved a series of fifteen lithographs of earlier paintings of famous horses, which he published himself. Among them are a few racehorses, usually standing alone in a landscape, showing with marvellous realism his sympathy for the character of each proud beast. It is for his ability to ennoble animals without sentimentality that Ward should be remembered.

1 A Series of Lithographic Drawings of Celebrated Horses, with dedications. Seven (out of the fifteen plates) are of racehorses.

    (1) Soothsayer – a racehorse belonging to George IV.
    (2) Primrose and foal – belonging to the Duke of Grafton.
    (3) Walton – a racehorse belonging to Sir John Shelley.
    (4) Phantom – a racehorse belonging to Sir John Shelley. (Derby, 1811). [*106*]
    (5) Leopold – a racehorse belonging to Mr John Lambton. (Derby, 1816).
    (6) Dr Syntax – a racehorse belonging to Mr Ralph Riddell. (Winner of 20 Gold Cups).
    (7) Moses – a racehorse belonging to HRH the Duke of York. (Derby, 1822). [*15, page 36*]

Lithographs by the artist. First published by the artist. Later printed by C. Hulmandell and published by R. Ackermann, Strand; (1), (2), (5)–(7) and by Rodwell and Martin, Colnaghi & Co. (1) April 1823; (2) 1 April 1823; (3), (5), (6) 1 April 1823; (7) 1 October 1823. Approx. 340 × 465 mm. Reissued by R. Ackermann.

WHEELER, John Alfred, 1821–1903
WHEELER, Alfred, 1851–1932

John Alfred Wheeler, the son of a stone-cutter, was born at Andoversford near Cheltenham. Raised by an uncle who disapproved of his wish to become a painter, he enlisted into the Queen's Dragoon Guards as a bandsman when nineteen years old. While serving with the Bays, as the regiment was known, John Wheeler obtained valuable experience of both horses and horsemanship; but he became ill and was discharged in 1847. He returned to Cheltenham, later moving to Bath in 1854 where he hoped to find more patrons for his paintings. In the same year he joined the Bath Troop of the North Somerset Yeomanry by whom he was commissioned to paint two pictures. He remained at Bath for the next twenty-three years painting equestrian subjects, dogs and a few portraits. In 1877 he was on the move again, this time to Hanwell on the outskirts of London, again attempting to find

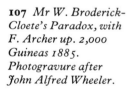

107 *Mr W. Broderick-Cloete's Paradox, with F. Archer up. 2,000 Guineas 1885. Photogravure after John Alfred Wheeler.*

new patrons and to be near the art galleries. It was not until quite late in his life, in the 1880s and 1890s, that he began to paint racehorse portraits, of which some were reproduced and published by Messrs Fores of Piccadilly.

Alfred Wheeler, the younger son of John Alfred, learnt to paint by watching his father at work. At the time of his marriage in 1874 he lived next door to him at 2 Raglan Villas, Bath and three years later also moved to Hanwell. While Alfred was less prolific than his father, he painted more racehorse portraits. Sadly, Alfred turned to drink. This may have been because he lacked commissions, with photography replacing the artist in recording the successful racehorses of the day.

There is often difficulty in separating the work of the son from the father since their styles are very similar; a problem not easily unravelled since Alfred sometimes signed his work J. A. Wheeler Jnr and, late in life, J. A. Wheeler Snr!

John Alfred Wheeler.

Racing

1 'Fores's Celebrated Winners'. See HAVELL 1; LUCAS-LUCAS 1; WHEELER, A. 1.

(1) Paradox. Portrait of a racehorse owned by Mr Broderick-Cloete. Winner of the 2,000 Gns and Grand Prix de Paris, 1885, ridden by F. Archer. With details of pedigree and performance. [107]

Photogravure. Published by Messrs Fores, 41 Piccadilly, London. 16 March 1891. Approx. 415 × 550 mm.

Steeplechasing

2 Zoedone. Portrait of a racehorse owned by Count Charles Kinsky, with Count Kinsky up. Winner of the Grand National 1883.

Count Kinsky served in the Austrian Embassy in London. There were only ten starters in the Grand National, 1883.

Painted with Isaac Cullin. Chromolithograph.

Alfred Wheeler

3 'Fores's Celebrated Winners'. See HAVELL 1; LUCAS-LUCAS 1; WHEELER, J. A. 1.

Ormonde. Portrait of a racehorse owned by the Duke of Westminster. Winner of the Triple Crown, 1886, ridden by F. Archer. In the 2,000 Gns, ridden by G. Barrett. With details of pedigree and performance.

Photogravure. Published by Messrs Fores, 41 Piccadilly, London. 1887. Approx. 425 × 570 mm.

WHESSELL, John, 1760–c1823

John Whessell was both an engraver and painter of some ability. Since he engraved many of his own paintings, a superior skill in the former department may have 'improved' any faults he may have had in oils – although a number of his racehorse portraits were exhibited at the Royal Academy between 1802 and 1808. His prints of Penelope and Parasol are of particular interest since these two horses helped to lay the foundations of the Dukes of Grafton's outstanding turf performances at the beginning of the nineteenth century.

Whessell seems to have been living in London for most of his life for many of his pictures were sent to exhibitions from an address in Paddington. Principally as an engraver, but also as a painter, Whessell must have been a successful artist during his life, of which we know so little.

1 Eagle, Brother of Spread Eagle. Portrait of a racehorse, trainer and lad, with details of pedigree and performance.

A painting of 'Eagle beating Eleanor, a match run across the Flat, Newmarket October Meeting, 1804' by Whessell was exhibited at the Royal Academy in 1805.

Stipple engraving. Painted and engraved by J. Whessell, 9 Winchester Row, Paddington. Published by J. Harris, Sweetings Alley, Cornhill and 8 Old Broad Street, London. 13 August 1805. Approx. 370 × 490 mm.

2 Portraits of Celebrated Running Horses, with the names of their owners.

Plate 1st.	
Plate 2nd.	Penelope – Duke of Grafton. [108] Published 29 May 1806.
Plate 3rd.	Bobtail – Earl of Egremont.
Plate 4th.	Parasol – Duke of Grafton. [109]
Plate 5th.	
Plate 6th.	
Plate 7th.	
Plate 8th.	

Plate nos. of: Dick Andrews – Viscount Sackville; Trumpator – Lord Clermont; Eleanor – Sir Charles Bunbury (Derby and Oaks, 1801); Meteroa – Lord Grosvenor (Oaks, 1805); and Violante – Lord Grosvenor, not known.

Portraits by Whessell of Penelope, Bobtail, Parasol, Dick Andrews and Violante were exhibited at the Royal Academy between 1805 and 1808.

Painted, engraved and published by J. Whessell, as above. Trumpator: 12 August 1808. Approx. 370 × 495 mm.
Republished by E. Orme, Bond Street, corner of Brook Street, London. 1 March 1809.

108 *The Duke of Grafton's Penelope. Stipple engraving by and after John Whessell.*

109 *The Duke of Grafton's Parasol. Stipple engraving by and after John Whessell.*

WOLSTENHOLME, Dean Snr, 1757–1837
WOSTENHOLME, (Charles) Dean Jnr, 1793–1883

Dean Wolstenholme Snr became an artist in middle life after losing his then not inconsiderable wealth in a property deal which went wrong. Before moving to London in about 1800 he had lived in Hertfordshire and Essex, pursuing a happy life devoted to foxhunting and coursing, painting a little for his own pleasure. In London he had to paint in earnest, bringing to the city (Red Lion Square) memories of his earlier years. He exhibited a painting of coursing at the Royal Academy in 1803; fox hunting in 1804; The Epping Forest Hunt the following year; and so on until shortly before his death in 1837. A large number of his hunting, coursing and shooting pictures were engraved, the later ones by his son. A single small set of 'The High Mettled Racer' was engraved and published by Dean Wolstenholme Jnr in 1817 from the Strand.

Dean Jnr was born at Waltham Abbey, Essex, in April 1798 during one of his father's many excursions back to the countryside he so loved. It was not long before Dean Snr was teaching his son to paint, and later the young man attended the Royal Academy Schools. As well as engraving the plates for 'The High Mettled Racer', Dean Jnr painted and engraved four racing scenes of his own which were published by Ackermann in 1834. These two sets are the sum total of the Wolstenholme's racing work. Wolstenholme Jnr lived to a great age, surviving for a further twenty years after he retired to Highgate in 1862.

The Wolstenholmes populated their landscapes with horses and huntsmen rather than painting commissioned equestrian portraits; and the pleasure of their work is their skill in depicting the English (Home Counties) countryside over a period of more than 100 years.

Dean Wolstenholme Snr

1 The High Mettled Racer. (With verses).

1. See the course throng'd . . .
2. Now Reynard's turned out . . .
3. Grown Aged . . .
4. At Length old, and feeble . . .

Aquatints engraved by D. Wolstenholme Jnr. Published by D. Wolstenholme, 279 Strand, London. 1, 2: 1 August 1817; 3, 4: 4 June 1817. Approx. 200 × 320 mm.

Dean Wolstenholme Jnr

1 Racing scenes.

(1) Preparing to Start.
(2) The Start.
(3) Running in Full Speed.
(4) Rubbing Down.

Aquatints engraved by the artist. Published by Ackermann & Co., 96 Strand, London. 1834. Approx. 180 × 260 mm.

WOMBILL, Sidney R., fl 1885–1890

1 Portraits of racehorses with jockeys up, winners of Classic and other races, with details of pedigrees and performances. See HUNT E. H. 1; POWELL 1.

(1) Melton – owned by Lord Hastings. Ridden by F. Archer. Derby, 1885. Published 7 August 1885.
(2) Ormonde – Duke of Westminster. F. Archer. Triple Crown, 1886. 1886.
(3) Bendigo – Major H. T. Barclay. Cambridgeshire, 1883 and Eclipse Stakes, 1886.
(4) Ayrshire – Duke of Portland. F. Barrett. 2,000 Gns and Derby, 1888. 26 June 1888.

Aquatints engraved by: (1) E. H. Hunt; (2)–(4) S. A. Edwards. Published by George Rees, 41, 42, 43 Great Russell Street, Covent Garden, and 115 Strand, London. Approx. 480 × 645 mm.

WOODWARD, Thomas, 1801–1852

Thomas Woodward was born in Pershore, Worcestershire, coming from an established and well known family in that district. The artist Benjamin West encouraged him to become an animal painter and at the age of eighteen he spent a year studying under Abraham Cooper (qv). At first working in London, he became a friend of Landseer who envied his skill in painting horses. Some of his pictures were engraved for *The Sporting Magazine* and he exhibited at the Royal Academy and British Institution from 1821 until his death. Sadly he was consumptive and had to move back to Worcestershire for the better air. He continued painting and also hunted with the local packs before he became too ill to do so. His choice of subjects was very wide including historical and military scenes, but the majority of his paintings were of horses, hounds, dogs and other animals, sometimes depicted in humorous situations which he had obviously experienced himself. He was commissioned to paint equestrian portraits by many of the Worcestershire hunting fraternity, but his pictures of racehorses are rare. He died at the early age of fifty-one.

His portrayal of horses is masterly, owing part of their style to the influence of Cooper, Sawrey Gilpin (*qv*) and James Ward (*qv*). He also had the ability to compose and populate his paintings so that they appeared entirely natural regardless of the limitations dictated in commissioned work.

1 Isaac. Portrait of a racehorse belonging to Mr Collins, with Sam Darling up. Darling's two sons in attendance. [*Plate 7*]

Isaac won 52 races between 1835 and 1845, including 18 in 1839 when owned by Mr Tomes. The painting for this print was exhibited in the Royal Academy in 1839.

Aquatint engraved by J. Harris. (*c*1839). Approx. 585 × 690 mm.

2 Plover. Portrait of a racehorse. Winner of the Derby at Chantilly, 1842.

Aquatint engraved by G. Hunt. 20 August 1842.

WOOTTON, John, c1683–1764

John Wootton was probably born at Snitterfield in Warwickshire. He assisted and then became the pupil of the successful Dutch artist Jan Wyck (*c*1645–1700) who was in great demand in decorating houses with battle scenes and what may be described as equestrian portrait groups in sporting surroundings. At first Wootton followed closely in the style of his tutor, but he quickly obtained commissions to paint more formal portraits of single racehorses and Arabian stallions. These are rather stiff in their handling but, with the exception of paintings by his contemporary Peter Tillemans (*qv*), his work was almost all that was available of any quality at the time. The aristocracy was looking for grandiose canvases to demonstrate their racing enthusiasm; Wootton supplied just what they wanted, for which he was paid an extremely satisfying fee. Among his patrons was Frederick, Prince of Wales and Wootton's paintings, mainly of hunting, can still be seen hanging in the places for which they were designed at Althorp, Longleat and Badminton.

Wootton also painted more 'extensive' racing scenes, thickly populated with strings of horses and armies of spectators, closer to the style of Tillemans. Anatomically, his horses are poorly painted. The landscapes, when not prettified in a Poussinesque manner, are very well composed and give a good idea of racing and training in his day. His portraiture of humans is disappointing, and there is evidence that he often called on others to supply the faces if not the figures of those who attended his race meetings!

Wootton was a popular man and no mere 'horse-painter'. He was a founder member of the Academy of Painting, and led a confident public life, accepted as an equal in the circle of his often noble patrons.

His eyesight failed towards the end of his life. At his instruction the remaining pictures in his studio were sold three years before his death, perhaps to provide some funds for his declining years when he was unable to continue painting. Next to Francis Barlow, Wootton was the founder and architect of the English school of sporting painting.

1 Part of a series of portraits of racehorses with the names of their owners. See ANON **1**; TILLEMANS **2**.

   (1)   Victorious – owned by the Earl of Portmore.
   (2)   Fox – Mr Panton.
   (3)   Silverlocks – Earl of Godolphin.
   (4)   Lampere – Sir William Morgan.
   (5)   Judgement – Sir William Morgan.
   (6)   Cartouche – Sir William Morgan.
   (7)   Coneyskins – Duke of Rutland.

Line engravings by J. Sympson Jnr. Sold by J. Sympson at The Dove, Russell Court, Drury Lane, London. *c*1730. Approx. 165 × 205 mm.

2 'A View of a Horse Match at Newmarket between Grey-Windham (a Horse belonging to his Grace the Duke of Somerset) and Bay Bolton (a Horse belonging to his Grace the Duke of Bolton) . . .'

Line engraving by J. Sympson Jnr. Sold by J. Sympson, as above. *c*1740. Approx. 260 × 430 mm.

3 Thirty-four racehorses with names of their owners and details of their pedigrees and performances framing the portraits. Some with coats of arms. See SEYMOUR **2**.

   26.   Silver Leg, owned by Nathaniel Curzon Esq.

Line engraving by R. Parr. Published by Thomas Butler. Pall Mall, London. Approx. 175 × 180 mm.

4 Portraits of racehorses.

   (1)   The Bloody-Shouldered Arabian.
   (2)   Pedlar – owned by Mr Henly.

Line engravings by R. Parr.

5 A series of Famous Sires. See STUBBS **20**.

   (1)   Darley Arabian.
   (2)   Match 'em.
   (3)   Flying Childers.
   (4)   King Herod.
   (5)   Byerley Turk.

Photogravures. Published by Messrs Fores. Approx. 280 × 355 mm.

ZIEGLER, Henry Bryan, 1798–1874

As a young man Ziegler became a pupil of the water-colourist John Varley (1778–1842); he also studied at the Royal Academy Schools. He painted landscapes and rustic subjects, turning more to portraiture at the end of his life. He was a drawing master including among his pupils Queen Adelaide and Prince George of Cambridge. Early in life, when living at Ludlow, he drew a panoramic scene of the nearby Worcester racecourse which he etched and had published locally.

1 Worcester Race-Course & Grand Stand, with dedication. [*110*]

Etched by H. B. Ziegler, aquatint by G. Hunt. Published by H. B. Ziegler, 40 High Street, Worcester. 9 December 1823. Approx. 320 × 575 mm.

110 *Worcester Race-course and Grand Stand. Aquatint after Henry Bryan Ziegler.*

SELECTED BIBLIOGRAPHY

Armytage, Julian, *Heritage of the Turf*, exhibition catalogue, 1986.

Beckett, Oliver, *J. F. Herring & Sons*, J. A. Allen & Co. Ltd, 1981.

British Racehorse, 1949–1978.

British Sporting Art Trust, *Catalogue Raisonné of Prints of Charlie Johnson Payne, Snaffles*, 1981.

British Sporting Art Trust, *Twentieth Century Sporting Art*, exhibition catalogue, 1983.

Cook, Sir Theodore Andrew, *A History of the English Turf*, 3 vols, H. Virtue & Co. Ltd, 1901–1904.

Coombs, David, 'The English Sporting Print c1650–1850', essay in *British Sporting Painting 1650–1850*, Hayward Gallery exhibition catalogue, 1975.

Egerton, Judy, *The Paul Mellon Collection. British Sporting and Animal Paintings 1655–1867*, The Tate Gallery for the Yale Center for British Art, 1978.

Egerton, Judy and Snelgrove, Dudley, *The Paul Mellon Collection. British Sporting and Animal Drawings c1500–1850*, The Tate Gallery for the Yale Center for British Art, 1978.

Fletcher, J. S., *The History of the St Leger Stakes 1776–1901*, 1902.

Graves, Algernon, *British Institution Exhibitors 1806–1867*, 1875.

Graves, Algernon, *Royal Academy of Arts Exhibitors 1769–1904*, 8 vols., 1905–06.

Graves, Algernon, *Society of Artists of Great Britain Exhibitors 1760–1791*, 1907.

Green, Reg, *A Race Apart*, Hodder & Stoughton, 1988.

Houfe, Simon, *The Dictionary of British Book Illustrators and Caricaturists*, Antique Collectors' Club, Revised edition, 1981.

Lambton, the Hon. George, *Men and Horses I Have Known*, J. A. Allen & Co. Ltd, new edition, 1963.

Lane, Charles, *Sporting Aquatints and Their Engravers*, 2 vols, F. Lewis Publishers Ltd, 1976–78.

Mackenzie, Ian, *British Prints*, Antique Collectors' Club, 1987.

Mallelieu, Huon, *The Dictionary of British Watercolour Artists up to 1920*, Antique Collectors' Club, 1976.

Mitchell, Sally, *The Dictionary of British Equestrian Artists*, Antique Collectors' Club, 1985.

Mortimer, Roger, *The History of the Derby Stakes*, new edition, 1973.

Mortimer, Roger; Onslow, Richard; and Willet, Peter, *Biographical Encyclopedia of British Flat Racing*, Macdonald and Jane's, 1978.

Munnings, Sir Alfred, *An Artist's Life*, 1950; *The Second Burst*, 1951; *The Finish*, 1952, Museum Press.

Redgrave, Samuel, *A Dictionary of Artists of the English School*, Kingsmead Reprints, 1970.

Ruff's Guide to the Turf and the *Sporting Life Annual*.

Selway, N. C., *The Golden Age of Coaching and Sport*, F. Lewis Publishers Ltd., 1972.

Siltzer, Frank, *The Story of British Sporting Prints*, Hutchinson & Co., 1929.

Slater, J. Herbert, *Engravings and Their Value*, Upcott Gill, 1891.

Snelgrove, Dudley, *The Paul Mellon Collection, British Sporting and Animal Prints 1658–1874*, The Tate Gallery for the Yale Center for British Art, 1981.

Taunton, Thomas H., *Portraits of Celebrated Racehorses, 1887–1901*.

Titley, Norah M., *Bibliography of British Sporting Art*, British Sporting Art Trust, 1986.

Walker, Stella A., *British Sporting Art in the Twentieth Century*, The Sportsman's Press, 1989.

Walker, Stella A., *Sporting Art: England 1700–1900*, Studio Vista, London, 1972.

Welcome, John and Collens, Rupert, *Snaffles: The Life and Work of Charles Johnson Payne*, Stanley Paul & Co. Ltd., 1987.

Wilder, F. L., *English Sporting Prints*, Thames and Hudson Ltd., 1974.

Wood, Christopher, *The Dictionary of Victorian Painters*, Antique Collectors' Club, 1971.

Wood, J. C., *A Dictionary of British Animal Painters*, F. Lewis Publishers Ltd., 1973.

INDEX

The Work of the Engravers, pages 67 & 68, not included. Main reference to an artist's work is shown in **bold**.